The History of Place Names in England

The History of Place Names in England and Worcestershire

Dr Mike Jenkins

To, Nicky

Happy Time Travelling

Best Wishes,
Mike

YOUCAXTON
PUBLICATIONS

ISBN 978-1-913425-78-4
Published by YouCaxton Publications 2021
YCBN: 01

YouCaxton Publications
www.youcaxton.co.uk

To my wife, Sue, for her steadfast support and to my grandchildren, Arthur, Tabitha, Alexander and Tess who one day may become generalists or specialists but hopefully never partialists!

Foreword

'Dwell on the past and you will lose an eye. Forget the past and you will lose both'.
Old Russian saying, Alexander Solzhenitsyn. The Gulag Archipelago 1973

IF you live or are reading this book in any part of England you are bound to be surrounded by a myriad of place names. We can often take them for granted, at face value or perhaps completely ignore them. If you do bring to mind the names of the places around you, peruse a road atlas or your local Ordinance Survey map you can begin to appreciate their deep and multifarious character. Some you may find quite ordinary, some quaint, some comical or rude, some strange or mysterious and some even alien. You may have wondered why place names seem so different from one another, when and by whom were they created and what can they tell us about their creators? You may have even pondered whether you are related to the folks who crafted them?

Understanding the reasons behind the great diversity and linguistic richness of the place names of England, their origins and their meanings is the key to answering some of these questions. This is because the main determinants of the form that place names have been given are the people, their languages and cultures who first coined them and those who later modified them. As a collective study, the vast array of place names around us are able to provide insights into almost every aspect in the lives of the folks who came before. Place names can help identify the language, dialects and culture of their originators, why they chose the particular name, how they lived, worked and died, their leaders, what they valued, their religious beliefs, their relationship with their neighbours locally and across borders, and even the ancient natural history and environment of the locality at the time. Numerous place names illustrate the social structures and legal customs of early societies with all ranks of a community represented, from royalty to humble peasants. Together they provide penetrating insights in to the lives, distributions and movements of ancient populations over thousands of years. They can also point to how the successive migrations into Britain of these people have led to us, in short, who they were and where we come from. Indeed, in place names you find almost every aspect of humanity highlighted and recorded like a beacon in time. Some of the echoes of these voices of the past will be heard loud and clear, no doubt who the originators were. Some are faint, almost inaudible and distorted, leaving uncertainty about their identity and what they are trying to convey. However, when we are able to understand the meaning of a place name, we can begin to imagine more about their originators. We can start putting faces to places. Perhaps surprisingly, discovering the original intended meaning that our ancestors gave to places is still useful and relevant today for a number of reasons that I will come to explain.

The modern and familiar place names of England are related to many place names found in Europe and beyond. So, I explore the history of place names as the main portal for telling the story of the people who first coined them and those who later modified them. Thus, I set the place names and people of England, and in more detail Worcestershire, in a wider historical perspective to underline connections and continuity.

I have also woven into the narrative threads from many other disciplines. Using a multi-disciplinary approach helps to develop a fuller picture of these people, their languages and even their cultural and genetic ethnicity. I complete the scene by describing their environment and the natural history that surrounded them at the time. In addition to the study of the origins of place names, toponymy, I encompass the specialties of linguistics, history, anthropology, archaeology, cultural evolution, ancient DNA and genetic population studies. By using a multi-disciplinary approach, a more complete story unfolds that may underline the continuity and connections from the past to you. The 2015 study by Stephen Leslie, The Fine Scale Genetic Structure of the British Population, published in the journal Nature proposed that this is particularly relevant to individuals whose relatives were included in the first National Census of England of 1801. Before the Industrial Revolution of the Eighteenth Century, on the whole, people worked, lived and died where they were born. So, the people included in this first census are most likely related to those who lived in the area in the more distant past and to the people whose families have continued to live in the area. This approach also uncovers links between people, events and entities which, at first glance, seem entirely distant and unrelated. such as the links between place names, language and both cultural and genetic ethnicity.

In Part One, I lay down the foundations for a basic understanding of place names including their nature, origins and importance and their intimate relationship with the evolution of language. I also delve thousands of years into the past to listen for the faint echoes of some of the oldest place names detectable.

In Part Two, I describe the wider and deep time picture of some of the global trends in human migration and the successive immigrations in to southern Britain since the end of the last Glacial Period. These elements of the story provide the background for understanding the origins, meanings and creators of the place names of southern Britain, including what was to become England. Thus, Part Two provides the background and general story that the reader, with a little more research, can continue into any county or locality of England and explore the place name evidence these folks left behind.

Finally, in Part Three, I move the story into Worcestershire to demonstrate the extraordinary potential of place names to reveal the lives of the local people, their cultures and their languages who once called the area their home. Place names surround us and are a tangible gateway into local history and a link to people's common origins and ancestry. In chapter 24 I provide the guidance and resources, a kind of 'history tool kit', that shows how you can explore the origins and meaning of your own local place names and discover who owned these 'Voices of the Past', when the names were created and what they are saying - bringing relevant, local history to your doorstep and 'faces to places'. Armed with an Ordnance Survey map, insights into the meaning of these place names and the identity of their originators you are ready to 'walk the talk'! Visit these sites, where there is public access, view for yourselves and start imagining why they were given these names and in what circumstances. The reward is both an enjoyable and satisfying experience by connecting to the past in your locality and discovering how people lived and related to the landscape that surrounds you now. It is a moving experience to stand at a place and understand the original intended meaning that different people and cultures, speaking different languages have given the location many centuries and even millennia ago. You can begin to understand why they gave the place that particular name. To stand on 'the hill where wolves live', 'the ridge of Puck the hobgoblin,' in 'the valley of wild garlic', 'the hill of the watch tower', or 'the palace of the Hwicce tribe' and 'the farmstead by the water meadow where the cranes live' and to imagine how the creators of these names lived is an intimate and personal journey. The spirits of our ancestors are locked in the meaning of the places they named and that still surround us today. They are waiting to be unlocked and can come alive again if we breath our energy and attention into them. This is vivid, intimate history at your feet.

The consistent theme of this book is how the study of the origins, history and meaning of place names and the people who coined them can further our understanding of both general and local history. It can provide an insight into the connections and continuity between the people who have successively migrated in to this region of north west Europe. It makes sense to explore the history of people alongside the history of place names. Putting 'faces to places' helps us understand their 'authors' and their relationship with ourselves.

As the book crosses the boundaries of many areas of enquiry it is ideal for the general interest reader who enjoys gaining insights into other disciplines of knowledge and research. This is not a book aimed at experts and academics. I have not used the institutional language which is required for discourse in academic organisations and research. I have avoided specialist and technical jargon as much as is meaningfully possible. However, I have provided supporting evidence and up to date peer reviewed references for those who care to explore these multiple aspects more deeply. I have acknowledged controversies and uncertainties and concentrated on continuity and connections.

The 'Voices of the Past' seem to call us, demand and deserve our attention. If we listen, they will tell us their story. A fascinating story because, at least for the last 60,000 years (some anthropologists argue for the last 150,000 to 200,000 years), we have far more basic biological, genetic, physical, physiological, cognitive and emotional aspects in common with our ancestors than differences! Indeed, the main difference, particularly over the last 60,000 years or so, are related to our cultural evolution.

Cover
There is circumstantial evidence from a number of locations around the world that the names given to some topographical features have survived from over 8,000 years ago. The earliest attested settlement names survive as cuneiform texts and hieroglyphs from the Middle East and dated to around 5,000 years ago. Similarities in the names given to settlements, topographic features and particularly rivers widely across pre-Roman Europe reflect the strong influence of the Celtic languages. Likewise, many names given to the physical features of the landscape of England still resonate from Celtic tongues possibly originating from around 500-400 BC. These include the Malvern Hills from 'moel' and 'fryn' meaning 'bare hill'. The earliest Anglo-Saxon place names originate in south east England from the 5th century AD. Rippel in 680 (Ripple), Heanburg in 691 (Hanbury), Ueeogorna civitate in 691 (Worcester), Fledanburg in 692 (Fladbury) and Chronochomme in 709 (Evesham) are some of the earliest attested Old English place names in Worcestershire.

Contents

Definitions of Abbreviations
OE - Old English Language
OS - Old Scandinavian Language
OF – Old French Language
PIE - Proto-Indo-European Language

PART 1
THE FOUNDATIONS

~

Chapter 1 The Nature of Place Names.

"The names of places carry a charge of the people who named them."
John Steinbeck

THERE are challenges in studying place names. Like most words, they invariably change and evolve overtime, so the current name may be derived from a distant, unknown and often unwritten language. The original place name can be of such antiquity that the derivation and meaning is likely lost forever and analysis becomes at best an informed or, at worse, a wild guess! They share the destiny of most languages, most words within languages and most biological species - they become extinct. This is one of the reasons why proportionately more meanings and origins of place names are known from the New World compared with the much longer human occupancy of the Old World. We are, of course, dependent on the earliest scribes who eventually first committed the names to paper and on the interpretation of the sounds they heard. Before this, the names of places would have been passed down through oral history and some transculturally via foreign languages. However, by gaining an insight into the methods our ancestors used for naming places you can at least have an informed guess as to the likely intended meaning. Some elements of place names can remain little changed in form but change in meaning or have several meanings depending on the context and setting of the place. Indeed, the same element can have the same or different meaning in different languages. A further confusion is that the identical modern form of some place names may have entirely different origins and different originally intended meanings because of convergence over time! More often, however, place names which had identical origins and meanings diverge to very different modern forms for any of many reasons!

Place names found on maps, even over the last few hundred years are not static but dynamic, changing slowly over generations and centuries. The evolution of a place name can occur suddenly when an incoming culture creates their own name, or mistakes or dislikes the sounds of the elements used by the previous culture. Incoming cultures, however, often adopt and modify a name that the indigenous culture had previously given a place. Changes can also occur by errors of interpretation and transcription of important documents. Even the Doomsday Book, transcribed by Norman administrators describing the demographics of Anglo-Saxon society contain errors by mistake or by intent!

The origin of many place names, therefore, have long been forgotten and lost. However, it is often possible to establish likely meanings through consideration of earlier forms of the name. An important principle of place-name etymology is that early name forms start the process of understanding the original meaning. Other facilitating factors include knowledge of the people and their language living in the vicinity at the time and the recognition of regional and local dialects in the choice of place names. Also, taking account of the physical features, geology and past natural history of a locality can help elucidate the original meaning of a name. It pays, and of course is great fun, to 'walk the talk' and actually visit and stand on the site under consideration to assess the topography and environment.

Place names have some important features in common. They are invariably demotic, originating from living units of speech, coined by our distant ancestors hundreds and sometimes thousands of years ago. Some of these 'Voices of the Past' can be heard loud and clear. Others are only faint echoes, linguistic fossils shining like dim beacons from the deep past. Modern place names invariably contain an original meaning often hidden within the modern form. However, on further examination and interpretation they can often be found bursting with information about themselves, almost becoming adjectives, describing their own characters so well.

Place names not only identify human settlements but also the enduring features of the landscape, knowledge of which, would have been vital for the survival of our ancestors. Indeed, these are often the oldest place names, some perhaps coined by the first nomadic hunter-gatherers before permanent settlements. They include rivers, mountains, hills, valleys, lakes, springs, marshes, forests, bays and seas. Many prominent natural landmarks and waterscapes that were useful for humans to know about, identify and pass on to each other, would have been given names. Fresh water was of major importance to the early inhabitants of an area, not only for sustenance, but travel and religious beliefs. River names are thought to be some of the oldest surviving place names and this may well reflect their vital importance to people in the past. Indeed, as we will see, words associated with water have been identified as some of the oldest 'core' words in vocabularies.

Ancient populations, particularly those since the Neolithic period, tended to be born, live, work and die in one locality so a particular physical feature near, whether a hill, river or lake, was the most relevant to them in their daily lives. The name they gave this natural feature was often the generic word used for that feature in their language. Thus the place name literally meant 'the hill', 'the water meadow', 'the river' or 'the high fortification', without any other distinguishing element or word. This principle explains why, in Celtic languages there are many river names known simply by the Celtic word 'afon' meaning 'river' and hills known simply by the Celtic word 'bryn'. Likewise, in many Indo-European languages, including Old English, settlements situated near water or rivers, such as Eton and Eaton (literally meaning 'water town) contain the ancient root 'ea', meaning 'stream' and 'to flow'. The root also appears in the contemporary names for many British rivers and streams as in the common river name 'Rea". A similar phenomena is found in the many names for hills found in England known simply as 'Berrow' which is derived from the Old English word 'beorh' and 'beorg', meaning 'hill' or 'tumulus'. This linguistic process seems to have been a characteristic of naming physical features, especially rivers and streams, for many thousands of years in early and probably even pre-Celtic European (thus pre-Indo-European) languages.

Another characteristic in the choice of names used for places, particularly natural features, is that an incoming culture would borrow a word that the previous culture used for the same feature and then incorporate it into their new name. So, the incoming culture unknowingly added a generic word of the indigenous language having exactly the same meaning for the feature in their own language. There are many examples of this process of accretion that produce some amusing tautologies. Thus, in a literal sense we will meet many place names formed by contributions from two different cultures literally meaning for example, 'river, river' or in three different cultures with three different languages contributing that eventually over the centuries have accumulated the form and meaning of 'hill, hill, hill'! Figure 4.

There are some recognisable patterns of the naming of places depending on exactly what or who is being described. One of the commonest types of names found are 'habitative names' which signify the original intended use of the settlement, as a cottage, homestead, farmstead, enclosure, hamlet, village or stronghold. Examples of this type of place name in the Old English language, you will probably recognise as they contain the elements of 'ton' originally meaning 'village' and 'ham' originally meaning 'farmstead'. Another common type of place name is one that describe people, an individual, a leader or tribe, known as 'folk names'. Many that we will meet were Anglo-Saxons, but Celts, Romans, Scandinavians and Normans all contribute. The third type is named after an obvious topographic feature of the locality, such as the Celtic 'pen' meaning 'head of' or 'hill'. However, most place names are actually a combination of two or all three of these groups and can include a personal name, the function of the place and a local physical feature. Thus, this combination offers a highly descriptive insight in to the past.

There are a number of trends in the way place names change and evolve of over time. For practical reasons, names have often become abbreviated, such as Colonia Lindum becoming Lincoln and Weogoran Ceaster to Worcester. Similar words in a language, initially with different meanings, can become corrupted and mistakenly applied over time, The Old English word 'dun' meaning 'hill' or 'fort' (loaned from a Celtic word) and 'denu' meaning 'valley' have been corrupted through Middle English. Thus, the name for the highest mountain in England and Wales, is known as Snowdon (from Old English 'Snawdune' meaning 'Snow hill'). The name of the town of Croydon, however, (early form 'Craudena' derived from 'denu') does describe exactly its valley location! One of the most dramatic transformations of a place name occurs when modified by a new incoming language, so sometimes the old meaning is completely lost. This may be the case with Derby from Old Scandinavian 'djura' meaning deer and 'by' meaning 'village'. However, the Roman name for the settlement was Derventio. This was likely related to the Common Brittonic river name, Derwent, which still flows through the city. As is often the case, the name is derived from the older river name, in this case the Brittonic Celtic meaning, so becoming 'valley thick with oaks. There were also many places with identical and very common names such as Stoke, from Old English 'stoc' meaning 'settlement dependent on a larger nearby settlement', and 'ham' which came to mean 'village'. To avoid confusion in an increasingly connected world settlements given common names have tended to be qualified by a second name such as Stoke Mandeville, a Norman feudal family name, or by the addition of a reference to their geographical location such as in Southampton or by the addition of the superlatives 'lesser' and 'greater'.

However, one of the main challenges of studying place names is that they transform over time for all the many reasons discussed above and sometimes with few or no written ancient forms. Although often the present-day form of a place name may give some clues, to have the best chance of understanding the original intended meaning it is vital to search for the earliest written evidence of the name and as many of the evolving forms of the name over time. In ancient unwritten languages it is important to focus on likely pronunciations represented in later written forms. Indeed, information from many sources are used to aid understanding. These are the basic procedures underlying the study of place name etymology known as toponymy or toponomastics.

I remember breaking these rules once and regretting it. A presenter asked his audience, in a rather playful way, what was the derivation of Hornyold Road, Malvern. Fortunately, it was a genuine question because he did not know the answer himself. The audience remained silent, so I took a stab at it, knowing that the majority of Worcestershire place names are derived from Old English and that 'horn' was the Old English for 'hard' assuming that the word was also used then as a meaning of 'difficult' or in this context 'exhausting' to climb in Old English. Thus, I made a series of ill-judged assumptions. Later, when I went through the correct etymological procedures, I realised I was spectacularly wrong! In fact, Hornyold Road, Hornyold Avenue and the Hornyold Arms Hotel all take their name from the lords of Hanley Castle, a Roman Catholic family named the Hornyolds! Also, if I had 'walked the talk', I would have realised that the thoroughfare is dead flat!

Fortunately, there are rich resources of expertise available in the discipline of toponymy and I have invariably used these for the interpretation and meaning of ancient place names. My main role within this book has been to integrate relevant and interesting aspects of the history of naming places, identify their 'authors', place them in their environmental and historical context and reveal continuity and connectedness.

Chapter 2 A Brief History of Language.

<table>
<tr>
<td>

"And little words of languages long-vanished,
Lithe words once lively on the lips of men,
And pretty in the prattle of small children,
No tongue will ever utter them again."

</td>
<td>

"A geiriau bach hen ieithoedd diflanedig,
Hoyw yng ngenau dynion oeddynt hwy,
A thlws i'r clust ym mharabl plant bychain,
Ond tafod neb ni eilw arnynt mwy."

</td>
</tr>
</table>

Waldo Williams from *Cofio* (Remembrance)[*]

THE study of place names is the study of the languages of the past, their form, meaning, context, how languages are related and how they have diverged. Thus, some grounding into the nature of language is an important part of understanding the nature of place names. This, of course, is easier when the language is written but there has also been a strong tradition of oral history and rote transferred between generations and, as we shall see, even between cultures. Indeed, all pre-historic languages are themselves the embodiment of an oral tradition passed from the old to the young. Of course, to name a place meaningfully needs both speech and a language. Speaking is the default modality for language in all cultures, our preferred method of communication in the past, though theoretically at least, it could have been written or sign.

There is ongoing debate as to when speech and language evolved and whether it is unique to humans, and thus up to 250,000 to 350,000 years old, or shared with our hominin ancestors over several million years. The evolution of language requires the appropriate anatomical apparatus, neurophysiological function, a gene set that includes FOXP2 (very rare mutations of which are known to cause an inability of the brain to construct complete sentences) and the ability to process information symbolically. Humans' unprecedented use of the tongue, lips and other moveable parts sets us apart from any other living species. All are features of 'modern' humans and what distinguishes us from all other life on the planet. Evidence suggests that all these requirements were likely in place by at least 60,000 years but some experts extend this back to 150,000 to 200,000 years ago and possibly even before. Either way, the evolution of language has been a long process intimately involved with the evolution of the brain and unwritten for well over 95% of our species' history.

The timing of the acquisition of the full complement of modern human behaviour is the subject of hot debate among anthropologists. Some have championed the idea that fully modern behaviour occurred in a relatively recent and rapid 'burst' around 50,000 to 40,000 years ago. This proposition is supported by finds such as the Lion Man of Hohlenstein Stadel, southwest Germany dated at 40,000 years ago and the ivory Venus of Hohle Fels dated at between 35,000 to 40,000 years ago. These certainly are exquisite and beautiful pieces of symbolic art which would be admired in any modern gallery and that a modern artist would be proud to have produced. Other experts suggest a much earlier origin of modern human attributes around 80,000 to 100,000 years ago. Certainly, there has been a growing array of artefacts found and dated to these times, including the Skhul Cave jewellery beads in Israel and the Blombos Cave Paint Studio kit found in South Africa, both from around 100,000 years ago and both suggesting symbolic thinking. The Blombos Cave Engravings are some of the oldest sub-Saharan African art and dated to over 72,000 years ago. Again, these artefacts suggest that their makers understood symbolism and abstraction. Indeed, some cruder finds including the Venus of Tan-Tan sculpture, from Morocco, has been dated at over 200,000 years ago and may be the work of one of our closely related hominin cousins and thus a pre-Homo sapien species.

Current evidence, including fossils found in Africa, suggest our species may be up to 350,000 years old. Several lines of research point to our ancestors migrating out of Africa in relatively small groups in separate waves. One group around 120,000 to 90,000 years ago arrived around the eastern Mediterranean area and seemed to have not survived. Another wave of migration, around 65,000 years ago, are the ancestors of all humans outside Africa. These migrations out of Africa involved relatively small populations compared to the total population of Africa at the time. This would explain why the genetic diversity of indigenous Africans is greater than all other indigenous populations of the world. Indeed, African populations also show greater cultural, linguistic and phenotypic diversity. Some recent research suggests the main catalyst for this exodus may have been a rapid increase in African human population at this time. Many experts agree, they would have spoken a language and separate waves migrating out of Africa probably spoke different but related languages. As we will see, languages are constantly evolving and a thousand years is a very long time in the course of the evolution of a language.

Linguistic scholars group languages together into relatively few families - probably less than twenty worldwide at present. Languages are linked to each other by shared words or sounds or grammatical constructions. It is likely that members of each linguistic group or family have descended from one, or at least very few languages, a common ancestor(s) perhaps hundreds of thousands of years ago and almost certainly in Africa.

Historical linguistics is the scientific study of language change over time particularly with regards to a specific language or groups of languages. Currently, linguists estimate that there are just over 6,900 languages spoken on the planet. However, around half these languages are spoken by less than 3,000 people and both the United Nations Educational, Scientific and Cultural Organisation (UNESCO) and linguistic experts predict that about half of today's languages will become extinct over the next 50 to 100 years. About one-third of the world's languages are found in Africa, the most likely origin of languages.

The earliest languages reasonably confidently identified through computer enhanced comparative methods are Proto-Afro-Asiatic. We can never know for sure, but by comparing the change over time of different modern languages we can be reasonably confident that some shared ancestor to those languages existed around 15,000 years ago.

The first languages were most likely simple. Pidgins are significantly simplified languages with only rudimentary grammar and a restricted vocabulary. They have appeared in historical times when two or more groups do not have a language in common. In their early stage, pidgins mainly consist of nouns, verbs, and adjectives with few or no articles, prepositions, conjunctions or auxiliary verbs. Often the grammar has no fixed word order and words have no inflection.

Like many great scientists Charles Darwin, in the middle of the 19th century, not only made some astounding advances in science, he also constructed and initiated new disciplines of scientific enquiry and his predictions in these different fields have proven invariably correct. He started the debate on how human sounds may have originated, writing in 1871 in his book The Descent of Man, and Selection in Relation to Sex: "I cannot doubt that language owes its origin to the imitation and modification, aided by signs and gestures, of various natural sounds, the voices of other animals, and man's own instinctive cries." Of course, much has been written since and many theories proposed, some of which appear in the references.

Darwin also commented on the similarities between the transmission of heredity and language. More recently, linguists have noted more specific similarities between the two. Language is a living entity in constant evolution. Words appear and disappear, the lifespan of words varying greatly from tens, hundreds, to many thousands of years. The ongoing struggle between words within a language and between different languages is a process very similar to evolution. A word, like a gene, will travel and prevail according to its usefulness and adaptation to perform a function. The fitness of a word to survive may derive from being attached to a desirable and important new invention or substance, or simply from being an amusing or useful concept. Genes and words tell us about different aspects of our human history. The 'gene book' tells a biological story that is even older than the story of the 'word book' that emerges from it - thousands of millions of years compared with at most several million years. The gene story unfolds because of mutations, gene recombination and variation over generations shaped by natural selection. Languages and words like species, have origins, diverge, thrive or become extinct, though not necessarily by the same mechanisms. Like species, far more languages have become extinct than are extant. It seems to take only a few centuries for a language to diverge with increasing geographical isolation as we will see in later chapters. Computer algorithm modelling can analyse and compare the rate of change of words in English and the 440 related Indo-European family of languages that share a common heritage. Researchers have found that the frequency with which a word is used relates to how slowly it changes through time, so that the commonest and most useful words tend to be the oldest ones. Linguists have identified some important and basic words, called core vocabulary, often related to every day relationships and everyday life. By studying cognates, words that sound similar and mean the same thing in different languages, linguists have used statistical modelling to discover some of the oldest words in current use. The researchers identified the most frequent cognates across seven language groups. These included words such as 'thou, I, not, that, we, to give, this, what, man, he, old, mother, black, to hear, fire, to flow, to pull, bark and ashes' which may be up to 15,000 years old. Note that one of these ancient words, 'to flow', is related to water and gives us an inkling of what kind of 'places' were among the first to be named.

The word 'lox' is a rare and fascinating example of a word that has not thought to have changed in sound or meaning for 8,000 years and thus spoken by some of the first Neolithic farmers in an ancestor of our Indo-European language! Then it meant 'salmon' and in Modern English 'smoked salmon'. Salmon is a fish that migrates from the sea to reproduce in fresh water. There are only a few places in the world where this occurs, so by the analysis of other words in these languages and the absence of words such as 'palm trees, elephant, lion or zebra', researchers have been able to locate the origin of the word to the area around the Black Sea. It has also been proposed that the very wide and successful spread of modern Indo-European languages to the east and west from this region, probably around about 6,000 years ago, was facilitated by the domestication of the wild horse, indigenous to the area, and wheeled transport. This new means of more rapid locomotion may have been one of the key factors in the dominance of this family of languages in its spread to the Far East and Western Europe.

The science of linguistics has been attempting to reconstruct the common ancestor of the Indo-European languages or Proto-Indo-European language (PIE). Since the speakers of the PIE language did not develop a writing system, we have no physical evidence of it. Although an accurate reconstruction of it seems impossible, there is a general picture of what Proto-Indo-European speakers had in common, both linguistically and culturally. The most widely accepted proposal for the homeland of the PIE language is the steppe hypothesis, which puts the archaic, early and late PIE homeland in the Pontic–Caspian steppe around 6,000 years ago.

The first published reconstruction of PIE was in 1868 by August Schleicher who composed a narrative using a text that represents what PIE may have sounded like and might have been spelt if it had been written. Schleicher's Fable is entitled *'Avis akvāsas ka'* 'The Sheep and the Horses'. There have been many revised editions of the fable each using more refined techniques to improve the accuracy of reconstruction of PIE. The story is, of course, a 19th century construct, but as you read the hypothetical words you may be making sounds similar to those of our Neolithic ancestors over 6,000 years ago. At this point you might like to look around - if there is no one else in ear shot or you know the people around you well - read aloud the following:

'*Avis akvāsas ka.*
Avis, jasmin varnā na ā ast, dadarka akvams, tam, vāgham garum vaghantam, tam, bhāram magham, tam, manum āku bharantam. Avis akvabhjams ā vavakat: kard aghnutai mai vidanti manum akvams agantam.
Akvāsas ā vavakant: krudhi avai, kard aghnutai vividvant-svas: manus patis varnām avisāms karnauti svabhjam gharmam vastram avibhjams ka varnā na asti.
Tat kukruvants avis agram ā bhugat.'

The Modern English translation is:

'*The Sheep and the Horses*
On a hill, a sheep that had no wool saw horses, one of them pulling a heavy wagon, one carrying a big load, and one carrying a man quickly. The sheep said to the horses: "My heart pains me, seeing a man driving horses." The horses said: "Listen, sheep, our hearts pain us when we see this: a man, the master, makes the wool of the sheep into a warm garment for himself. And the sheep has no wool." Having heard this, the sheep fled into the plain.'

The earliest possible end of PIE linguistic unity is believed to be around 5,400 years ago. Although Neolithic Anatolia has been proposed as the homeland of the Indo-European language family, linguists now tend to favour a later origin in the steppes north of the Black Sea. However, it is clear that the Anatolian languages, are the earliest attested branch of Indo-European and have been spoken in Anatolia since at least 4,000 years.

The most widespread family of languages today is the Indo-European, spoken by half the world's population. Ranging from the northern Indian subcontinent and Iran to the British Isles and from Finland to Portugal it includes all but one of the modern European languages. It is believed to be descended from the language of a tribe of nomads roaming the plains of eastern Europe and western Asia (in modern terms centered over the Ukraine, Caucasus and Southern Russia) that then spread to most of the rest of Europe. The language also penetrated far into Eastern Asia - occupying the Iranian plateau and later much of India. From about 5,000 to 6,000 years ago people speaking Indo-European languages began to spread west through Europe, eventually reaching the Atlantic coast and the northern shores of the Mediterranean. The Indo-European languages would have displaced and facilitated the extinction of the languages of the indigenous hunter-gather inhabitants of Europe, the so called Old or Paleo-European languages. However, there is evidence that some of the Germanic branches of the Indo-European languages loaned some words from these more archaic languages. During this expansion, the Indo-European language diverged forming a large family tree with at least twelve branches by around 3,000 years ago. Some of these languages became extinct but the surviving branches gave rise to all but one of the current European languages. The main branches include Hellenic, Italic, Indo-Iranian, Celtic, Germanic, Armenian, Balto-Slavic and Albanian.

The modern Celtic languages diverged further into two subfamilies: the Goidelic (or Gaelic) Q-Celtic and the Brittonic or (Brythonic) P-Celtic languages. The Goidelic languages would later evolve into Irish and Scottish Gaelic and Manx. The Common Brittonic language evolved into Welsh, Cornish, Cumbric, Breton and was also probably used by the Picts of northern Scotland. It was thought that although the Picts later spoke a Celtic dialect, inscriptions carved on their monuments hint of an earlier possible non-Indo-European (Paleo-European) language. However, this view has been challenged by improved understanding of Ogham inscriptions. The Pictish language is thought to have become extinct around the 11th century.

The Celtic languages are among the oldest of European languages, evolving before the Germanic languages and after Anatolian (the oldest) and Hellenic. The oldest attested Celtic language is Lepontic spoken in Switzerland and northern Italy from at least around the 6th century BC and known from inscriptions on coins and stone tablets. Place names, demonstrate that a Celtic language was spoken widely across Europe in the first millennium BC. Welsh is one of the oldest Indo-European languages. J. R. R. Tolkien wrote "Welsh is of this soil, this island, the senior language of the men of Britain; and Welsh is beautiful". He may, however, have been a little biased considering his interest in ancient Celtic and Old English languages. In a 2017 survey of the most beautiful sounding languages of the world the most popular were (from highest votes), Italian, French, Spanish, Portuguese, Chinese (Mandarin), English, Russian, Finnish, Japanese and Arabic.

The Germanic languages are a large branch of the Indo-European family whose common ancestor was Proto-Germanic, spoken in Scandinavia around the middle of the 1st millennium BC. The languages have further evolved into a Northern Germanic subbranch including Danish, Norwegian and Swedish and a Western Germanic subbranch that include, German, Dutch and English. Over half of the English language is made up of loan words from around 350 other languages. So, English might be called a 'language of languages' and this seems to be one important factor in its success. About 20% of the world's population speak English or about 1.5 billion people. About 360 million people speak English as their first language, about 4.6% of the world population. This short summary of the evolution of languages of Europe is important to understand, because as we shall see, these are the attested languages that have contributed to the place names of the British Isles derived from this great Indo-European family.

It is interesting to note that even if we take a late time for the evolution of language at 50,000 years ago, even the languages of 5,000 years ago, should not be considered as 'primitive'. They were 90% the way, at least in time, to evolving in to their present forms!

We are now in a better position to understand the context and languages of the cultures who successively migrated into southern Britain and their influence on modern-day place names.

Chapter 3 The Oldest Known Place Names

One fleeting moment as the sun is setting,	Un funud fach cyn elo'r haul o'r wybren
One gentle moment as the night falls fast,	Un funud fwyn cyn delo'r hwyr i'w hynt
To bring to mind the things that are forgotten,	I gofio am y pethau anghofiedig
Now scattered in the dust of ages past.	Ar goll yn awr yn llwch yr amser gynt

Waldo Williams *Cofio* (Remembrance)[†]

Rivers of Time

There is something special about rivers and the names they have been given. They tend to be the oldest attested place names; perhaps even more so than the names of other ancient topographical features. This might tell us something about the special relationship and importance of rivers to early people. From the end of the Palaeolithic period, around 10,000 years ago, 90% of Central and Western Europe including peninsula Britain were to become covered in forest. Thus rivers, as well as providing sustenance, supporting daily living, and in some cultures bestowing religious meaning, also facilitated transport. Indeed, as we have seen words relating to rivers, such as 'water' and 'to flow' are among the oldest words and part of core vocabulary.

Several authors have investigated the hydronyms of European rivers. The consensus view is that many of these river names are ancient and probably of very early Indo-European language, probably early Celtic, origin. Krahe identified the ancient patterns of river naming, often using common roots and extending from Scandinavia to southern Italy and from Western Europe, including the British Isles to the Baltics. He also recognised a similar pattern of naming European mountains and mountain ranges, the study of oronyms, often with names beginning with the letter 'K', as in the 'Karpatan' and 'Karawanken'. Indeed, it might be that these names are related to a similar name meaning 'mountain' in a Proto-Celtic or earlier language. Among his European inventory of over 10,000 ancient river and stream names, Krahe included the Yealm, Alaw and Hayle in the South West as some of the oldest named rivers in England.

There are recognisable patterns in the use of word elements of older languages which have then been loaned and modified by succeeding languages. These older elements often seem to be words loaned from a previous language that are related to the properties of rivers with meanings such as 'water' and 'flowing'. The Danube is an ancient European river name thought to be derived from 'danu' in a Proto-Indo-European language and may be a generic name for 'river' in these early languages. Other river names from the same root include the Don, Dnieper, Donets, Dunaj and Deatnu. The Finnish word for Danube is Tonava, which likely derives from the same name of the river in Swedish and German, Donau. In Sami, a Northern European language, Deatnu, likely the same derivation, means 'Great River'. The root 'ea' is particularly related to 'water' in many Indo-European languages. Sanskrit was an Indo-Aryan language of the Indian subcontinent related to the Indo-European family of languages. Fortunately, it survives in written form as the Vedas religious texts, around 3,500 years old, and provides a deep insight into the evolution of languages. In Sanskrit, 'danu' means 'fluid', 'drop' and 'swift' and in Avestan, an early Iranian language which diverged from Sanskrit, the same word means 'river'. In the Rigveda ('rgveda' meaning 'praise' and 'veda' 'knowledge'), a collection of Sanskrit hymns dated to over 3,200 years ago, 'Danu' is the mother of Vrtra, a dragon that blocks the course of rivers.

Many Sanskrit words are recognisably related to those in the modern Indo-European family of languages including English and, indeed, modern Celtic languages. Words of most similarity tend to be the oldest words and these tend to be the words for important every day relationships and things. These are, therefore, the most stable words that have changed the least over the millennia and a selection are listed in Table 1.

This relationship between languages accounts for the similarities between modern river names over wide geographic regions as far apart as India and Britain. Thus, these river names, including some in modern England, have common origins attested to at least four thousand years ago. The river Stour is a common river name in southern England. The known etymology of the Worcestershire Stour, the most northern, is: in 686 AD Stur, in 866 AD Sture and in 1300 AD Stoure. In modern India, the common root is found in the river Sthavard and in Italy and Germany several rivers have the same Sanskrit root, 'Steu', all meaning 'the strong one'.

Similarly, the English rivers Thames, Teme, Tame and Tamar all share the Sanskrit root Tamus, meaning 'the dark one'. The Tamus, is the contemporary name of a tributary of the great River Ganges of India. There are many likely cognates in European rivers, including the modern river names; the Tamega, in Portugal, Tamaran in France, Tammaro in Italy and Teifi in Wales. The etymology of the Thames can be traced backwards from Middle English, Temese, Old English, Temes, from the Latin Tamesis and possibly from Proto-Celtic 'tamesas' meaning 'river', 'water' and 'darkness'. Some river names are unattested and based on comparative linguistic methods.

Most European hydronyms, including over two-thirds of rivers in modern England, are Celtic in origin, meaning their first known and traceable names were given to them in a Brittonic Celtic language. Apart from those mentioned above, the major English rivers Avon, Wye, Derwent, Trent, Tyne and very many other smaller rivers and streams are all of Common Brittonic Celtic origin. Indeed, this may not be that surprising considering the influence of the Celts in Britain for around 1,200 years before the arrival of the Anglo-Saxons. The river Humber is interesting as it is probably derived from the Common Brittonic Celt root 'com-bero' ('coming together') giving the Modern Welsh toponym 'cymer', a common place name in Wales found at the confluence of two rivers. Thus, Humber may be derived from 'cym(b) er'. This is supported by the known Celtic to German sound change rule, 'K' to 'H' known as Grimm's Law and the fact that the Humber estuary is formed at the confluence of the tidal rivers Ouse and Trent.

There are patterns discernable in the origin of place naming relating to topographic features. Successive new cultures arriving in a region rarely seem to ignore the names used by the previous inhabitants but loan them and often modify them into their own language and 'map' of the landscape. Thus, there seems to be a different and slower rate of change for these topographic place names that are often geographically separate and socially distanced from the relatively faster rate of change of and within human settlements. The names of the enduring physical features of the landscape seem themselves to be enduring survivors.

The generic word or common noun meaning 'river' in one language, is often adopted as referring to a particular river in the newer language to the area. For example, the Celtic word for river, *'afon'* was loaned by the Anglo-Saxons into Old English and used as the name for specific rivers, as in the

Hampshire and Warwickshire 'Afons', later under the influence of Norman Old French, becoming one of the many rivers named 'Avons' in England, as there was no 'v' in the Celtic or Old English language.

Another manifestation of the antiquity of river names is that settlements established on or near rivers very often take their names from the earlier named river. The reverse process is rare. The Brittonic Celt name for water, 'dyfr', was given to several rivers and streams and adopted and written as 'dofer' in Old English. Examples of the use of the word are found in Dover, Kent and Doverdale in Worcestershire.

Place Names in Pre-History

There is increasing recognition and accumulating evidence that oral history can provide insights into events, natural history and the names given to places by people in the distant past. The references to place names handed down over millennia often describe incidents that have had monumental impact on ancient people, their land and waterscapes. Over the last few decades improvements in geological techniques and dating methods have provided data able to explain many ancient stories in terms of specific events at specific locations. The sudden appearance of unpredictable and catastrophic natural phenomena such as earth quakes, volcanic eruptions, tsunamis and comets would have been disruptive and sometimes lethal for a local population. These unpredictable, bewildering events that befell a tribe seem to have been communicated through many generations, together with a supporting explanatory account often related to the beliefs of that culture and which we now call myths and legends.

Some North American cultures contain descriptions in their oral traditions that strongly resemble hairy mammoths. If true, these must have been passed down for at least 4,000 years or around 150 generations after the species had become extinct. Another oral tradition in the Klamath people of Oregon in western North America describes a time when a large volcano which towered over their territory erupted and collapsed forming Crater Lake that is present today. The traditional story warns each new generation the importance of avoiding the lake in case the gods are annoyed and the volcano erupts again. We now know from analysis of the local geology that the volcano erupted around 7,600 years ago.

There are several examples from Australian Aboriginal oral tradition that recent improvements in scientific dating techniques have collaborated. South Australian Aboriginal stories tells of a bird taller than a man which was hunted in the vicinity of volcanoes. The extinct species was probably Genyornis newtoni known to have lived at the same time as volcanic activity in the area and geologically dated to around 5,000 to 10,000 years ago. There are over twenty coastal Aboriginal traditional stories from a variety of locations around Australia that seem to describe a coastline that was much lower than that of today. Most are interpreted as memories of a time before the rise of the sea level we now know occurred after the end of the last Glacial Period. At one such location in eastern Queensland, Fitzroy Island lies three miles off the coast. The local Yidindi Aboriginal name for this island is 'gabar' meaning, the 'lower arm' of a former mainland promontory. We now know that rising sea levels around 9,960 years ago caused the island to appear. This indicates that the initial description has been passed down by oral tradition for almost ten millennia or around 400 generations. These oral traditions act as a mental repository of 'libraries' in non-literate cultures transferred from one generation to the next through song, dance and performance. These cultural traditions are more than engaging entertainment. They also provide the information, knowledge and skills vital for the survival of a population in a harsh and changing environment.

There have been significant archeological discoveries of Palaeolithic and Mesolithic human settlements over the last few decades. One of the oldest well-preserved archaeological sites is at Ohalo near the Sea of Galilee. It was occupied by hunter-gatherers, probably seasonally rather than continuously and radiocarbon dated to around 25,000 years ago. The oldest constructed remains of dwellings on the site were huts made of mud and branches around 19,000 years ago, with some evidence of small scale 'trial' cultivation. We can be fairly confident that even a settlement of this antiquity would have been given an original name by their occupants but known only to them. A recurring theme, however, in ancient cultures is for the choice of a place name to be related to a physical characteristic of the locality. The name chosen is often the word in that language for that particular physical feature such as 'lake', 'water' or 'hill'. However, given the particular context, culture and time, this is only an interesting speculation.

Damascus is one of the oldest continuously inhabited cities in the world, with evidence of habitation dating back at least 11,000 years, the name, however, is only 3,500 years old. Similarly, excavations at Jericho suggest habitation from around 11,000 years ago and reveal it is one of the oldest walled cities in the world. The name is first mentioned in cuneiform tablets about 5,000 years old. Aleppo, in Syria, has been continuously occupied for 6,000 years and was referred to as Yamhad, a tribal or folk name, again from about 5,000 years ago. The city was later called Halab, an Arabic name meaning 'gave out milk', derived from the ancient tradition that Abraham gave milk to travellers as they moved through the region as written in the Old Testament Genesis 18:8. around 1,450 BC (3,400 years ago).

With the emergence of written language by the Sumerians of southern Mesopotamia (a topographical descriptive place name meaning 'the land between the rivers') around 5,500 years ago we can be more confident about the original name a place was given. The earliest proof of the written Sumerian language is the cuneiform Kish Tablet discovered in Iraq. The first known sentence written in the Egyptian language was found in a tomb and dates back to 4,690 years ago.

One of the earliest known folk place names refers to Anatolia as the 'Land of the Hatti' appearing on Mesopotamian cuneiform tablets from the period of the Akkadian Empire (4,350- 4,150 years ago). Around 3,000 years ago the Greeks called the Anatolian peninsula Ἀσία' (*Asia*).

A clue that a word or place name may be ancient and derived from an older and often extinct language is if it contains an element that is not found otherwise in the more recent language. A more recently evolved language loaning a word from an older language is quite common. This has been proposed in a number of European and English river names and some of which may have elements of words from Paleo-European languages rather than from more recent Proto-Celtic and Celtic origins. Likewise, similar origins have been proposed for some settlement place names in England.

As I have already mentioned, the source of place names and events from the past is from oral history, mythology and tradition. The Rigveda texts were written as hymns in Sanskrit around 3,500 years ago but passed down the generations by oral history and rote for about 2,000 years before appearing in written form. The basis of Homer's works, the Iliad and the Odyssey, are also thought part of a detailed oral descriptive poetry tradition spanning over 400 years before appearing in writing. Research comparing mythologies between cultures such as the Greek and Norse gods are similar enough to have likely originated in the ancestral cultures who spoke the Proto-Indo-European-Language. One of the oldest shared myths in Indo-European cultures are about 'dragons' and biblical-like 'flood' stories that may reflect real historical events that were experienced by those cultures.

TABLE 1 Some Sanskrit Words and their Modern English Cognates	
Sanskrit	**English**
matr	mother
ma	me
pithr	father
duhitr	daughter
bhrathr	brother
sunu	son
naama	name
na	no
dhama	domicile
thri	three
ghas	grass
lubh	love
hrit	heart
nara	nerve
sarpa	serpent
naas	nose
raja	royal
gau	cow
navagatha	navigation
jan	gene
akstha	axis
sthuga	thug

PART 2 POPULATING BRITAIN

~

"Time is the longest distance between two places."
Tennessee Williams, The Glass Menagerie

Introduction

IN this part I outline some of the characteristics of the early cultures that have successively migrated into southern Britain since the last Glacial Period. These were the founders of the place names of Britain and some of their muted echoes may, even now, be audible to us. Table 2 is a working guide for the general interest reader. I have estimated the duration of occupancy of the main cultures in relation to their opportunity for creating place names in their own language, be they physical features of the landscape, tracks, and seasonal or even permanent settlements. Of course, these pioneering place names have mostly been lost in time but perhaps with some exceptions. In relation to the duration of main occupancy in southern Britain, when a culture predominated and thus had an opportunity to name places in their own language, their effectiveness for doing so varied. There are many factors involved in this process including, of course, how long ago this opportunity was and how many cultures have appeared in Britain since. Considering the Roman period of political and military ascendancy lasted around 367 years only a tiny few of their place names have survived. The Normans whose more recent occupation lasted around 271 years faired a little better in surviving place names in their Old French language. Considering the Scandinavians and their Danelaw spanned only around 95 years, a remarkably high number of present-day place names in England are of Old Danish and Old Norse origin. This may be related to their closer linguistic relationship to Old English than to Norman Old French. Brittonic Celt was the main language spoken in southern Britain for between around 600 to 800 years before the Roman invasion and thus around 1,000 to 1,200 years before the influence of the Anglo-Saxons. Some modern English place name settlements are of Brittonic Celt origin but their main legacy is the high proportion of names for topographic feature derived from the Brittonic Celt language and still used today.

There is an increasing body of evidence that with successive waves of immigrations into Britain since the end of the last Glacial Period, around 12,000 years ago, the indigenous cultures did not immediately disappear but were slowly assimilated into the new expanding cultures. Thus, it is increasingly acknowledged that Britain has been a multi-cultural and multi-lingual society for much longer than was once thought.

Chapter 4 The Palaeolithic Hunter-Gatherers of North West Europe

"Dear books, please take me to the places where my feet can't take me."—
Hikaru Midorikawa

THE naming of places is both ancient and vital. They may have been among some of the first words that appeared in languages alongside other important everyday words describing family relationships, the human body and common objects. The importance of giving names to features of the landscape is demonstrated by the hunter-gatherer aborigines of Australia who reached that continent about 65,000 years ago towards the beginning of the Upper Palaeolithic period.

All the practical knowledge and survival skills had to be carried in the heads of individuals within small groups. Expanding areas of research in anthropology are studies of living non-literate hunter-gatherer societies. Some of this research is focused on how groups accumulate knowledge and skills of the use of bio-resources, of materials and their surrounding environment and landscape. Some anthropologists consider these hunter-gatherers assimilate and have a working factual knowledge comparable or even more than the working memory of the average human living in a technologically advanced society today. There is a long tradition within these Palaeolithic cultures of the use of oral history to communicate important information to peers and to transfer down generations. These oral traditions were translated as 'dreaming tracks' in the Australian Aboriginal societies and coined 'Songlines' by Chatwin in 1987. Songlines identify the route taken by 'created-beings', across the land and sky, during the 'Dreaming'. The Dreaming or Dreamtime represents a cultural construct of origins, when ancestral spirits were thought to have progressed over the land, and the creation of life and of the physical features of the world. These paths are recorded in traditional songs, stories, dance and art and are the basis of ceremonies within an animist belief system. However, Songlines also have a far more pragmatic aspect. They include oral maps of the landscape and night sky, enabling the transmission of navigational skills down the generations in non-literate cultures. The naming and orientation of useful topographic features within a vast landscape would have been vital for use on long distance hunting and trading journeys. Songlines often contain mnemonics and practical applications such as the ability to predict tides, as well as navigation, time keeping, and the maintenance of a calendar. In short, they are a vital part of Aboriginal culture, a survival strategy and a practical connection to the landscape. The transmission of knowledge using song has been documented within other indigenous populations.

It is interesting to speculate if similar strategies of orienteering and identification of directional markers in the landscape were used by Palaeolithic hunter-gatherers as they expanded into north-west Europe around 45,000 years ago. This was during the middle of the Last Glacial Period (115,000 – 11,700 years ago) when we know bands of hunter-gatherers roamed the region following herds of wild horses, deer, hares, mammoth, rhino and hyena. During the colder periods a peninsula of north-west Europe now corresponding to Britain would have been almost devoid of any life. During warmer periods, however, when the glaciers receded, they would have hunted in the area we now call southern Britain. This nomadic, foraging way of life, has occupied over 95% of the whole-time span of our human species existence.

The landscape on this peninsula was then treeless tundra with glaciers covering northern and sometimes southern Britain. During warmer periods hardy grasses and some trees would have expanded into the peninsula. Generally, the Late Palaeolithic, from 40,000 until around 10,000 years ago, is characterised by blade tool industries; a proliferation of artefacts in bone, antler, and ivory; and the emergence of rich symbolic art in the form of paintings, engravings, sculpture, and personal body adornment. The presence of small groups of Upper Palaeolithic hunter-gatherers into southern Britain is known from about thirty sites in the south and south east where characteristic flint tools have been found. At one of these, a jawbone discovered at Kents Cavern, South Devon, in 1927, was re-dated in 2011 to between 41,000 and 44,000 years old. The most famous find from this period is the burial of the 'Red Lady of Paviland' (actually now known to be a young man ritually dyed and buried in red ochre) in modern-day coastal South Wales, which was dated in 2009 as 33,000 years old.

About 13,000 years ago, towards the end of the last Glacial Period, these Palaeolithic people created the earliest known cave art in England at Creswell Crags in Derbyshire. A collection of 12,500-year-old butchered human bones have been excavated in Gough's Cave, Cheddar, which suggests some of our ancestors were cannibals. These early modern humans were Magdalenians, a cultural group of Cro-Magnon hunter-gatherers. These were the people who drew some of the oldest cave paintings in Altamira, Cantabria, Spain 36,000 years ago and in Lascaux in the Dordogne, France around 30,000 years ago.

We can be certain these Palaeolithic people spoke a language, as the evolution of language is at least 150,000 - 200,000 years old or more. The hypothetical languages they spoke are called Paleo-European languages, or Old European languages. They are the mostly unknown languages that were spoken in Europe prior to the spread of the Indo-European family of languages.

A characteristic of hunter-gatherer languages is that many different, distinct and seemingly unrelated language communities can appear on a continent. This reflects migration over an extended period and a life style supporting a relatively low-density population and therefore a greater chance of groups and tribes remaining isolated from one another. This was found in the native North American Indians whose languages are both numerous and diverse. At the time of the first European contact there were over 300 distinct language communities. They are in no way primitive, displaying all the complexities of languages elsewhere in the world. Some can be grouped into families but others are language isolates with no known relatives. This is caused by successive cultures migrating through a vast region or continent over an extended period of time. In the American continent, with the discovery of the skeleton of a boy found Alaska, the estimated time span of human migration into the New World has increased from 14,000 to around 20,000 years.

The migration of Palaeolithic cultures in to Western European speaking Paleo-European languages would have played out over around 35,000 years before the emergence of cultures speaking the Indo-European languages that were to eventually dominate in Euro-Asia. Time enough for these Paleo-European languages to have considerably diverged and become language isolates.

Table 2 Successive Migrations into Southern Britain Since the Last Glacial Period				
Culture	Beginning	End	Duration of Main Occupancy	Language
Mesolithic	11,000 years ago	6,000 years ago	5,000 years	Unknown labelled a Paleo-European
Neolithic	6,000 years ago	4,500 years ago	1,500 years	Unknown labelled a Paleo-European
Bronze Age	4,500 years ago	2,800 years ago	1,700 years	Possible Proto-Celt
Celts	2,800 years ago	1,977 years ago	823 years	Brittonic Celt
Romans	43 AD	410 AD	367 years	Latin
Anglo-Saxons	420 AD	1066 AD	646 years	Old English
Scandinavians (mainly Danes and Norwegians)	865 AD	960 AD	95 years	Old Scandinavian (Old Danish and Old Norwegian)
Normans	1066 AD	1337 AD	271 years	Old French
English	1337 AD	To Present	683 years	Middle and Modern English

Chapter 5 The Mesolithic Hunter-Fisher-Gatherers of Europe

"I am the willing heathen, I worship everything
I will add new words to my language and write them on the wind"
Ralph McTell, First and Last Man

THE Mesolithic Period in Britain (Middle Stone Age) spanned from the end of the last Glacial Period, around 12,500 years ago, to around 6,000 years ago. The climate was becoming warmer and dryer, the ice started retreating for the last time and trees were on the move. During this warmer period there was an expansion of birch trees, shrubs and grasses and eventually oak woodland. This advance north occurred at different rates depending on the lightness and mobility of the species' seeds. Poplar and willows transport their light seeds over half a mile per year. Birch, maple, hornbeam, ash and conifer seeds are heavier. Some species, including conifers, employ winged seeds that with high winds can fall up to one mile away. Heavy fruit producers, such as oak, chestnut and beech are much more limited in this northward migration. If conditions are favourable beech can extend by a 1/4 mile per year. Thus, after the last Glacial Period, most of Britain would have become forested over the following several hundred years with particularly birch, oak, pine and alder expanding to cover around 90% of Britain. Elm and lime were also much more common in lowland England at this time. These 'Wild Woods' would have been interspersed with grassy clearings and separated by grasslands and heathlands. This more wooded landscape was less suitable to the large herds of reindeer and wild horse that had previously sustained Palaeolithic hunters. Those animals were replaced in Mesolithic diets by less social animals such as elk, red deer, roe deer, wild boar and aurochs (wild ox), while the wetlands created by the warmer weather provided fish and wetland birds. Around 9,300 years ago, during the early Mesolithic Period, the last fossil evidence of the tarpan or wild horse are found. These changes led to the

Mesolithic people becoming the first to continually inhabit this peninsula of north west Europe. In the Early Mesolithic Period before the formation of the North Sea and English Channel these hunter-gathers would have walked across the low Dogger Hills or followed the river Rhine followed the River Rhine to the north west. At this time the rivers Thames and Rhine were confluent becoming the river Channel that eventually flowed into the North Atlantic.

Mesolithic hunter-gatherers developed more sophisticated tools than their Palaeolithic predecessors typically small, sharp shards of flint. These would then be mounted in composite tools, with multiple tiny microliths embedded into a wooden tip or shaft to form spears, arrows, sickles, barbs and harpoons. The distribution of tool finds suggest those hunting inland seemed to have had a predilection for wooded valleys. Some research has focused on the use of woodland clearings by Mesolithic people. Frans Vera, in Grazing Ecology and Forest History, provides evidence that a semi-open landscape was common during this period. Indeed, the berries and nuts and edible roots of woodlands are predominantly found at edge habitats and grasslands. The main source of food in woodlands is game but hunting in dense woodland is challenging. Vera describes clearings which are encouraged by hunter-gatherers by burning to promote grazing by aurochs and wild horse. By concentrating animals in a confined place, they are easier to hunt and kill. The tell-tale signs of an early assart (from the French 'essarter' meaning to clear and grub up trees and bushes) is the curving front edge of what is, in effect, a one sided 'hedge' which partly blocks the path of hunted animals from escaping into the adjacent woodland.

Although Mesolithic people spread to all parts of Britain, evidence of the earliest continuous occupancy of a site comes from Starr Carr in North Yorkshire around 11,000 years old and a round house near the village of Howick in Northumberland dated at 10,000 years old. We can be confident that these early human settlements would have been given names but names known only to themselves. A recurring behaviour of cultures in pre-history and early history is that they tended to give names to the enduring features of their landscape and thus these are among the oldest names. These physical features include rivers, mountains, hills, valleys, lakes and forests. These topographic features played an important part in their nomadic or semi-nomadic lifestyle as directional markers and would, therefore, have been given names. There was also a tendency for cultures to use the generic word in their language for these features. We will see this repeatedly in successive cultures who migrated into Britain. At the Starr Carr site a large wooden platform has been discovered nearby on the shore of a former lake – the earliest known example of carpentry in Europe. Thus, the Mesolithic name for the settlement may have contained the word for lake or water in their language. This would have been one of the Paleo-European languages (before the appearance of the Indo-European language in Western Europe) which we know almost nothing about.

However, there is a tantalising echo of a Mesolithic place name which may be from at least eight thousand years ago! St Michael's Mount, that beautiful iconic tidal island off the coast of south Cornwall, was occupied by Benedictine monks after the Norman Conquest. They built a monastery there and called the island after its name-sake in Normandy, Mont Saint-Michel. In the Cornish branch of the Celtic family of languages, however, the landmark was known as 'Karrek Loos yn Koos'. This literally means, "the grey rock in the wood" and may represent a folk memory passed down by oral history describing a time before Mount's Bay was flooded by the formation of the English Channel around 8,000 years ago. Remains of trees have long been seen at low tides following storms. Radiocarbon dating confirms the submerging of these hazel wood thousands of years ago. This suggests the passing by oral history of a place name trans-culturally from Mesolithic to Neolithic to Celtic people and eventually to us! This Old Cornish name is remarkably similar to the Modern Welsh equivalent – 'Y Carreg Lwyd yn y Coed', and demonstrates close linguistic connections between these Celtic languages that, as I will explain later, have a common origin.

Evidence from Genetic Studies

We gain a penetrating insight into the genetic ethnic continuity of the Mesolithic people from a well-preserved skeleton dated to around 9,100 years old found in 1903 at Gough's Cave at Cheddar Gorge and who became known as Cheddar Man. Evidence suggests he met a violent death. During this period there was a strong tradition of ritual communal burial in caves. DNA can survive in bones and teeth for extraordinary lengths of time given the right environmental conditions. The oldest hominin DNA analysed so far has been dated to around 400,000 years ago but the oldest genetic protein related information gathered is that of a Homo erectus dated at 1.7 million years and a Homo antessor at 800,000 years. DNA survives less well in bones from temperate climes, but cave environments seem to provide protection from degradation. There was good preservation of the DNA retrieved from Cheddar Man. This is the first time the full genome of a Mesolithic Briton has been sequenced and the oldest almost complete skeleton found in Britain. His mitochondrial DNA (mtDNA) belonged to Haplogroup U5. Within modern European populations, U5 is now concentrated in North-East Europe, among members of the Sami people, Finns, and Estonians. This distribution and the age of the haplogroup indicate that individuals belonging to U5 were among the first people to resettle Northern Europe, following the retreat of ice sheets from the end of the last Glacial Period about 11,500 years ago. It has also been found in other Mesolithic remains in Germany, Lithuania, Poland, Portugal, Russia, Sweden, France and Spain. Members of U5 may have been one of the most common haplogroups in Europe, before the spread of agriculture from the Middle East.

DNA analysis in 2018 identified one of Cheddar Man's direct descendants as a local history teacher. Indeed, these original indigenous Mesolithic people have an estimated 10 % of descendants living in Britain today! Thus, there is increasing evidence of genetic ethnic continuity of the previous occupants of Britain rather than total replacement by successive cultures. A process of diffusion and interaction rather than ethnic replacement. Studies of the analysis of nuclear DNA have shown that Mesolithic Britons were closely related to those in Western Europe at the time. This is not an unexpected result given the land bridge that existed between Europe and Britain for much of this period. The study also suggested that the Mesolithic people of Britain probably had pale-coloured eyes, lactose intolerance, dark curly or wavy hair and dark skin.

Chapter 6 The Neolithic Farmers Arrive

"The discovery of agriculture was the first big step towards a civilised life."
Arthur Keith

THE first cultures to abandon, for the most part, hunter-gathering and move towards an agricultural way of life appeared in the Near East around 10,000 - 8,000 years ago. There followed a monumental expansion of these Neolithic Agriculturalists across Europe which took around 3,000 to 4,000 years to reach Western Europe. The Neolithic period in Britain arrived later, introduced by migrants from Europe around 6,000 years ago and continued until about 4,500 years ago. These were the first farmers of Britain and used larger lithic tools, including axes, made from flint or hard igneous rock hafted on to wooden handles. During this period the first pottery technology appeared in Britain. They brought with them new agricultural techniques as pastoralist and horticulturalists. They farmed sheep, cows and pigs, pulses, barley and emmer wheat, but in addition still relied on wild food and natural resources. However, some evidence suggests earlier Neolithic people did appear to be semi-nomadic. These changes in lifestyle were associated, at least initially, with a sharp increase in the Neolithic British population.

An unfortunate consequence of this agricultural revolution, and indeed for humans ever since, was the increase in infectious diseases associated with the close and continual husbandry of animals - the zoonoses. As hunter-gathers became shepherds and farmers the seeds of many diseases were also sown. Pathogens prolific in animals were transferred to humans so we now share about 65 microorganisms with animals. Pigs and ducks brought influenza, horses transmitted rhinovirus and thus the common cold, tuberculosis from cattle and measles from canine distemper. Cats, dogs, ducks, hens, mice, rats and reptiles introduced salmonella. Polluted water from animal faeces spread polio, cholera, typhoid, viral hepatitis and diphtheria.

Now, between one third and one-half of all infectious diseases of humans have a zoonotic origin. Unfortunately, these pathogens often cause some of the highest infection fatality rates in humans. Indeed, 75% of the new infectious diseases identified in humans over the past 10 years, such as the West Nile virus from birds via mosquitoes, SARS from bats and civet cats, Ebola from Fruit Bats and jungle meat and HIV from Old World monkeys from West Africa are zoonoses causing serious infections. We are currently in the grip of a pandemic caused by SARS-CoV-2, the virus responsible for COVID-19 disease. This coronavirus is definitely a zoonosis and the balance of research, at the moment, points to a very recent species 'jump' involving bats and pangolins to humans. This is not only evidence of a long evolutionary adaptation of microorganisms to humans but also demonstrates our connectivity and continuity with our ancestors. Indeed, we know that however difficult modern times are, our ancestors experienced worse. Much worse in relation to the suffering, mortality rate and general decimation in all age groups by infectious disease pandemics of the past. Reflecting on these truisms does not, however, help those that have lost or nearly lost loved ones in our current pandemic.

Neither, it seems, was farming a seamless transition to a better quality of life. Studies comparing skeletal structure of Mesolithic hunter-gatherers and Neolithic farmers have shown that Neolithic skeletons are typically several inches shorter than their Palaeolithic precursors. Over reliance on one or several starchy crops in times of crop failure can mean risk of malnutrition and increased mortality.

The previously almost untamed landscape of Britain was changed forever by these Neolithic people in several ways, as they created imposing new marks upon the British landscape. The first of these were the chambered tombs of the Early Neolithic and later Megalithic stone circles such as Avebury, and its more famous sibling, Stonehenge. Many more stone circles litter the countryside, a reminder of the innovation and power of the Neolithic peoples. These monuments are taken to reflect ideological changes, with new ideas about religion, ritual and social hierarchy. Burials at this time were often communal.

These changes to the landscape also included some of the earliest permanent settlements and the earliest evidence of large-scale woodland clearance and timber management. These coincided with the introduction of Neolithic agriculture between 5,100 and 4,900 years ago. At the start of the Neolithic period around 90% of Britain was covered in woodlands. Towards the end of this period the coverage was reduced to around 60-70%.

The landscape transformations occurred relatively quickly within a period of 400 years. The population of Britain in the Late Neolithic era about 4,500 years ago (2,500 BC) had increased to around 250,000 people. If they survived infancy, most people could expect to live to their 40s or 50s.

Evidence from Genetic Studies
There has been a lively debate in archaeology as to whether these new cultures appearing in Europe and Britain represent the arrival of new people or the spread of waves of innovations and ideas. The archaeological community have debated whether the Neolithic Revolution was brought to the British Isles through adoption by natives, or by migrating groups of continental Europeans who settled there. The relatively new areas of research into Population Genetics and Ancient DNA analysis have been supported by new methods of molecular DNA testing technologies which have contributed to this debate. These techniques are capable of identifying genetic similarities and differences between populations. These techniques include quick whole genome analysis, comparison in protein polymorphism of autosomal DNA, Y-chromosome DNA (male line of decent) and mitochondrial DNA (female line of decent). Together they are providing new evidence and a fresh perspective into the people of the past of these islands. The studies can then compliment and be correlated with evidence from written history, archaeology and linguistics.

The genetic evidence suggests this was a true migration of farmers into Britain and not just the transfer of the knowledge and practice of farming to the indigenous Mesolithic culture. As soon as these Neolithic cultures start to arrive, we see a big change in the ancestry of the British population. The analysis of ancient human DNA has shown when the Neolithic culture arrived in a region of Europe, it appeared alongside new genetic ancestry that came from the Middle East. This suggests that it was not just farming cultures that swept across the Continent, but farmers too.

Early studies by Cavalli-Sforza used polymorphisms from proteins found on human blood cells including the ABO blood groups and Rhesus blood antigens to compare populations. This study suggested that the majority of genetic diversity of Europeans can best be explained by immigration from the Middle East by the first farmers in to the region.

The People of the British Isles (PoBI) project 2015 suggests there was a substantial migration across the channel after the original post-ice-age settlers, but before Roman times. DNA from these migrants spread across

England, Scotland, and Northern Ireland, but had little impact in Wales. As this Neolithic population moved west, there are cumulatively increasing levels of the local hunter-gatherer signatures in the genetics. So, this does not show one population wiping out the other. This evidence suggests the migrants were genetically mixing with the indigenous population.

More recent developments in genetic research demonstrate the R1b haplogroups of the Y- DNA that dominant in modern Western European populations came from Steppe migrants from the Middle East (north of the Black Sea), rather than from Iberia or France. This suggests that farming was brought to the British Isles by sea from north west mainland Europe, by a population that was, or became in succeeding generations, relatively large. The R1a also entered Europe with this migration. The second most common R1b subclade in England is R1b-S21, which is most common in eastern England, the Netherlands and Denmark. Ireland is also dominated by R1b-L21 ("Celtic"), which is also found in north western France, the north coast of Spain and western Norway. This subclade is also common and dominates in some parts of England.

It is not known definitely what language these early farming people spoke. However, it seems likely that British Neolithic farmers spoke a pre-Indo-European language or languages (labelled Paleo-European). Linguistic experts have thought likely that the massive expansion of Neolithic Agriculturalists across Europe between about 9,000 to 6,000 years ago probably caused the extinction of many more archaic languages in their path. I mentioned earlier that all the current languages of Europe are Indo-European except one.

Euskara is the language of the Basques and the only current thriving language that could possibly qualify as a Paleo-European language. Linguists have identified Euskara as a language isolate, pre-Indo-European and unrelated to any other language in Europe or the World. In addition to the linguistic uniqueness of the Basques, scientists, as long ago as 1937, have noted the unusual distribution of blood group types in their population. They have a very high frequency of group O Rhesus negative, in general around 50%, but an even higher prevalence in the remoter areas where the language is best preserved. In this they resemble the Icelanders, the Scots, the Irish, the Welsh and the Sardinians. However, more recent genetic analysis has revealed the Basques differ from all other populations in Europe by their very low frequency of the B gene. This indicates they are more closely related to the original Neolithic farmers who occupied the Iberian Peninsula than any other peoples. Today, in genetic terms, the Neolithic population of Europe substantially survives in only one place – Sardinia. As we will see, the genetic evidence suggests these Neolithic populations were not to have a large impact on the genetic make-up of modern British populations.

Chapter 7 The Bronze Age Immigrants

THE Bronze Age in Britain spanned between 4,500 - 2,800 years ago (2,500 and 800 BC). Around 4,000 years ago (2,000 BC) the Bell Beaker people migrated into Britain introducing a new style of bell-shaped drinking pottery and the first metal weapons and jewellery. Initially the metal used was copper, but by about 2200 BC bronze (an alloy of copper and tin and other metals) was being worked in Britain.

Large megalithic monuments similar to those from the Late Neolithic continued to be constructed or modified. From about 3,700 years ago (1700 BC) the Bell Beaker culture devoted their energies to creating physical land boundaries: walls, banks and ditches, sometimes on an enormous scale. Due to the effects of more recent and intensive lowland farming these are now best preserved in upland areas. During the middle and Late Bronze Age, landscapes were divided up by great field systems and permanent round houses were built, often grouped into villages such as Grimspound in Devon. Competition for land and a need for security prompted the construction of the earliest hillforts. The remains of roundhouses have been found within massive boundary walls. During this period woodland clearance extended into higher elevations though the great majority of the country remained forest.

By 2100 BC, Britons were mining metals. Trading ships travelled to mainland Europe carrying copper, tin and precious objects made by metalworkers. By around 1600 BC, the southwest of the island was experiencing a trade boom as British tin was exported across Europe.

In the Middle Bronze Age around 1,500 BC there was an increase in permanent settlements. There is evidence of a ritual deposition of personal items into watery places towards the end of the Bronze Age. Their dead were cremated, their ashes placed in pottery urns, and buried in small cemeteries beneath barrows and mounds near each settlement.

The Bronze Age also shows innovations including the taming of horses and by 1000 BC they had learned to make carts with wheels pulled by horses or oxen. By the end of the Bronze Age (800 BC) the population of Britain had doubled since the Neolithic to about 500,000. These Bronze Age settlements, monuments and extensive field systems would likely all have been given names. However, although the ruins and foundations of some settlements and the boundaries of some Bronze Age fields have survived, their names and even their language has not. We do not know definitely what language the early British Bronze Age people spoke on their arrival around 4,500 years ago. They may have spoken a pre-Indo-European language (Paleo-European) but there is a possibility their language may have been more closely related to an Indo-European language such as early Celtic (Proto-Celtic).

The Evidence from Genetic Studies
The Bell Beaker culture appearance was marked by an enormous population turnover. These immigrants displaced more than 90% of Britain's Neolithic gene pool ancestry. A 2017 ancient DNA study has demonstrated the Beaker people themselves had large amounts of Bronze Age Eurasian Steppe ancestry (including the R1b haplogroup) and at least some of the new arrivals came from the area we now call Switzerland. A study by Olalde, suggested the Bell Beaker culture migrated from the lower Rhine to Britain and brought with them a high level of Steppe ancestry. This resulted in a huge transformation of Britain's gene pool amounting to a replacement of 90% of the previous Neolithic derived lineages between 4,200 to 4,000 years ago (2,400 and 2,000 BC). Modern autosomal genetic clustering is testament to this fact, as the British and Irish cluster genetically very closely with other North European populations, rather than Iberians, Galicians, Basques or those from the south of France.

These studies decide the debate among archaeologists as to whether the "Beaker people" were a culture who migrated to Britain en masse from the Continent, or whether a Beaker cultural "package" of goods and behaviour diffused to Britain's existing inhabitants through trade across tribal boundaries. The former hypothesis now seems very likely. These findings may not indicate a direct clash of a metal-based culture with one based on stone but perhaps a consistent competitive edge.

Chapter 8 The Migration of Celts to Southern Britain

"I swear by the gods by whom my people swear and if I break my oath, may the land open to swallow me, the sea rise to drown me and the sky fall upon me"
An Insular Celtic oath.

THE traditional view of Celtic cultural identity is that they appeared as a collection of tribes in central Europe that shared a similar language, traditions and religious beliefs. Celtic culture started to evolve as early as 3,300 years ago (1,200 B.C.) typified by the Hallstatt site in Austria and later by La Tene in Switzerland. More recently some experts propose Celtic roots arose in the Beaker period in the 3rd millennium BC and others from an Atlantic Bronze Age culture contemporaneous with the Hallstatt culture but centered in the western Iberian Peninsula and western France. Recent genetic studies, however, support the theory that the Celts, as many cultures before them, were descended from people who migrated west and originated in the Steppes north of the Black Sea.

Between 750 BC to 12 BC, the Celts were the most powerful people in Central and Northern Europe, including Britain. They would stay in ascendancy, including their influence on place names, for well over 1,000 years until the expansion of the Anglo-Saxons in the 4 - 5th century AD. Their legacy is seen in the large number of names of towns, cities and regions spread widely across Europe of Celtic origin. These names can be found from the north of Britain on Hadrian's Wall (Uxellodunum), via its name-sake on the Dordogne, France to the southern Iberian Peninsula south of Lisbon, (Caetobriga) and from south west England (Dumnoniorum, now Exeter) to the river Danube (Singidunum, now Belgrade).

These names often have suffixes such as 'briga', meaning 'hill' and 'dunum', meaning 'fort'. There was a Celtic tendency for choosing superlative names to describe settlements, such as 'sego', meaning 'powerful' and 'uxello', meaning 'high'. So Celtic toponyms still echo their shared cultural origins across north west Europe, including Britain. The greatest concentrations of Celtic place names in Europe now occur in Britain, Gaul and Western and Central Iberia. There are smaller concentrations along the Danube, southern Russia and Anatolia.

Although the Celts brought their Celtic Indo-European language to Britain around 800 BC, it is not certain they were the first to do so. There is a possibility that the Beaker people may have spoken an Indo-European language closely related to Celtic (Proto-Celtic). The written existence of the European Celts was first documented by the Greeks in the seventh or eighth century BC and called Keltoi, which was thought to be the Greek name for 'Barbarians'. However, the etymology of the term Keltoi seems unclear. Possible roots include Indo-European 'kel', 'to hide', present also in Old Irish ceilid, kʲel 'to heat' or 'kel' to 'impel'. Some linguists suggest the meaning to be "the tall ones". Herodotus, writing in the 5th century BC, noted of the Celts, 'they lived where the river Istros (Danube) arose, further west of all people, other than the Cynetes' (people of Portugal).

The earliest known Central European Celtic inscriptions, from 575 BC to 1 BC, were found near Lake Como and Maggiore, in the heartlands of the Lepontii tribe, now northern Italy. Herodotus also noted at the same time he had heard a rumour of Atlantic islands known as the Cassiterides where commercially important tin could be found. It was understood that the Cassiterides, or "tin islands" were part of the British Isles, probably Cornwall. Thus, Britain was certainly known to the Classical world by many written references. Indeed, the Greeks, Phoenicians and Carthaginians traded for Cornish tin in the 4th century BC. The Carthaginian sailor Himilco is said to have visited the island in the 6th or 5th century BC.

The geographer Strabo, writing about Gaul towards the end of the first century BC, refers to the "race which is now called both Gallic and Galatic," though he also uses the term Celtica as a synonym for Gaul. He also reports Celtic peoples in Iberia, and uses the ethnic names Celtiberi and Celtici for peoples there, as distinct from Lusitani and Iberi. Pliny the Elder cited the use of Celtici in Lusitania as a tribal name, which epigraphic findings have confirmed. Latin 'Gallus' (pleural Galli) might stem from a Celtic tribal name, perhaps loaned into Latin. The root may be from Proto-Celt 'galno' meaning 'power, strength', as the use of superlatives to describe themselves was common in Celtic culture. In Irish, 'gal' means boldness, ferocity and in Modern Welsh 'Gallu' means 'to be able, power'. The tribal name of Gallaeci and the region of Galatia in Anatolia most probably has the same origin.

Although the word 'Celt' is a modern name, first attested in 1707 in the writing of the academic scholar Edward Lhuyd, it does seem an appropriate label given the historical evidence. The earliest known written reference to the inhabitants of Britain comes from 4th century BC records of the voyage of Pytheas of Massilia, a Greek geographer who explored the British Isles between 330 and 320 BC. Pytheas called the islands collectively (hai Brettaniai), or the Brittanic Isles; he also used the term Pretannike. The peoples of these islands were called (Prettanoi), Priteni, Pritani or Pretani. Pritani is a Celtic word that might mean "the painted ones" or "the tattooed folk", referring to body decoration and may have reached Pytheas from the Gauls, who possibly used it as their term for the inhabitants of the islands. British toponyms are another type of evidence, recorded in Latinised forms by Ptolemy's Geography. His surveyed map of the British Isles is remarkably accurate for the most part. Pytheas uses the same name as all classical writers who did not apply the terms 'Keltoi' or 'Celltae' to Insular Celts but to the Continental Celts. Caesar commented that Celtae is the Gauls own word. To the Greeks they were known as 'Galatia', and in Latin the 'Galli'.

There are many classical accounts that offer us insights into how these ancient Celts lived. Ptolemy reported that his friend prince Alexander, who later became king of Egypt, had met the Celtic ambassadors at a reception on the coast of the Adriatic in 335 BC. They were "big men both in stature and in opinion of themselves", he said. The historian, Diodorus Siculus, in the 1st century BC, notes the Celts are "physically tall, lithe and fair, often their hair artificially bleached with lime, the nobles sporting moustaches that covered their mouths. Their language sounded deep and harsh."

The late 1st century BC is the earliest period for which we have first-hand written sources for the history of Britain to supplement what we know from archaeology – a confluence that marks the end of prehistory. Together they hint at a complex world of power and intrigue set in a land of Celtic tribal kingdoms. It is thought that the Celts came to Britain in several waves as Iron replaced bronze as the material used to make tools and weapons, while religion, art, daily life, economics and politics changed dramatically. However, the patterns of land use in this new age did not appreciably change from the Bronze Age, suggesting this was a process of assimilation rather than displacement. With these stronger tools, they began large-scale woodland clearances to provide more land for cultivation and for grazing. This process of felling, burning and grazing animals on coppice regrowth continued into Anglo-Saxon times. The many artistic innovations of the Celts included intricate stone carving and fine metalworking. Elaborately crafted Celtic designs have been found on artefacts of gold, silver and precious gemstones. Some of the commonest Celtic finds are, however, coins and brooches. Clothes were mostly of wool or linen in the form of long-sleeved shirts (tunics) and long trousers, but silk was characteristically worn by the rich.

The earliest indisputably acknowledged language spoken in the British Isles belonged to the Celtic branch of the Indo-European family. The first Celtic immigrants to the northern British Isles may have been the q-Celts who spoke Goidelic Celtic and this may be an older Celtic language. A later wave of Brittonic speaking Celts migrating into southern Britain are called p-Celts as harsh sounding words such as 'cenn' became 'penn'. There is some debate that the Late Bronze Age immigrants may have had Celtic cultural characteristics and may have spoken a Celtic or Proto-Celtic language and thus an Indo-European language. Common Brittonic Celt shows a significant influence from Latin during the Roman period, and especially so in terms related to the Church and Christianity, which are nearly all Latin derivatives. No documents written in Common Brittonic have been found, but a few inscriptions have been identified. The Bath curse tablets, discovered in the Roman reservoir at Bath, contain about 150 names, about half of which are undoubtedly Celtic (but not necessarily Brittonic). There is an inscription on a metal pendant discovered in 1979 in Bath, which seems to contain an ancient Brittonic curse.

By the first half of the first millennium BC, Brittonic Celt was already diverging into separate dialects or languages. By the sixth century AD, the language had split into the various Neo-Brittonic languages: Archaic Welsh, Cumbric (extinct by around the 11th century), Cornish, Breton and probably the Pictish language. The Goidelic language of northern Britain evolved into Irish, Scot and Manx. Old Welsh was a stage in the evolution of the Welsh language about 800 AD until the early 12th century when it developed into Middle Welsh before Modern Welsh appeared. Thus, very many place names in modern Ireland and Scotland are of Goidelic Celt origin and many place names in Wales, Cornwall and Brittany of Common Brittonic Celt origin. Figure 1

The oldest surviving text entirely in Old Welsh is understood to be on a gravestone in Tywyn – the Cadfan Stone – thought to date from the 7th century. A key body of Old Welsh text also survives in glosses and marginalia from around 900 AD in the Juvencus Manuscript. Some examples of medieval Welsh poems and prose originated from this period, but are found in later manuscripts 'Y Gododdin', for example, is preserved in Middle Welsh and refers to an earlier Brittonic poet of the 6th century, Taliesin. A text in Latin and Old Welsh in the 'Lichfield Gospels' called the 'Surrexit Memorandum' is thought to have been written in the early 8th century but may be a copy of a text from the 6th or 7th centuries, placing it chronologically before the Book of Kells but after the Lindisfarne Gospels. Marginal entries indicate that the manuscript was in the possession of the church of St Teilo in Wales at some point in the 9th century and eventually came into the possession of Lichfield Cathedral during the 10th century.

The many Insular Celtic tribes of pre-Roman Britain gave their names to the territories in which they lived and are thus folk place names. Many Brittonic Celtic names derive from this period and thus hundreds of place names in modern England, especially in the west and north, are of Brittonic Celt (so not strictly Welsh) origin. Cumbric Celt place names include Carlyle, from 'Caer' meaning city of 'Luguvalos' and Penrith, from 'pen' meaning 'head of' and 'rhyd' meaning ford.

Many Brittonic (Celtic) place names in England survived for several centuries after the Anglo-Saxon invasion and some still remain intact. They are found sporadically in the east and with increasing frequently in the west of England. These names were of Celtic tribes or territories like Devon (territory of the Dumnonii) and Leeds (people living beside the river Ladenses, meaning 'strongly flowing'), important towns like Carlisle (Cair Luguvalos) York (Cair Ebrauc) and Dover (place at the river Dubras or 'water') and of hills and forests that were transferred to settlements like Crick, Penge and Lytchert. A Brittonic Celt word found commonly as an element in contemporary English place names is 'cruc' and 'crug' meaning 'a hill, mound' or possibly 'tumulus'. Examples are Creech in Dorset and Somerset, Crouch in Oxfordshire, Crich in Derby, Crook in Devon and Somerset and Crutch in Worcestershire. When the word is used for naming a hill it is commonly associated with the Old English word 'hyll', also meaning 'hill' so gives rise to another tautology or of the landscape that shouts 'Hill, Hill'. One not uncommon manifestation of this ancient Celtic name manifests itself in several villages in England now called 'Churchill' as in Oxfordshire, Worcestershire, Herefordshire and Shropshire. Indeed, the most frequent Celtic place names that survive are those describing natural features of the landscape such as rivers, hills and mountains. There are around six 'Eccles' and many more with the prefix 'Eccles' found in modern England. It is thought most likely a loan word from Brittonic Celt to Old English cognate with modern Welsh 'eglwys', Latin 'ecclesia' and in Modern English 'church'. There is a strong bias of this place name in the north west Midlands.

Evidence of the continuing presence of Celtic populations well after the Anglo-Saxon expansion can be found in place names that include the Old English element 'wealh'and 'walia' meaning foreigner or stranger. Such names are few but widespread across England. There are a smattering of villages around the Fenland town of Wisbech that hint of this meaning: West Walton, Walsoken, and the Walpoles, but these names are commoner in the west of England. Some villages that exhibit "Tydd" in their name, e.g., Tydd St Giles, may derive from an element of the Britonnic word for "small holding". Linguistic evidence for Celtic place names in present-day England is widespread and can be found in names such names Axminster, from Celtic 'iska', 'water', to Manchester from Celtic 'mamm', 'breast', (referring to the shape of a hill) to Wigan (Celtic folk name). In the Celtic speaking regions place names often commemorated local important individuals and families by the use of their personal names. These personal place names survive in Celtic parts but in England many of the Old English personal names did not survive after 1066. More evidence of spatterings of Brittonic Celt place names in England often contain the element 'pen' meaning 'head of' and are found in Penn, Buckinghamshire, Penn, West Midlands, Pendlebury (a hybrid name of Celt and Anglo-Saxon 'fortified hill') and Bryn, Greater Manchester, from Celtic 'bryn' meaning hill'. Many Celtic settlements took their names from the river they were situated on. Darwen, a market town and civil parish in Lancashire is an example taking its name from the river Derwent that passes through. It appears as 'Derewent' in 1208 from the Brittonic Celt 'derva' meaning 'oak' which is cognate to the Modern Welsh 'Derw'.

There are even around a half-dozen Goidelic place names in England, most folk names, such as Malmesbury from the Irish founder of the abbey Máel Dub and Fixby in West Yorkshire from the Gaelic Irish personal name Fiach. Some refer to Irish people, as in Ireby, Irby upon Humber and Ireleth.

The oldest Celtic place names, however, are those given to the enduring features of the landscape, such as rivers, mountains, lakes and forests. This is also a feature of place naming from the deeper past. In Britain it reflects the occupancy by Celts for over 1,200 years before the arrival of the Anglo-

Saxons who would themselves have a profound and lasting influence on the place names of England. So today, many ancient features have kept their Celtic names, especially in the north and west. Jackson surveyed the distribution of the river and stream names of Celtic origin in modern England and was able to classify four areas related to the duration of dominance of the Old English language. Overall, about two-thirds of England's rives including many major waterways such as the Avon, Dee, Derwent, Ribble, Severn, Wye, Thames, Tame, Tees, Trent, Tyne, Cerne and Itchen all have attested Celtic origins. The Brittonic Celtic root 'com-bero' meaning coming together gives the Welsh toponym 'cymer', which is typically found at the confluence of rivers in Wales. The derivation of the river Humber from 'cym(b)er is supported by the Celtic to German sound changes of K to H known as Grimm's Law, and the geographical fact that the Humber is formed by the confluence of the rivers Ouse and Trent.

The name of the river Trent is thought to be of Romano-British origin and related to a tendency to flooding. This may explain the presence of the Celtic element 'rid' in several place names along its course, such as Hill Ridware. The Modern Welsh word for ford is 'rhyd'. Clun is a small town in South Shropshire which takes the name from the river that runs through it, as do Clunbury, Clungunford and Clunton. The river name is Celtic derived from an earlier form 'Colun' and has the same root as rivers now known as Colne.

Some mountains in the north west of England such as Blencathra 'Summit Chair', and Helvellyn 'Pale Yellow Moorland' are of Cumbric Celt origin, as are the rivers Ehen and Cocker. Mountains of Common Brittonic Celt origin include Pen-y-Ghent 'Hill of the Wind or Border' in Yorkshire, the Malvern and Bredon Hills in Worcestershire and the Wrekin in Shropshire. During the Norman period the hill was called Mount Gilbert after a hermit who lived there before reverting to the Celtic name 'Wrikon'.

Many forests, valleys and lakes in England are derived from Celtic names. In central England these include the Forest of Arden and the Wyre Forest. The Charnwood Forest in Leicestershire is an upland area rising to 278 m scattered with exposed rocks and barren areas. The first element derives from the Brittonic Celt word 'carn' meaning 'rocks' or 'stones'. A characteristic of incoming cultures to an area is that they would often use the name given by a previous culture for a specific physical feature and then incorporate this older name or name element into a new hybrid name. There was also a trend in early Indo-European languages, including Celtic and Anglo-Saxon, of using the generic word for that feature in the language within an element of the place name. An example is Bredon on the Hill in Leicestershire which derives from the Brittonic Celt 'bryn', meaning 'hill' and from Old English, 'dun', meaning hill but later corrupted to 'don'. Thus, the place name becomes a tautology or pleonasm, as the name has three elements all having the same meaning in three different language - Brittonic Celt, Old English and Modern English - thus Hill, Hill, Hill!

The population of southern Britain boomed in the centuries before the Roman invasion and so did tribal identities, with intense rivalries and alliances. The Romans were to make full use of these political dynamics to improve their chances of a successful invasion and occupation of Britain.

Evidence from Genetic Studies

We gain an insight into the identity of the people of pre-Roman Britain from the study of Population Genetics. The University of Oxfords's People of the British Isles (PoBI) project was initiated by Sir Walter Bodmer in 2004 and published in Nature in March 2015. The study aimed to create the first ever detailed genetic map of a country. The story of the United Kingdom's history is, as I have described, of successive immigrations and invasions, so the genetic make up of modern British people is likely to be varied and complex. The study compared variations in the genomes of over 2,000 volunteers in rural locations around the country whose grandparents had all been born in the same area and included in the first National Census of England in 1801. The analysis, therefore, shows a snapshot of clusters of genetic variation in the early 19th century when people were less likely to migrate far from their place of birth. The results, indeed, reflected historical waves of migration by different populations into Britain and produced the most detailed map of genetic variation ever produced, uncovering distinct geographical groupings of genetically similar individuals across the UK. There appeared no single 'Celtic' genetic group, in fact the Celtic parts of the UK (Scotland, Northern Ireland, Wales and Cornwall) are among the most genetically different from each other. The Cornish are much more similar genetically to other English groups than they are to the Welsh or the Scots. The Welsh appear more genetically similar to the earliest settlers of Britain after the last ice age (the Mesolithic hunter-gathers) than do other people in the UK. So genetic ethnicity is not always associated with cultural ethnicity. People travel, match, mix and change their identity. Modern autosomal genetic clustering is testament to this, as both modern and Iron Age British and Irish samples cluster genetically very closely with other Northern European populations.

The Welsh and Scottish samples are consistent on average with 30% Anglo-Saxon ancestry with a large spread. Previously, historians have postulated that the European Atlantic populations of Orkney Islands, Scottish, Irish, British, Bretons, and Iberians (Basques, Galicians) have a common origin. More recent genetic evidence does not support the notion of a significant genetic link between these populations, beyond the fact that they are all West Eurasians. Sardinian-like Neolithic farmers did populate Britain (and all of Northern Europe) during the Neolithic Period; however, recent genetics research has claimed that, between 2400 BC and 2000 BC over 90% of British DNA was overturned by a North European population of ultimate Russian Steppe origin as part of an ongoing migration process that brought large amounts of Steppe DNA (including the R1b haplogroup) to North and West Europe. Modern autosomal genetic clustering is testament to this fact, as both modern and Iron Age British and Irish samples cluster genetically very closely with other North European populations, and somewhat limited with Galicians, Basques or those from the south of France. Such findings have largely put to rest the theory that there is a significant ancestral genetic link, beyond being Europeans, between the various 'Celtic' peoples in the Atlantic area. They are related in that male lines are brother R1b L151 subclades with the local native maternal line admixture explaining the genetic differences.

Chapter 9 Roman Britain

"The interior of Britain is inhabited by people who claim, on the strength of their own tradition, to be indigenous. The coastal areas are inhabited by invaders who crossed from Belgium for the sake of plunder and then, when the fighting was over, settled there and began to work the land; these people have almost all kept the names of the tribes from which they originated. The population is extremely large."
Bellum Gallicum *(The Gallic War)* Julius Caesar 58-52 BC

DURING the first century BC British Celtic culture was influenced by the Romans through diplomatic, trading and educational links. After the conquest of Britain (from 43 AD and was mostly completed by 84 AD) a Romano-British culture emerged. The cultural introductions to Britain were numerous and included improvements in agriculture, transport, political administration, architecture, plumbing, sanitation, a universal currency, a new way of time keeping (the Julian calendar) writing and, of course, a new language. Latin and British Vulgar Latin appear and coexisted with Brittonic (Brythonic) Celt.

While Britain formed part of the Roman Empire, Latin became the principal language of the elite and the official written language of government and administration especially in the more Romanised south and east of Britain. In the less Romanised north and west, Latin and British Vulgar Latin never substantially replaced the Brittonic language of the indigenous Britons and died out in western Britain by around 700 AD. By the end of the 4th century the vast majority of the population of Britain, estimated at 3.6 million, were rural and spoke Brittonic Celt. Only about 240,000 people lived in Roman influenced towns and cities. Thus, the Romans had surprisingly little lasting influence on place names considering an occupation of 435 years and very few pure Latin place names still exist in modern England. The Romans did not create new place names only Latinise native names. Many Celtic place names were Latinised, particularly those related to military settlements., however, after Roman power and influence disappeared only a few Roman place names survived. Thus, Brittonic Celtic names, though usually Latinised in written sources, continued to be used throughout this period in everyday life and were not replaced. Over 200 place names from the Romano-British period are known and their location identified from contemporary maps. However, only around thirty-five to forty remained in use after the Roman period. In modern times a few names like Catterick (from 'cataracta' meaning 'waterfall') and Lincoln from Lindum Colonia (meaning 'Roman colony (for retired legionaries) by the lake') contain Latin elements. Lichfield has a Romano-British origin and appears early as 'Letocetum' meaning 'the grey wood'. This can be compared with the Modern Welsh equivalent 'Llwyd coed'. The name in Old English became 'Lyccid' to which the Old English 'feld' meaning 'open country' was added.

The 2,000 miles of paved trunk roads that formed one of the most impressive features of Roman engineering in Britain, are today all known by Anglo-Saxon names as their original Roman and Celtic names have been lost. The three longest are Watling Street, at 276 miles, from the Kent port of Rutupiae, now Richborough, Kent, to Viroconium (Wroxeter). The name derives from Old English ' Waecelinga Straet' itself named after an Anglo-Saxon tribe, the Waeclingas who occupied a territory around current St Albans. The Fosse Way, named after the ditch alongside the road, is 230 miles long from Exeter (Isca Dumnoniorum) to Lincoln. Ermine Street, at 193 miles, ran from London (Londinium) to Lincoln (Lindum Colonia) then onto York (Eboracum). The name is from the Old English, 'Earminga straet' in 955 AD and named after an Anglo-Saxon tribe called the Earningas who inhabited the area around modern Cambridgeshire. Some Latin words were adopted by the Celts early and long before the arrival of the Anglo-Saxons. These loan words include topographical elements of place names such as 'fossa' (Celt 'fos', meaning ditch), 'portus' (Celt 'porth', meaning port). During the 5th century, following the Anglo-Saxon immigration, Latin and Celtic place names were anglicised, some beyond recognition. Londinium to London, Dubris to Dover, Colonia Lindum to Lincoln and Bangertium to Bangor, Eboracum to York and Pons Aelius to Newcastle. The Latin influence under Roman occupation is distinct from the influence of Latin in the medieval period when it became the language of the church and administration. Latin affixes were then commonly used, such as 'Forum' meaning 'market', 'Magna' meaning 'great' and 'Regis' meaning 'of the King' to distinguish places with identical names.

Evidence from Genetic Studies

DNA studies have found little evidence of a Roman genetic legacy in Britain as relatively few Romans settled here and thus the Roman contribution to the current genetic make up of the British population is probably very small. However, this may be in part, a function of the sensitivity of current genetic testing and sample size. Interestingly, a family with the surname of Revis, who are visibly white, and are thought to originate from Yorkshire have been found to carry Haplogroup A1a which is characteristically only found in Africa. It has been suggested that the Revis family has African ancestry which may date from the Roman occupation of Britain when Africans and Romans of African descent are known to have settled in Britain. Another 2016 study by Martiniano analyzed nine ancient genomes of individuals from northern Britain, with seven from a Roman-era cemetery in York, and the others from earlier Iron Age and later Anglo-Saxon burials. Six of the Roman genomes showed affinity with modern British Celtic populations, such as Welsh, but were significantly different from eastern English samples. They also were similar to the earlier Iron Age genome, suggesting population continuity, but differed from the later Anglo-Saxon genome. This pattern is thought to reflect the profound impact of the Anglo-Saxon migrations of the period. It is, indeed, exciting to reflect that more interesting and surprising insights into our past may emerge by the refinement and expansion of this genetic research.

Chapter 10 The Anglo-Saxons

"I remember the time, when mead we took,
what promise we made to this prince of ours
in the banquet-hall, to our breaker-of-rings,
for gear of combat to give him requital,
for hard-sword and helmet, if hap should bring."
Beowulf Old English Poem 10th-11th century

THIRTY years or so after the Roman departure of Britain in or around 410 AD, a diverse group of German-speaking people started appearing on the east coast of England from north west continental Europe. Their Germanic languages were related to Old Friesian, Old Norse and Old High German and were to form the basis of the Anglo-Saxon identity and the emerging Old English language.

Gildas, a 6th century British monk, notes that Saxon war tribes were hired to defend Britain when the Roman army left and implies some were originally invited immigrants. The Venerable Bede, a monk from Northumbria writes in his, Ecclesiastical History of the English People completed in 731 AD, they were mainly Saxons, Angles, and Jutes. They came from different parts of Germany and Denmark – the Angles were from Angeln, which is a small district in northern Germany; the Saxons were from what is now Lower Saxony, also in northern Germany; and the Jutes were from Jutland, now part of Denmark. According to Bede the Angles settled in East Anglia, the Saxons in southern England, and the Jutes in Kent and the Isle of Wight. The Saxons called themselves Seax or Sax from the characteristic dagger they wore. It is worth noting that the migration of Germanic people to Britain was part of a more extensive expansion of Germanic tribes, including the Goths, Vandals and Franks widely across Europe and known as the Migration Period or 'Volkerwabderung' between 375 to 800 AD.

Historians debate the most accurate description for the appearance of

Anglo-Saxons in to the British Isles, as invasions, migrations, settlements, diffusions or integrations. There is no doubt there was conflict but also perhaps a combination of all these interactions. One current theory outlines the manipulation by a small number of warrior elite upon a larger indigenous Celtic population. This political and social dominance may have been achieved by preferential rewards of those who could claim Germanic descent and speak Old English without Latin or Brittonic inflection. So, language may have been a key indicator of ethnicity that gave important advantages in freedom of law, access to patronage and the use of weapons.

The immigration of the Anglo-Saxons into Britain would have the most profound cultural effects of any immigration, in terms of architecture, political and social systems, writing, language and genealogy. Many of these changes and the expansion and domination of the Anglo-Saxons are reflected in the nature and distribution of place names. Indeed, the vast majority of modern settlements in England have their origins in Old English formed between the 5th and 10th centuries. Many of these place names are documented in the various charters (legal documents recording the ownership of property and rights) that appear in England in the 670s.

There are some, but very few, Old English words loaned from Brittonic Celt or Vulgar Latin origin, indicating very little influence from these languages. The place names of Celtic origin in England are certainly still evident but are only a few percent of the total, and are often present in an anglicised form. They tend to be names related to topographic features and found rather peripherally to the centre of populations and social change.

Many of the old Brittonic kingdoms began to disappear in the centuries after the Anglo-Saxon immigrations. The Celtic kingdom of Ceint (modern Kent) was the first to fall in 456 AD. The Anglo-Saxon Chronicle, a collection of annals in Old English recounting the history of the Anglo-Saxons, tell us about these events. The original manuscript was created late in the 9th century, probably in Wessex, during the reign of Alfred the Great (871–899). The Chronicle records the Anglo-Saxon kingdom of Wessex was founded in 494 AD and the area we now know as Worcestershire fell after 577 AD. By the 9th century the Anglo-Saxons had completed their dominance of southern Britain and were on the way to achieving a common cultural identity. Indeed, by 786 AD George, bishop of Ostia, travelled to England to attend a church meeting, and he reported to the Pope that he had been to 'Angul Saxnia'.

The Anglo-Saxon cultural and military dominance had some important effects on place names in southern Britain and beyond, that reflect these powerful social changes. Firstly, these events represent the expansion of a heathen society into a Christian society. The first Christian communities in southern Romano-Celtic Britain appeared in the early years of the 3rd century AD. Christianisation intensified with the legalisation of the Christian religion under Constantine the Great in the early 4th century and had even by then produced its own heretic in Pelagius, a British theologian. The first Anglo-Saxon king to accept baptism was Æthelberht of Kent around 597 AD. The conversion of the Anglo-Saxons in England was a process spanning mainly the 7th century, but was not a smooth process and suffered numerous setbacks. It was essentially the result of the Gregorian mission of 597 AD, sent by Pope Gregory the Great and which was joined by the efforts of the Hiberno-Scottish mission from the 630s AD. The Anglo-Saxon expansion of the 5th century seeded from south east Britain spread slowly outwards over several hundred years. Place names of heathen origin related to gods and shrines mirror this expansion like an incoming tide which ebbs around the centre of England. Many of these pagan shrines were purposefully destroyed during the Christianisation of the Anglo-Saxons of the 7th century, but their echoes still reverberate in the forms of place names. These pagan place names include those associated with the god Woden as in Woodnesborough in Kent, Wansdyke in Wiltshire and Wensley in Derbyshire, Wednesbury in Staffordshire. Place names derived from the god Thunor are found as Thundersley in Essex, Thunderfield in Surrey, Tiw and Tysoe in Warwickshire and Wye in Kent. The Old English word 'weoh' means idol or 'shrine'. Old English place names associated with pagan shrines include Puckeridge in Hertfordshire, Hascombe in Surrey from 'haegtesse' meaning 'witch' and 'hearg'. Harrow. In contrast, in the Celtic west, from Penzance (Holyhead) to Holyhead in Anglesey (St Cybi's Head), there are many place names associated with Christian beliefs.

Secondly, as the culture and language of the Insular Celts fragmented, a significant number migrated to mainland Europe and established kingdom colonies in Brittany, the Channel Islands and Britonia in modern Galicia, Spain, where in the 7th C a British Celtic Christian church was established. The Temple of Breton still stands in Bretona and is considered the heir to the ancient capital of the Britons of Galicia. Britonia seems to have disappeared by 900 AD.[1]

---

[1] The migration of Brittonic Celts to north west France combined with a residue of Gaulish (Celtic) speakers formed the kingdom of Brittany, meaning 'lesser Britain' (in Modern Welsh Llyddaw). The name Great Britain evolved to avoid confusion with Lesser Britain. In turn, not to be confused in modern times with the TV series 'Little Britain'!

Thirdly, the expansion of the Anglo-Saxons towards the west and north of Britain created a wedge between the tribes of the Brittonic Celts and may have further catalysed the divergence of the Common Brittonic Celt language into Cornish, Welsh, Breton and Cumbric Celt. The Cumbric language of the Hen Ogled, 'the Old North' and southern Scotland, became extinct after the 11th century. The remnants of the Pictish language in the north of Scotland eventually disappeared as the Scoti invaded from Ireland. In the 5th and 6th century the related language of Goidelic Celt, in northern Britain, was splitting into Gaelic Irish, Scot and Manx. It does not seem to take long for languages to significantly diverge when populations are geographically isolated. Evidently, sometimes less than a few hundred years.

Celts who stayed in England were gradually assimilated, rather like the name of the town, Much Wenlock. It gets its 'Much' from the Anglo-Saxon Old English 'mycel', meaning 'great' or 'much'. Wenlock comes from Celtic 'wininicas', meaning 'white area', and the Old English 'loca' meaning an 'enclosed place'. There are a good many other hybrid names, consisting of a Celtic word to which an Old English element has been added as in Lichfield, Manchester and Bredon. These Celtic names incorporated into hybrid place names can sometimes reflect the survival of a British population within the occupied areas. Lichfield is another Celtic-Anglo-Saxon hybrid name. Place names such as Eccleshall in Staffordshire, Eccleswall, Herefordshire and Exhall in Warickshire are all formed from the Old English 'ecles', itself a word borrowed from the Celtic word 'eglwys' meaning 'church'. This suggests that Celtic Christian churches continued their role within the community after the Roman era and were recognised by the pagan Anglo-Saxon settlers.

In the study of the origins and meaning of place names we are very indebted to the numerous Anglo-Saxon charters; even those that did not survive were fortunately copied. These documents date from the Early Medieval Period spanning the 5th to 11th centuries. This period was formerly labelled the 'Dark Ages', meaning an intellectual darkness when compared to periods of intellectual and conceptual revolution which became known as 'The Enlightenment'. However, the industrious and particular Anglo-Saxons were very busy writing charters, typically relating to land grants or recording privileges, so there is no 'darkness' in relation to contemporary information. The earliest surviving charters were drawn up in the 670s and these contain grants of land to the Church. From the 8th century charters were increasingly relating to the granting of land to the lay people. The Early Medieval Period was also a time of both great Old English place name formation and documentation. The Anglo-Saxons were competent organisers with efficient administration and elaborate legal systems and avid recorders. Indeed, many law codes were written down from the early 7th century and began the ground work towards democracy, predating the Magna Carta by 600 years. They were also skilled artists as shown in many of their manuscripts such as the Lindisfarne Gospels or the Benedictional of Aethelwold and skilled craftsmen reflected in the metal, glass and gold artefacts found at Sutton Hoo and in the Staffordshire Hoard.

The oldest Old English place names are found in the south and east England from the 5th century and reflect the direction and progress of the Anglo-Saxon expansion. They have a pragmatic, direct, no-nonsense ring to them! We are again indebted to their authors for their descriptive richness which provide details about their way of life and the nature of the places they lived. Thus, many modern English place names can be traced back to these charters, among other sources, and many reflect the surge in the activity of place-name creating between the 5th and 10th centuries. Table 3 lists some of the common Old English words still found in modern English place names. However, when these early places were originally named, the Old English language was not generally a written one. Therefore, spellings of the same place even with the same intended meaning could change significantly over time.

Table 3 Old English Words Commonly Found in Modern English Place Names and their Meaning	
burg, byrig	fortified settlement
beorg, beorh,	hill
broc	brook, badger
ceaster	settlement by a Roman fort
dun	hill
ham	homestead, village, often by a water meadow
heah	high
holt	woodlands, often of single species trees
ingas (-ing)	the people of
leah	woodland clearing
stoc	secondary settlement dependant on another
tun	village
wic	a specialised farm or trading settlement, often dairy
worthing	enclosed settlement

Within England there is a recognisable variation of place names of Old English origin which reflects the different tribal dialects and sometimes different meanings of the same words. The word 'ham' in most of Anglo-Saxon England meant a small settlement and can also mean a flat piece of land in the bend of a river. However, in Worcestershire and Gloucestershire, the area settled by the Anglo-Saxon tribe the Hiwicci, it is specifically related to a settlement on a river or stream in a water meadow. Many modern place names in England reflect the different language trajectories taken by different regions and their dialects. 'Ley' is practically nonexistent south of the Worcestershire Avon but 'ham' and 'ton' are common. Swanage appears as Swanawic in the Anglo-Saxon Chronicle under 877, Swanwic in the Doomsday Book in 1086 and Swanewiz in 1183, Old English 'swan' meaning 'herdsman' and 'wic' a specialised farm or trading centre. This change from the suffix 'wic' to 'age' is common in southern England contrasting to little change in other areas where 'wic' to 'wick' is common. Place names with the suffix 'ge' Old English 'district' are common in the south east. However, Cressage, in Shropshire is Cristesache in 1086 from Old English 'Crist' meaning 'Christ' and 'ac' meaning 'oak', probably relates to a place where missionaries preached. Thus, place names from very different origins can converge to a similar form.

Although the new Anglo-Saxons immigrants had a tendency to avoid Roman towns and urbanisations, preferring settlements in a rural landscape, they did frequently use the sites of old well-positioned Roman fortifications. Settlements would then grow up around these areas and would invariably include the Old English word 'ceaster' from the Latin 'castra' meaning 'military camp'. Examples from the Midlands are Worcester and Gloucester but in other regions the word 'chester' was used as in Colchester and Dorchester. The archaeological evidence suggests that for most of the 5th and 6th centuries Britain was a rural society and the towns and cities of post-Roman Britain were depopulated. Anglo-Saxon settlements that were established between 450 and 550 were strikingly non-urban in character.

A common type of settlement name in both Celtic and later in Anglo-Saxon England were folk names, most reflecting personal names. The Old English 'ingas' means 'descendants, followers or people of'. So, Reading is Old English 'the people of Reada' and Hastings means 'the people of Haesta' the latter keeping its pleural form. Toponymists have traditionally assessed place names that include the element 'ingas' as the oldest English settlements but this has been more recently challenged. It can be found forming a compound name with a local feature of the landscape as in Avening, Gloucestershire, meaning 'people of the Avon' and Epping from 'the upland people'.

The regional dialects within Anglo-Saxon England is demonstrated by comparing the first line of the Lord's Prayer in the years after their conversion to Christianity:

West Saxon	Faeder ure, thu eart on heofonum
Mercian	Feder ure, thu eart on heofenum
Northumbrian	Faeder urer, thu art on heofonu

Thus, the wide variety of dialects found in current English regions are related to this initial divergence from the three slightly different original dialects of the Saxons, Angles and Jutes.

The location of many of the 2,000 miles of Roman roads in Britain are known but only by their Anglo-Saxon names, such as Akeman Street, Deer Street and Portway. Stretton, literally meaning in Old English 'town on a street' describes a town on a Roman Road. Of the nineteen 'Strettons' in England, seventeen are on a Roman Road.

As commerce and social interactions between nearby villages of the same name became more frequent, they were often distinguished by additional elements to a place name as in Upper and Lower Slaughter from the Old English 'slohtre' meaning 'muddy place' or 'ravine, deep channel'.

Most Anglo-Saxons (including children over 10 years of age) worked on the land. This agricultural society is reflected in the many place names with the suffix 'leah' meaning 'woodland clearing', as in Barnsley, Bromley and Crawley. It has been estimated that woodlands covered about 30% of England by the Early Medieval Period (three times more woodland coverage than now). The Anglo-Saxons were also skilled craftsmen, their close relationship with timber revealed by the variety of words for the management of woodlands such as 'holt, a single species wood and 'graef' meaning 'coppiced trees'. There were many names given to hills that described subtle differences in shape and position. A wood on a sloping hill was known as a 'hangra' and a wooded hill a 'hyrst'. Some topographical words were loaned from Celtic such as the Old English 'cumb' meaning 'valley' from Celtic 'cwm' and 'pen' meaning 'hill'.

Some words can have many different meanings depending on their location such as 'wich' and 'wic', these forms can also have different meanings in several languages. It is used in Old Norse meaning 'farm' as in Keswick (cheese farm) and in Old English, 'wic' meaning a specialist farm, but in Roman Latin 'wich' represents 'victus' meaning 'place' but a 'wick' in a coastal setting is often Old Norse denoting a 'bay' or 'inlet' as in Lerwick.

Place names can also give hints to the quality of land and how it was used. A word of Celtic origin 'fryhth(e)' means land overgrown with brush wood by the edge of a forest, of less agricultural quality and now commonly found in the names Frith and Thrift. The first field names which still survive were coined by the Anglo-Saxons, although it is likely that Neolithic and Bronze Age farmers also gave names to their fields. Linguistics expert Dr Paul Cavill describes many of the 45,000 field names in his book, the New Dictionary of English Field Names.

In the 10th century just when England was first united the new kingdom was divided into shires. These were administrative areas with a court and bailiff or reeve whose task it was to represent the king within those bounds and became known as the sheriff. Thus, the names of the counties of England are derived from this time.

Old English place names extend beyond the border of modern England into south east Scotland and south east Wales. An excellent, and much later example, of the association of place names and ethnicity is demonstrated by the Landsker Line which runs through south west Wales. The word is derived from Old English meaning a visible border between two tracts of land. The Landsker Line demarcates a boundary between the English speaking population of south Pembroke shire and south Gower, associated with many English place names (sometimes called Little England Beyond Wales) and a Welsh-speaking population living predominantly in settlements of Welsh place names to the north. The boundary is also marked by a series of Anglo-Norman and Welsh castles and defensive systems constructed during the 11th and 12th centuries. More recent genetic population studies have also demonstrated this north-south divide in a genetic ethnic sense. So, the evidence of these ethnic cultural divisions has persisted for almost a millennium.[2]

Evidence from Genetic Studies

Several recent genetic studies have consistently demonstrated the effect of Anglo-Saxon migrations on the composition of the genetic make-up of modern England. Anglo-Saxon contributions to the gene pool vary by region, tending to be highest in eastern, southern, central England and Yorkshire with up to 50% recorded. These genetic signatures concord well with the known initial expansion and distributions of Anglo-Saxons in southern Britain during the 5th and 6th centuries. These studies show that the Anglo-Saxons have had by far the greatest impact on our ancestry and also settles a historical controversy in showing that the Anglo-Saxons intermarried with, rather than replaced, the existing populations.

---

[2] The western seaboard of Britain has witnessed movements of many different cultures and languages which are reflected in place names. These include, in addition to English, Roman, Viking, Scandinavian and Irish influence. During the 4th and 5th centuries, the Irish landed on the coasts of Cornwall, Wales and western Scotland. In south west Wales they founded dynasties in Dyfed and Brycheiniog (Brecon), both place names of Irish (Gaelic) origin. Some Irish words were adopted into the Welsh language, including 'cnwc', meaning 'hill', often found in names of peaks in the Preseli Mountains in Pembrokeshire. The word 'feidr' is thought to derive from Gaelic and is found in several road names in Pembrokeshire including Feidr Brenin (the Kings Road), Feidr Ganol (Central or Middle Road) and Feidr Wynt (Road of the Wind). Irish Gaelic died out as a living language in Dyfed sometime in the 7th century.

Two studies published in 2016, based on data collected from bodies found in Iron Age, Roman and Anglo-Saxon era burials, concluded that the ancestry of the modern English population contained large contributions from both Anglo-Saxon migrants and Romano-British natives. In Schifells studies Anglo-Saxon genetic samples were closely related to modern Dutch and Danish populations while Iron Age samples share ancestors with multiple North European populations including Britain.

Since 2010, use has been made of technologies which can test hundreds of thousands of possible mutation points (SNPs) in the rest of the human genome (the autosomal DNA). The results of these large studies have shown that the main patterns of relatedness between European populations are simply geographical, meaning that the British and Irish are most genetically related to the people in neighbouring countries.

Chapter 11 The Scandinavians in Southern Britain

Of life and goods did the grim warrior
rob men wrongfully;
by the way which was watched by him,
no quick wight ever came
The lay which now learned thou hast
thou shalt speak and spread 'mongst the quick:
the Sun Song, which in sooth will be
found to be lying the least
Extract from *The Sun Song* (Sólarlióth), Old Norse Poem, 1200 AD

THE first documented account of a Viking raid on England was a landing on the Isle of Portland in 787. Many were to follow including the looting of Lindisfarne in 793, Jarrow in 794 and Iona in 795. Monasteries and minster churches were targeted as they contained easily portable wealth. Raids were a regular occurrence over a wide distribution of coastal England in the period to 850. The Scandinavian invasions, comprising mostly Norwegians and Danes and some Swedes, occurred over the 9th, 10th and 11th centuries. The Old Norse word 'vikingr' was initially used for someone of any ethnicity who went on expeditions abroad by sea and usually in a group, so the equivalent of a modern day 'sailor'.

In 865 'The Great Heathen Army' appeared on the East Anglia coast. Following on from this successful invasion, the Anglo-Saxon Chronicle tells us that Viking warriors, having previously sought treasure 'proceeded to plough and support themselves'.

The Danes settled mainly in East Anglia, the East Midlands and most of present-day Yorkshire and the Norwegians colonised mainly the north west including present-day Lancashire and Cumbria, the north west Scotland, many of the Western Isles and Isle of Man.

The ensuing conflicts between the Danes and the Anglo-Saxon kingdoms of Mercia and Wessex waxed and waned over several decades. Wessex was invaded by the Danes in 871, and Alfred was compelled to pay them Danegeld to leave. Similar events were playing out in Anglo-Saxon Mercia where in 874 King Burgred was toppled and a 'puppet' placed on the throne. The Danes re-invaded Wessex in 876, but were forced to withdraw but in 878, they forced Alfred to flee to the Somerset levels but were eventually defeated at the Battle of Edington in the same year. After the battle the Viking leader, Guthrum, converted to Christianity, and 886 Alfred took London from the Vikings and fortified it. The same year he signed a treaty with Guthrum which partitioned England by a line drawn approximately between Chester and London. The eastern side of this boundary was under Danish rule for the next two centuries and this colony became known in the 11th century as Danelaw, where people were subject to Danish laws and Alfred became king of the rest of England.

On several occasions Viking Armies ventured deep into Mercia. In 894 AD they over extended themselves and met a combined army of Mercians and Celts at Buttington near Offa's Dyke, Welshpool. Several Viking kings were slain and much of the army lost and this reverse weakened the Danes in England. In commemoration of this battle the locals planted the Buttington Oak which survived until 2018 after being badly damaged by a storm in 2017. Thus, there is very little evidence of occupancy of the Danes west of Danelaw. An exception is Danesford on the River Severn just south of Bridgnorth, Shropshire. A Danish army over-wintered there in 896 in an attempt to take Bridgnorth. The Saxon Chronicle tells us "they made their way overland until they arrived at Quatbridge on the Severn, and there they constructed a fort. They then sat that winter out there". However, the Danes were not allowed to build a permanent settlement as Ealorman Aethered kept harrying them on behalf of King Alfred until they moved on. This gives an interesting insight into the origins of a place name. Even though a Danish army occupied the locality for one winter, it was thought significant enough to name the place Danesford.

Alfred's grandson, Athelstan, became the first true King of England by leading an English victory over the Vikings at the Battle of Brunaburh in 937 and his kingdom included the Danelaw for the first time. In 954, Eric Bloodaxe, the last Viking king of York, was killed and his kingdom was taken over by English earls. By 960 the Danes had been all but overthrown in England and their power dissolved.

Their Old Danish and Old Norse languages though, both of Germanic origin, referred to as Old Scandinavian, left their mark with hundreds of Old Scandinavian place names still discernible in England today. As implied by the brief history of the Viking and Anglo-Saxon conflicts, Old Scandinavian place names are rare in the West Midlands and in southern England. Some Scandinavian place names in southern England, such as East Garston and Swainston, may be named after Scandinavians who belonged to the bodyguard of the kings of Wessex such as King Cnut or Edward the Confessor.

Table 4 lists some common Old Scandinavian words found in place names of modern England. There are around 1,400 place names in England of Scandinavian origin mainly in the area of what later came to be known as Danelaw. Many names are entirely of Scandinavian origin include Kirkby, Lowestoft, Scunthorpe and Braithwaite. A recurring memento of Danish occupation is the element 'by' meaning 'farm' in continental Europe. However, in the Old Scandiavian of Anglo-Saxon England it meant 'homestead' as in Derby, Kirkby and Whitby. This became a loan word into Old English and today it has come to mean 'locality' as in our bye-laws and bye-ways. Another loan word into Old English is the Old Scandinavian word for island 'ey' which is now found widely in England. It also describes inland 'islands' far from the coast - often describing slightly higher and firmer ground surrounded by a marshy area. There are many examples of place names containing this element such as the villages of Eye, found in Cambridge, Suffolk and Herefordshire. Other examples of the 139 known loan words from Old Scandinavian in to OE include 'berserkr', berserk (originally meaning a Viking warrior who charged into battle with no armour and wearing only animal skin!), 'myki', muck and of course, our day of the week 'porsdagrr', 'Thor's Day' or Thursday.

Some are hybrid names, a mixture of Old English and Old Scandinavian such as Durham (from Old English 'dun', hill, and Old Scandinavian 'holm', island) and Welby (Old English 'wella', spring or stream and OS 'by', farmstead') and Woolthorpe (Old English person name Wulfstan and Old Scandinavian 'thorpe', an outlying village dependent on another village).Other place names might be from either language reflecting the similar words and common historical origins of the languages - Snape (Old English 'snaep', boggy piece of land or Old Scandinavian 'snap', poor land). Some place names such as

Carlton, are not found in Scandinavia so most likely a Scandinavianisation of the Old English Ceorlatun and Kettleburgh (Old English name Cetel but with the Old Scandinavian 'k' and Old English 'beorg').

Place names can sometimes provide an insight into how different cultures lived when in close proximity to one another. This is particularly useful when supported by archeological evidence. In north west England there is some evidence of social stratification between Anglo-Saxon and Scandinavian settlers. Fellow-Jenson in a 1985 study revealed a pattern of Scandinavian farmers occupying land over 800 feet and associated with poorer agricultural soil than their Anglo-Saxon neighbours situated in the valleys below. A similar pattern has been identified in modern Lincolnshire and Nottinghamshire where the place name evidence strongly suggests that the Old English named villages are situated on the most desirable agricultural land compared to the Old Danish named settlements.

Table 4 Common Old Norse and Old Danish Words found in Modern England	
beck	stream
by	settlement
ey	island
firth	inlet
gill, ghyll	gully
kirk	church
lund	grove
ness	promontory, headland, (literally 'nose')
tarn	lake
thorpe	secondary settlement dependant on another
thwaite	clearing, meadow
toft	homestead, particularly on a hill

Viking raids and sometimes occupation on the west coast of Britain have left their imprint, especially on islands such as Orkney, Anglesey (Ogull's island),

Skomer (Cloven Island), Lundy (Puffin Island) and also of major towns such as Swansea (Sveinn's island), Lerwick (Mud Inlet) and Stornoway (Steering bay).

Orkney is particularly interesting as the Romans were aware of and probably circumnavigated the islands which they called the "Orcades". This was originally a tribal Pictish name meaning young pigs or young boar. Norwegian settlers arriving over a thousand years later in the late 9th century reinterpreted the name orc as the Old Norse name orkin 'seal' and added 'eyjar' meaning 'islands' so becoming Orkneyjar. It is now thought unlikely that it derives from 'orc' the Latin name for whale. Indeed, fossil and archeological finds have confirmed the presence of wild boar on the island in the past.

Probably, best known for their navigational skills and marine technology, colonisers and traders they were also experienced farmers, carpenters and metal workers; hacksilver is a characteristic find marking these times. Their artwork was highly stylised, with animal shapes and abstract patterns often adorning functional objects such as drinking horn finials. They affirmed their religious beliefs through jewellery, many wearing Thor's Hammer relating to a belief that Thor defended the order of the gods against their foes using the might of the hammer.

The Evidence from Genetic Studies

Another important Viking influence was the long-standing connection between North Eastern England and Denmark, part of the Danelaw territory during the Early Medieval Period. Although the Normans were partly descended from Vikings, some studies have suggested no obvious genetic signature of the Danish Vikings, even though, as we have seen, they controlled large parts of England for around two hundred years. However, an ancient DNA study by Margaryan published in Nature in 2020 noted samples from Denmark showed similarities with samples from modern Denmark and modern England. This study also suggested that modern British populations carry about 6% of 'Swedish-like' ancestry that was present in Danish Vikings. The People of the British Isles (PoBI) project found the population in Orkney emerged as the most genetically distinct, with 25% of DNA derived from Norwegian ancestors. This shows clear evidence of invasion with diffusion, assimilation and intermarriage with the indigenous Orkney population and with no evidence of significant replacement. Another study into the Norwegian Viking ancestry of British and Irish people found evidence of particular concentrations in certain areas, especially the North Sea islands of Shetland, but also to a lesser extent the Western Isles, including Skye in Scotland, Anglesey, the Isle of Man, the Wirral, West Lancashire and Cumbria. This recent genetic data is consistent with the story told by historical records.

Chapter 12 The Normans

"Life yields only to be conqueror. Never accept what can be gained by giving in."
William the Conqueror.

THE significance of the year 1066 is widely known. There is probably less awareness that it took the Normans around six more years to subdue the population, neutralise foreign threats from the Danes and Scots and for William to achieve relative security of his throne. The Norman war machine was efficient and, at times brutal but even so occasional revolts continued until 1075.

There were many consequences of the conquest. William eliminated the old English aristocracy and dispossessed Anglo-Saxons of their lands. Only a handful of English sheriffs remained in office. Similarly, he took over control of the Catholic Church in England replacing all but two Anglo-Saxon bishops with Norman bishops. Another consequence of the invasion was the introduction of a new type of feudal system to England. Although William set about allocating parcels of land to his family, his Norman lords and the church, their legal status were tenants-in-chief who occupied the land but ownership was kept by the king. This type of feudal land tenure provided great honours to the holder but also many responsibilities of homage, reverence and submission to the king including providing knights and men for military service. Indeed, the peasantry was not as adversely affected by the Norman Conquest as the nobility. Anglo-Saxon commoners were given the legal status Englishry, from the Old French 'Englescherie' meaning a person of native Anglo-Saxon stock. The 'presentment of Englishery' was particularly important in relation to the administrative district, or hundred, when an unknown man was found slain. If it could be proven that the slain man was English then the hundred would not be fined. Otherwise, it was presumed he was a Norman and the hundred fined accordingly.

Norman motte and bailey castles were erected, initially of wood and later of stone and these introductions reshaped warfare at the time. Rural life was organised around these castles or manors as serfs and villeins worked for their lord's estate in a system called manorialism. Many of these lords also owned estates in Normandy, so England and France became historically connected and trade between England and the Continent was greatly increased.

Between 1086-1087 a very detailed and systematic catalogue of the assets and wealth of England was ordered by William the Conqueror and compiled in the Domesday Book, (in Latin 'Liber de Wintonia' or the 'Book of Winchester'). The information accumulated in this 'Great Survey' has become extremely helpful in place name studies including some 13,000 settlements, mostly in England but also included some settlements in parts of Wales.

As were the circumstances in previous invasions of Britain, by the Romans and by the Anglo-Saxons, the Normans were vastly outnumbered by the indigenous population. Historians estimate that Norman landlords numbered only around 8,000, with 200 Norman nobles and 100 bishops and monasteries among a population of 1.5 to 2 million which increased significantly between 1050 and 1300.

An important change was the introduction to England of the Old French language which was not closely related to the Germanic languages spoken in England's recent past. This change in vocabulary, syntax and pronunciation would have long lasting effects on place names. An interesting consequence of the different languages spoken by the Norman conquerors and the Anglo-Saxon conquered were the words used to describe the different aspects of essentially similar items. The expensive end stage of meat production became known by words related to the Old French as used by the consumers. Examples are 'boef', 'veel', 'porc', 'muton', 'puoletrie' and 'venesoun', in Modern English 'beef, veal, pork, poultry and venison'. The production end of the process, as carried out by predominantly Anglo-Saxon farmers, used Old English derived words such as 'cu, cealf, 'swin' and 'picga', 'hen', cicen and 'deor'. In Modern English 'cow, calf, pig, piglet, hen, chicken and deer'. However, the number of English place names of French origin are relatively small and are mostly related to the Norman aristocracy, their castles, estates and their monasteries such as Battle (named after the Battle of Hastings), Belvoir, Grosmont, Richmond and Beaumaris.

The Normans inherited the Anglo-Saxon shire administrative systems gratefully as they were superior to their own. However, the Normans referred to the old shires as counties.

The names of towns and villages on land owned by the great French speaking feudal families often acquired the family names. They were particularly used to distinguish places with the same name such as Kingston Lacey and Stanton Lacey. Often Norman families added their own names to place names of Old English towns. So, the Old English names of Shepton, Stoke and Thurrock became Shepton Mallett, Stoke Mandeville and Grays Thurrock. Some hybrid names have been compounded as in Herstmonceux and Stogursey. The Norman church often added an ecclesiastical name to an Old English place name such as Bishopsbourne and Abbotsham to signify that they had become the new owners of the land.

The Normans found Old English a rather coarse language and had difficulty pronouncing its words. Scribes often changed words to soften them, so the Norman influence on the form of place names is significant. A notable example is the change from 'ch' to 'c' and the loss of the 's' before 't', substitution of 't' for Old English 'th' and 'v' for 'f'. Many words became softened, Old English 'burg or byrig', pronounced 'burx', becoming 'bough' and later 'borough'. The city of Nottingham is a good example, first recorded in the late 9th century as 'Snotengaham' and in the Domesday Book of 1086 as 'Snotingeham'. Both are of Anglo-Saxon origin meaning 'Homestead of the family or followers of Snot'. The settlement lost the 's' in the 12th century as the Norman had great difficulty pronouncing the original Anglo-Saxon name! Indeed, some pronunciations in Old English did not exist in Norman French.

The Evidence from Genetic Studies
There is little genetic evidence to suggest, like the Romans before them, that more than a relatively small number of elite Normans settled in Britain. Thus, there has been little effect in subsequent generations. It is the written records, archaeological evidence and place name studies that reveal the wider impact of 1066.

Chapter 13 Late and Post-Medieval England

WE have already met the original insular Anglo-Saxon Old English language. The language spoken by the majority of the population between the 11th to 15th century is known as Middle English and there are many place names that originate from this period. One of the characteristics of place names in the Late Medieval period relates to the increasing use of Latin as the main language of the church and administration. Latin elements were introduced primarily to distinguish settlements with identical names by affixing Forum 'market', Magna 'great' and Regis 'of the king'. Indeed, there has been a long tradition in England of royal patronage. There are about a dozen places in England that have been granted the title 'royal' by royal charter or similar authority initiated by the monarch. Kingston upon Thames was the site of the Coronation of Aethelstan in 924/925 and Eadred in 946 and described as a royal town in a charter. Most other royal towns were granted after 1500 and include Sutton Coalfield bestowed by Henry VIII, Leamington Spa in 1838 and Tunbridge Wells in 1909.

However, surprisingly few place names are of post-Medieval origin (after 1500), but those that did appear in this period often commemorated important people and memorable events. These include famous military men such as Wellington and Nelson and innovative engineers such as Telford and Brunel. Important battles were also marked as in the towns of Waterloo and Blenheim. Biblical names, such as Bethlehem (1588), Bethesda (1823) are common in the west of Britain. Westward Ho! is unusual as the name is taken from the title of the historical novel by Charles Kingsbury published in 1855 and used to promote tourism to the town.

A handful of names are associated with the Industrial Revolution and the arrival of railways in particular Fleetwood founded by and named after a local MP. Landowners are commemorated as in Camden Town and immigrants as in Chinatown.

In the past many street names were given a functional element relating to some of the activities that went on there. Thus, Pudding Lane, where the Fire of London started in 1666, Old Fish Lane, Church Street and Mill Lane all provide clues as to important activities of life that were conducted there. In 'red light' areas where prostitution was common 'Grope Street' was not uncommon and for reasons of social sensibilities these are often re-labelled as Grape Street without any historical basis. However, it is reassuring to witness new building project developers acknowledging local historical events, famous local people and natural features.

When two cities, towns or districts have been amalgamated for practical socio-political reasons rather than to create a new name their original names are often preserved such as in Telford and Wrekin and when Hinckley merged with Market Bosworth to become Hinckley and Bosworth. This both helps dealing with the sensitivities inherent in such mergers and also retains the historical origins and symbolic nature of place names.

Another characteristic feature of modern place naming is to convey a particular atmosphere to an area. New residential developments are often given the addition of 'Village' or 'Green' to create a rustic image. Sometimes a place is named to give an air of sophistication and prestige by choosing a symbol of 'high status' such as Bloomsbury or Knightsbridge originally districts in the West End of London

It is likely all these trends will continue into the future and place names will commemorate contemporary notable people, events and historical locations, reflect social change, changes in the use of localities and technological advances. I can well imagine that in the future a locality where the public embark on journeys into space is designated by an appropriate eponym, local event or topographic feature followed by 'Space Port'.

Chapter 14 The Call of the Wild

"We are not separate from Nature, it is not a place to visit. It is home."

THE primary evidence for the former occurrence of now extinct species is archaeological, or when available, documentary. However, the natural history of past times is also well described in place names and reflects our ancestor's close relationship with and dependence upon their surrounding and local natural resources. There are elements of old place names for fauna and flora including trees, plants, animals, birds, fish and even insects. Some place names in England are called after the species or types of wildlife that lived there at the time. Some of these species have since become extinct and thus these historical markers can provide an indicator of suitable locations for reintroductions, an important element of rewilding.

There are many examples that provide insight into the historical landscape and wildlife of the past. We are fortunate, indeed, that these place names were often coined using very descriptive terms so that even now we can built-up a picture of a locality and the environment at the time. There are over 500 hundred places named after species of trees and plants alone! Trees are found in elements of place names as in the very common name in Acton (Old English 'ac' or 'aec', oak and 'ton' enclosed settlement) Oakley (Old English 'ac' or 'aec' and 'leah' a woodland clearing), and Lindridge (Old English 'lind' and 'hrycg', the ridge where the lime trees grow) and Ashby (Old Scandinavian from 'askr' and 'by' farmstead or village where the Ash trees grow) and Ashford Old English with elements 'aesc', meaning ford by the ash trees. Sale is derived from 'Salic' Old English 'sealh,' 'willow' and many villages with a prefix of Old English 'hath' such as Hatherton mean 'farmstead where hawthorn grows'.

Croydon derives from the Latin word for crocus, borrowed into Old

English as 'croh', and don from Old English 'denu' meaning valley. The species of saffron called Crocus is not native to Britain and was imported and cultivated in Britain by the Romans for medicinal use. Saffron (from the Arabic 'zaeacran') was also imported after the Crusades and Saffron Walden from Old English 'walh', pleural 'wala' foreigner and Old English 'denu', valley, so 'valley of the British' and later 'where the saffron grows' became a centre for cultivation.

Romsley Worcestershire is Old English 'hremes' and 'leah' so 'clearing of wild garlic' and Dulwich originates from Old English 'dile' and 'wich' giving 'meadow where dill grows'.

Place names containing the element wolf are very widespread in England and Britain with 200 names across most counties. Most names derive from the Old English word 'wulf' from 450 onwards, or the Old Norse 'ulfr' from 900 onwards. They occur mostly in upland areas but not necessarily areas that were wooded at the time of the Doomsday Book. Several studies have used place names to map the distribution of wolves in Anglo-Saxon England and the findings have been collaborated with archaeological finds. Wolves were thus common when the Anglo-Saxons were naming their settlements and landscape, from Wooly Green (Wolfs Wood) in Berkshire, to Woolacombe (Wolfs Valley) in Devon and Wlfstanes (Wolfstones) North Yorkshire. There are no wolf reintroduction programmes in England underway as yet.

Only around 20 place names contain an element of the beaver (OE 'befer' and 'beofer), confirming they were in decline after the 5th/6th century. Beaver place names, not surprisingly, are associated with names related to water as in Beverley Brook and Beverley Lock. The change from 'f' to 'v' is due to the Norman influence. The most recent native beaver sighting was reported in Bolton Percy North Yorkshire in 1789, the same year as the beginning of the French Revolution, when a bounty was paid for its head. Following successful reintroductions in Knapdale and the river Tay in Scotland, The River Otter Beaver Trial in Devon started in 2015 as a 5-year study to assess the effects of Eurasian beaver re-establishment. The report demonstrated benefits to landscape, wildlife and people with three kits born in the first season. One of the best places to view these engaging creatures is outside the village of Otterton! In August 2020 the UK government made a ruling that they could legally stay. This decision represents the first time an extinct native mammal has been legally reintroduced in to the wild in England.

Several place names including Barlow and Barsham commemorate the previous habitation of wild boar as the prefix is from the Old English word 'bar'. The species became extinct in Britain in the 17th century but has since been re-introduced.

Places relating to the red fox, Vulpes vulpes, are very numerous in England often appearing with the prefix as in Foxton and Foscombe, and in Worcestershire as in Foxlydiate.

Some place names refer to rabbits as in Warren Row, Berkshire and Warren Street in Kent from Old French and Middle English.

The badger, Meles meles, is also found in many place names that include the Old English word 'broc' which is probably derived from the Celtic word (Irish 'broc' and Welsh 'broch'). In England examples are Brogborough, Bedfordshire, Bagshaw Derbyshire and Brockhall Lanchaire.

The Old English word for cat is 'catt', but the interpretation of place names is complicated by the use of similar words for personal names. There are records of people named 'Wigga' meaning 'beetle' and 'Putta' meaning 'kite'. Catesby, Northamptonshire, is Old Scandinavian meaning farmstead or village of a man called Katr and Caterham, Surrey, from Celtic 'cadeir' meaning chair-like hill but Catmore, Berkshire, is Old English 'pool frequented by wildcats' and Cathanger, Hampshire, means Old English 'sloping wood frequented by wild cts'. There are a few dozen place names in England which include the suffix cat. The locations of these place names confirm that the wild cat was once widely distributed over Britain but is now limited to the mixed woodlands of north and east Scotland. Although there may be several thousand individuals in the wild, because of hybridisation with domestic cats, only a minority are estimated to meet the morphological and genetic criteria of pure wild cats. The European lynx was hunted to extinction in Britain between 500 to 700 AD primarily for its valued fur. Some place names may be a reference to the lynx rather than the wild cat and the lynx may well be the next top predator to be assessed for a reintroduction programme to areas of northern Britain.

There are around 500 place names in Britain likely to be related to the golden (Old English cognate 'earngeap' and Gaelic 'iolaire') and white-tailed eagles ('yarn'). The ancient distribution of the golden eagle and white-tailed eagle in Britain has been estimated from place names locations and further correlated with archaeological evidence. Some of these place names have origins from over 1,500 years ago. Their distributions in the past have been extremely wide spread and overlapping. As expected, the place names associated with golden eagle include the higher altitude sites such as

Arncliff, North Yorkshire, Earn Gragg, Westmorland and Arnberg Scar, West Yorkshire but also lower locations as in Arley Worcestershire, Arnewood, Hampshire, Ernesborough, Devon and Arne beside Poole Harbour in Dorset. White-tailed eagle locations are also widespread but are more closely related to woodlands, rivers and valleys and include Yarnscombe, Devon, Yarnshaw Hill, Cheshire and Yarnfield, Wiltshire. The Anglo-Saxon names, however, may not always be specific for eagle species as they may not have correctly distinguished between the golden and white-tailed eagle. These sites have correlated well with archeological evidence of species finds and show the white-tailed eagle sites are of earlier origin. These studies indicate that the white-tailed eagle was common in southern Britain in Roman and Anglo-Saxon times and there is no reason to question its reintroduction to southern Britain on historical grounds. In fact, this evidence contributed to the reintroduction of the white-tailed eagle to the Isle of Wight in 2019, 230 years after the species became extinct in southern England.

There are several hundred place names with the prefix 'cran' in England reflecting how abundant and widespread cranes were in the past, including Cranford, Cranbrook, Cranmore and Cranefield in Bedfordshire which is derived from Old English 'cran feld', 'open country frequented by cranes'. There are also many place names in England derived from the Old Scandinavian roots 'trana' or 'trani' that refer to cranes as in Tranmere, in Cheshire, Tranwell in Northumberland and Tranholme in North Riding.

During the festivities to enthrone Archbishop Neville of York in 1465, around 2,500 guests consumed 204 cranes and also on the menu were 4000 pigeons and 4000 crayfish, 2000 chickens, 104 peacocks, 100 dozen quails, 400 swans and 400 herons, 113 oxen, six wild bulls, 608 pikes and bream, twelve porpoises and seals! This menu continues with another 22 species of wild creatures served during the event! The changes in cultural norms makes this sad reading nowadays but probably salivating reading to them. At Henry III's Christmas meal in 1251 he and his guests consumed 115 cranes, accompanied by a menu of bitterns and ducks! Unsurprisingly, cranes became extinct as a breeding bird in the UK in the 17th century as a result of hunting and the draining of wetlands. Standing in a lowland field in Anglo-Saxon England, it would have been difficult to ignore these once plentiful, beautiful birds with their loud trumpeting calls and complex courtship dance. Fortunately, The Great Crane Project, between 2010 to 2014, has successfully re-introduced about 180 birds to England's wetlands, so now cranes live close to their historical namesakes again. This represents, in historical terms, the first breeding in the wild of cranes in England since Queen Elizabeth I occupied the throne!

In Anglo-Saxon Old English, a slang word or nickname for a tall, lanky person with long legs was a 'cran' which is thought to be the root of the surname Crane. Other Old English words meaning Crane are 'cranuc', 'cron', 'cronuc', 'cren' and 'crenuc' but later came to include the word for a heron.

The village of Storrington in West Sussex, was known as 'Estorchestone', or 'homestead of the white storks' in the Domesday Book of 1086 and still uses a stork symbol on its signs. The last breeding pair in Britain was recorded on St Giles' Cathedral, Edinburgh in 1416. Roasted stork was also a popular delicacy in medieval banquets and, in the 16th century, there are records of each bird fetching up to 48 old pence at London markets. A symbol of rebirth and renewal it was persecuted by authorities at times because of a perceived association with rebellion! Fortunately, Storrington has also regained its full former status and true meaning as a result of the White Stork Project, founded in 2016. In season 2020 there was a successful breeding with three chicks hatched.

Many places are named after smaller birds as in 'Finchale' (finch), 'Gawthorpe' (cuckoo) and the more obvious meanings of place names include Rookwith, Swallowcliffe, Crowhurst and Larkhill.

Place names such as Fishlake and Fishbourne are straightforward, but less so are Ely and Alford both named after eels. Insects are represented as in Berwick and Becket (bees). Wigley is derived from the Old English 'wigga' meaning 'beetle' and lives on as our modern word 'earwig'. Gnatham means 'water meadow of the gnats' and Latchmere reflects that the lake was a source of leeches used for medicine.

The study of place names has a part to play in the reintroduction of previously indigenous species, and indeed, in the progressive approach to conservation called rewilding. This process includes the large-scale restoration of ecosystems and the reintroduction of missing species. Reducing human interference seeks to reinstate natural processes and encourage diversity. In short, reducing interference and allowing nature to take care of itself. By gaining an insight into what the landscape, habitats and ecosystems looked like thousands of years ago, we have a good idea of what rewilding is trying to achieve and if and when it has been attained.

Chapter 15 The Diversity of Place Names in Modern England

"The act of naming a place and the resulting diversity of place names is a unique manifestation of the human spirit"

ONE of the most striking features of modern-day England is the amazing diversity of place names that can be found. As we have seen, these reflect the deep tapestry of our common past. Many tongues from many different cultures and languages migrating into Britain are responsible for weaving these threads into something resembling a multi-coloured dream coat linguistic map. There are over 50,000 named cities, towns, villages, hamlets and suburban areas in England, not including all the sub-districts, named smaller areas and all the named features of our landscape. Many are engaging, some strange, some comical, some alien, some seem rude to us and most provide new insights and perspectives into our shared past. Many tell us a story of the localities but also, invariably of the originators and the later modifiers of these names.

The vast majority of these place names are of Anglo-Saxon origin, and therefore, coined in Old English between the 5th to 11th centuries. These Old English place names are particularly prevalent in parts of the country, such as southern and central England, where there has been long and continuous habitation by Anglo-Saxons. However, most of the cultures and languages that have successively occupied these lands are represented. There are discernible patterns of Old Scandinavian names in the north and east England, Celtic names in the north and west England and a scattering of Roman and Norman names particularly in southern England. These different cultures and languages also show themselves in multi-cultural or hybrid names and vary depending upon which was the dominant language in the area at the time.

Some of the most comical names must be Great Snoring, Gigglewick and Nether Wallop. Some strange names include Pity Me, Ashby-de-la-Souche and Ugley and others seem alien like Mamble, Hobby, Rhydd, Aingarth or Symonds Yat. Many place names reveal aspects of the people who coined them. Many farming communities in England are disadvantaged by their impoverished soil but only one place name resonates a plea passed down the decades - Pity Me. Few places in the world have official names written on birth certificates that vary from Botany Bay to Moscow, from California to Gibraltar and from Cupid's Green to Mesopotamia. A true celebration of differences!

Anglo-Saxon charters often define the boundaries of estates and thus many places take their name from these markers. These also add to the diversity found in place names and include 'treow' or 'tree' as in Coventry and 'Elstree', 'doc' or 'ditch' as in Shoreditch and Redditch and 'Stan' or 'stone' as in Bishopstone.

A popular aspect of place names, judging from the plethora of magazine articles on the subject, are those that seem rude or at least comical to our current sensibilities. Table 5 lists a selection of some of the most comical found in England. However, few explain the reasons for this affront which are often reactions based on misunderstandings between different cultures and languages. There is usually no intention of rudeness or even comedy by their originators. They used words in common usage at the time to convey the intended meaning. But the nature of language, even related languages, is that they change and diverge over time. Probably, some of the rudest, but not without mirth, place names found in modern Britain might be Scratchy Bottom in Dorset, Nob End in South Lancashire, Broadbottom in Cheshire, Brown Willy in Cornwall, Brokenwind in Aberdeenshire and Horny Old Road, Malvern! However, that is not to suggest that the Anglo-Saxons had no sense of humour, which they certainly did. Already mentioned is the Anglo-Saxon nickname for a tall long-legged person, Old English 'Cran' or 'Cranuc', meaning 'Crane', but also Old English calo' or 'calewe' meaning 'bare' and commonly found in hill names in England. However, in Anglo-Saxon England it was a nick-name for a bald- headed man and was still in use in the 13th century as 'le kalewe'. The Wheatear, an insectivorous bird of open country, is derived from the Anglo-Saxon, meaning 'white arse' after the prominent white rump found in most species. Comical to us but not to them, as those were the descriptive words used at the time. To understand the original intended meaning and how and why these names have arrived to their present form it is necessary to gather as many of the recorded intermediate variations as possible.

Diversity also derives from the many examples of multi-lingual or hybrid place names across England. As expected in the western most parts, Old English-Celtic hybrids predominate such as Much Wenlock, already mentioned, and Malvern a hybrid place name from Celtic 'moel' meaning bare and 'fryn', a variant of Celtic 'bryn' meaning hill. There is no 'v' in either the Old English or Celtic alphabet so this letter appears from an Old French Norman influence. Manchester is also an Old English-Celtic hybrid, in 1086, Mamecestre, from Celtic 'mamm' probably meaning 'breast-like hill' and Old English 'cestre' settlement by a Roman fort.

Old English-Old Scandinavian hybrid names are found in the region that was within the Danelaw as in Durham, in 1056 Dunholm, from Old English 'dun', hill and Old Scandinavian 'holmr' meaning island. Ashby-de-la-Souche is part Old English, part Old Scandinavian, part Old French! In 1086, written 'Ashby', so of Anglo-Danish origin, meaning 'farmstead where the Ash trees grow'. During the reign of Henry III in the 13th century Ashby came into the possession of the La Souche family.

An interesting choice of a place name element which also adds variety appears as an onomatopoeia. An example is found in Ludlow from the Old English words 'hlude' meaning 'noisy' and 'hldw' meaning 'mound', and refers to the waterfalls on the River Teme which flows around the beautiful town set on its hill.

Table 5 Some Unintended Comical Place Names in England		
Modern Place Name	**Language**	**Original Meaning**
Broadbottom, Cheshire	Old English	broad valley bottom
Brown Willy, Cornwall	Cornish Celt	from 'bronn ewhella' meaning 'highest hill'
Crackpot, North Yorkshire	Old Scandinavian Middle English	'kraka' meaning 'crow' 'pot' meaning 'cleft'
Land of Nod, E Yorkshire	Modern English	from the Bible, Genesis, 4:16-18
Mumps, Oldham	Middle English	possibly from 'mumper' slang for beggar
Pity Me, Durham	Modern English	expression for living off poor soil
Plucks Gutter, Kent	Modern English	named after, Ploeg, a Dutch drainage engineer
Nasty, Hertfordshire	Old English	place of the east enclosure
Nob End, South Lancashire	Old English	the end of a rounded premonitory
Scratchy Bottom, Dorset	Old English	a flat valley with rough scrub
Shitterton	Old English	place of an open effluent
Ugley, Essex	Old English	woodland clearing of a man called Ucga
World's End	Modern English	an area or field far away from a village

PART 3 THE PLACE NAMES OF WORCESTERSHIRE

~

Chapter 16 Populating Worcestershire

"Even places you know well can take on a touch of the unknown when you arrive there from a different direction."
Kate Milford from *Shadowhunters and Downworlders*

IN this part we go local, allowing history to arrive at our front doors! This means your front door in any English county or area if you follow and apply the guidance and the resources outlined in chapter 24. Each locality will have their own stories, all fascinating, many different and some unique and will help you get to know and understand why your local settlements and landscape were given their particular names and by whom. These will help you visualise their authors, what it was like to live at the time, their challenges and how they responded.

In Part One I presented indirect evidence for the naming of places in very ancient history, perhaps even 9,000 to 10,000 years ago. Is there any evidence of very ancient place names in Worcestershire, before the Celts brought their Indo-European language to the area? If there were, the places to most likely find them are in the names of the enduring features of the landscape.

Toponymists tend to suggest that the origin of the form of a place name is very ancient if it contains elements not usually found in that language. This finding is often related to the loan of a word or element from another language previously indigenous to the region. This should be, of course, a proposition rather than an assumption that place names difficult or impossible to interpret are necessarily from an unknown ancient language. Several such proposals have been made for some place names in Worcestershire. In order to set the scene, I describe the archaeological and environmental evidence of the periods before the appearance of the attested local place names.

THE PALAEOLITHIC PEOPLE IN WORCESTERSHIRE
The Archeological Evidence
The distribution of finds around the time of those at Kent's Cavern and Paviland Cave suggests that humans in this period preferred the uplands of Wales and northern and western England to the flatter areas of eastern England. Finds in Worcestershire from this time have included flint and Bert hand axes found near Upton-Upon-Severn, Alfrick and Kemerton. We can reasonably speculate that these small bands of Palaeolithic hunters who travelled through the land we now call Worcestershire would have known, named and used a significant topographic feature such as the Malvern Hills as a directional marker. First formed around 600 million years ago, these hills are 2,000 times older than the whole-time span of our species - they are truly enduring features of our landscape to us!

The View from the Malvern Hills in the Palaeolithic Period
If you stood on the Malvern Hills during one of the late Palaeolithic warmer periods (for this and subsequent visits I will grant you the use of binoculars!), you would see an open tundra landscape. Scattered trees, shrubs and sedges would be evident among an expanse of open grasslands with mosses and lichen on exposed rocks. You might make out herds of wild horses and deer, including elk and hairy mammoth. Due to an extremely low population density, you would be very unlikely to meet these Palaeolithic folks at close quarters. Occasionally, you might witness smoke rising from the fire of a small lone Palaeolithic hunting party set in a vast and uninhabited landscape.

THE MESOLITHIC PEOPLE IN WORCESTERSHIRE
The Archeological Evidence
Although Mesolithic sites are widespread in Britain there is a higher

concentration of known locations in the south east and north and few in the English Midlands. In south east Worcestershire, however, not far from the village of Broadway, a valley-floor settlement has been excavated and the site has provided evidence of over 60 pieces of worked stone, mainly fashioned from flint cobbles. These artefacts are thought to date to the later Mesolithic Period, and were produced between 8,500 and 5,400 years ago. The commonest Mesolithic artefacts found generally in Worcestershire consist of blades of long narrow flakes of flint. These blades are then further worked into microliths used in composite tools and weapons. Around 1,400 flint tool fragments have been found at Wribbenhall near Kidderminster, along with post holes, a hearth, bullies and a pit. These finds suggest a settlement, perhaps seasonal, which have been dated to around 8,800 years ago and thus the oldest yet identified in Worcestershire. Pollen evidence suggests that woodlands had been cleared at this site and crops grown.

The View from the Malvern Hills in the Mesolithic Period

Although the archaeological evidence of Mesolithic people in Worcestershire is sparse, we have enough accumulated evidence to imagine the scene standing on the Malvern Hills during the Mesolithic Period. The view would be mostly of woodlands, the original 'Wild Woods', with some bare hills rising above the Severn valley and some open areas within the forest encouraged by the grazing of indigenous large herbivores, such as aurochs, tarpan, wisent, elk and the omnivorous wild boar. At this time and, indeed, for most of the Post-Glacial period, the river systems here were tidal and subject to regular flooding, so large bodies of water may well be evident. Later, we will see how successive ancient cultures arriving in the area named these topographic features and it is likely the Mesolithic hunter-fisher gatherers also did so. The ancient Malvern Hills and the relatively young River Severn would have been given names but known only to these people. You may see smoke rising from below Bredon Hill, marking the valley-floor site of a Mesolithic community and which may have been a semi-nomadic, seasonally used settlement. You may see and hear the sounds of wolves, brown bears, lynx, elk and aurochs. Red deer herds were numerous and a prime food source. You may visually identify and hear some of the larger birds such as the crane and the golden and white-tailed eagle gliding above the hills or plying up and down above the River Severn and flood plains. Large flocks of migratory geese and duck would be seen and heard on the flood plains dwarfing the assemblies at the current Wildfowl and Wetlands Trust reserve at Slimbridge further down the estuary. You would be unlikely to directly encounter Mesolithic people themselves as the population density for the Hunter-gatherer way of life is low. Temperate deciduous woodlands are able to support about 0.16 hunter-gatherers per square kilometer and thus the area of current Worcestershire would support only around 300 individuals. What a wonderful feeling of space! Less population density than the current day Falkland Islands, the second least populated country in the world! However, times will change.

THE NEOLITHIC PEOPLE IN WORCESTERSHIRE
The Archeological Evidence

There is more extensive evidence for the Neolithic period in Worcestershire. More aerodynamic leaf-shaped flint arrowheads are found during this period and the largest type found in Worcestershire are the scrapers used for working animal hides. Stone axes from the Neolithic show extensive trade links, including examples from Brittany and northern Italy or Switzerland, as well as Cornwall, North Wales and the Lake District. Pottery finds also start in this period. Finds at Clifton and Severn Stoke, include Grooved ware pottery, axes, and burnt stones used to heat water for cooking or possibly a sauna. An axe head found at Bromsgrove came originally from Langdale, Cumbria. A macehead or shafthole adze was discovered in a stream in the Wyre Forest and a skull from this period at Worcester. Neolithic farming has left many traces, such as crop marks on gravel terraces. Settlements can be identified from post holes, for instance at Huntsman's Quarry, Kemerton. However, the most obvious Neolithic evidence comes from their ritual landscape. At Fladbury, five cursus ceremonial monuments have been discovered, structures that are found at many sites in England and excite much debate and speculation. At Whittington Tump the hill has been heightened to make another ceremonial or burial monument. The estimated population density of Neolithic farmers is around 0.6 people per square kilometre, therefore, Worcestershire may have supported up one to two thousand people at this time.

Linguistic experts have speculated if there are any place name remnants that originate from the Neolithic period or even earlier cultures? These people would have spoken the hypothetical Paleo-European languages and thus a pre-Indo-European language. If present they would most likely appear in river names, particularly those that cannot be easily explained in terms of Celtic or Germanic origin. They remain inaudible.

The View from the Malvern Hills in the Neolithic Period

The view from the Malvern Hills would have revealed a wooded landscape but less so than in the Mesolithic period. A reduction from about 90% to around 60-70% forest coverage and the first significant visual impact of a mosaic pattern on the landscape. The first small permanent settlements might be seen in these woodland clearings with evidence of livestock and arable farming activity. Rectangular wooden framed huts with pitched thatched roofs, finished with wattle and daub might be identified along with smoke rising from the cooking fires within. These would have been particularly in evidence in the Avon and Severn flood plains. You may be lucky enough to spot some Neolithic travellers on the trade routes that passed near modern day Worcester where there was a ford crossing the River Severn. This unknown but almost certainly named long distance thoroughfare was to form part of Ryknild Street improved by the Romans 3,000 to 4,000 years later. Thomas observed that some Neolithic communities did not seem to build megalithic monuments around them and this may apply to Worcestershire. However, to some extent this may be related to the relatively small number of excavations that have been undertaken in the county. Round barrows may have existed at this time on Bredon Hill, North Hill and Crookbarrow Hill at Whittington. The nearest well known Neolithic chambered long barrow is Belas Knap at Cleeve Hill on the Cotswold escarpment around 26 miles south. Belas is probably derived from the Latin word 'bellus' meaning 'beautiful' and the Old English word 'knap' meaning the 'top, crest or summit of a hill'. Most of the fauna and flora extant during the Mesolithic Period would still be evident. However, the elk and aurochs were on the brink of extinction and bears were becoming rare.

BRONZE AGE WORCESTERSHIRE

The Archeological Evidence

The Bronze Age population density had doubled since Neolithic times and Worcestershire would have supported between three to four thousand people. Bronze Age artefacts found in Worcestershire include flat metal axes from the Malvern Hills and barbed flint arrow heads. During the very Late Bronze Age hill forts appeared on Herefordshire Beacon and Midsummer Hill. The latest theories suggest these were used seasonally by local tribes for fairs, markets and religious ceremonies. The name Midsummer Hill itself supports the idea that Bronze and Iron Age tribes used the hill during the warmer seasons. There are a number of 'Summerhills' in Worcestershire possibly with similar origins.

The View from the Malvern Hills in the Bronze Age

If we stood on the Malvern Hills at this time the influences of the Bronze Age people on the landscape would be particularly evident. There would be fewer woodlands as the landscape was becoming predominantly agricultural. Cattle farming was common with recognisable field systems, some resembling modern field boundaries. Smoke rising from round houses of open settlements in the valley floors and burial mounds on Bredon Hill and Kempsey Common would be seen, in addition to the nearby hill forts on the Malvern Hills. The bellowing of the massive aurochs would no longer be heard nor the elk seen. Both driven to extinction by Bronze Age hunters and species such as bear had become rare. As is often the case, among the first species humans tend to exterminate in an ecosystem are the megafauna. In Britain the disappearance of brown bear, lynx, wolf, beaver and elk has been linked, in varying degrees, to hunting and loss of habitat as a direct result of human influence. Likewise, the Dalmatian Pelican disappeared around 2,000 years ago through drainage of habitat and hunting and the White Stalk, Common Crane and Great Auk were to follow. The disappearance of megafauna and the appearance of humans has been a suspicious and recurrent theme of the past, and indeed the present, and is very likely causative. Megamarsupials were disappearing in Australia around 50,000 years ago, from 10,000 years ago the giant sloth, mammoth and the saber-toothed cat Smilodon from North America, and around 6,000 years ago ground sloths and large monkeys in the Caribbean. These dates correspond to the appearance of human migrants to these regions.[3] There is growing evidence that our label as an unprecedented Global Super Predator that preys on other apex predators is well deserved. Our species seems to be good at it as we are likely to have had at least 60,000 years of practice!

We are now in an excellent position to understand the impact of different cultures on the many attested place names of Worcestershire, their origins

---

[3] Recent evidence has questioned the timing of human migration into Australia, with recent data suggesting an earlier appearance around 60,000 to 65,000 years ago. This calls into question if humans were responsible for the extinction of megafauna on the Australian Continent, as they seemed to have coexisted for thousands of years. What is sadly becoming more evident in present times, however, is the effects of human interference on the ecosystems of the planet. Increasing population, increasing consumption, expansion over land and sea, pollution and consequent global warming are reducing the biomass of the planet and increasing the natural background extinction rate by a factor of many hundreds. This is unsustainable.

and meanings and to get to know the people who successively migrated into the area, called it home and who may be your ancestors. We have followed the threads of continuity in the movements of people across southern Britain in the past, their boundaries, religions and ways of life. This continuity continues in the modern-day place names of Worcestershire. We will see how the Celts described the physical properties of the landscape, how the Anglo-Saxons tell us about the details of their lives and the cultural impact of the Normans, mainly through the places they named. The place names of the county reflect its multi-cultural history and hybrid place names may well mirror the cooperation and assimilation between these people. The studying of the meaning of place names allows us to paint a detailed and colourful picture of the activities and lives of the people who have inhabited the area.

Chapter 17 The Celts in Worcestershire

WE continue our journey from the deep past into Iron Age Britain. It might seem strange to start the last leg of our journey to present-day Worcestershire from as early as 500-400 years BC, about 2,500 years ago, but there is sufficient evidence to support the threads of connections and continuity in order to do so. These portals include evidence from place names, language, culture, religious beliefs, archeology, written records, tribal boundaries and, the more recent evidence of genetic population studies. In Worcestershire the biggest influences in creating this rich tapestry of history have been the Celts, Anglo-Saxons and Normans in chronological order.

We do not know for certain when the first people who spoke a Celtic language appeared in Worcestershire. There is evidence that the south east of Britain was under the influence of continental European Iron Age technology by the 8th century BC. Celtic hill forts began appearing in Wessex around this time but became prominent 550 - 400 BC. The Hallstatt culture emerged in south east Britain around the 6th century BC. The earliest chariot burials in Britain are dated to around 500 BC and in England are characteristic of the Iron Age Arras culture of the Parissii tribe. The Hallstatt culture has been tentatively associated with an Indo-European, Proto-Celtic language. Other scholars see Celtic languages as covering Britain and Ireland, and parts of the Continent, long before any evidence of "Celtic" culture is found in archaeology. The rampart and ditch of the Iron Age Midsummer Hill Camp have been dated to around 390 BC. British Camp is estimated to have been built in the 2nd century BC. There is evidence of the La Tene culture (late Iron Age) working tin in Cornwall before 300 BC and La Tène artefacts have been excavated at Beckford, Worcestershire. Two hundred metal money bars discovered near the Wyche Cutting suggests La Tène people inhabited the area around 250 BC. We do not know for sure but these people may have spoken the Brittonic Celt language.

In the centuries before the Roman invasion of Britain many Celtic tribal territories had been established but with some evidence of boundary changes related to invasions from the Europe. The Insular Celtic tribes of southern Britain shared a common language (Common Brittonic or Brythonic Celt), and indeed, they shared many traditions, ways of life and religious beliefs with their continental neighbours. Several Insular Celtic tribes shared the same names as their Continental Celtic neighbours and were probably related, including the Belgae and Atrebates of Belgium and France. Caesar noted that Diviciacus of Suessiones, a powerful king of the Belgic nation had ruled territories in much of Gallia Belgica, but also in Britain. The Parissii tribe of Gaul may also have had close associations, possibly by invasion, of the same named tribe on the East Riding Yorkshire coast.

Insular Celtic and Continental Celtic tribes shared a tradition of naming the area they lived from their tribal name and thus a folk name. They also shared a tendency to use quite bombastic, superlative names to describe themselves. Thus, the Catuvelleni meant the 'battle-excellent ones', the Ancalites, 'the very hard ones', the Brigantes 'the high ones' and the Parisii, 'the commanders' (the same derivation as in the Modern Welsh verb 'peri' 'to cause, command or have done'). It may be, the late Terry Jones, member of the Monty Python Flying Circus and excellent historian knew about these traditions and satirized folk names in the sketch of the medieval 'Knights Who Say Ni'. The Celtic Dobunni tribe (probably pronounced 'DO-BEE-NEE') inhabiting the Severn and Avon valleys at this time may have been unusual in this respect as one of their possible etymologies is from 'bunne', a vessel used in pagan ceremonies before their conversion to Christianity during the 4th century.

The Dobunni tribal boundaries extended to those of modern-day Worcestershire and Gloucestershire and also parts of north Somerset, east Herefordshire and west Warwickshire. Their northern border relates quite closely to modern Worcestershire, the Clents and Lickey Hills forming a natural boundary to the north. Their capital later acquired the Roman name of Corinium Dobunnorum, today known as Cirencester. This was a large tribal area that even today with modern roads and cars would take over an hour to travel - if you are lucky! There are seven references to the tribe in Roman histories and inscriptions. The Venerable Bede (672 - 735 AD), a Benedictine Monk in Northumbria whose most famous work was the Ecclesiastical History of the People of England (731 AD), refers to the Dobunni as occupying this area in the pre-Roman era. We do not know when, how or from where exactly the Dobunni tribe formed. During the Iron Age there is evidence of salt production at Droitwich, a pottery industry in Malvern exporting to the surrounding area and Wyche Cutting, a pass through the Malvern Hills, was used in the Iron Age as a salt route to South Wales.

So, it may be the echoes of the Dobunni that can still be heard in modern Worcestershire settlement and topographic place names of Celtic origin and listed in Tables 6 and 7. They seemed to be a peaceful tribe as they agreed to Roman subjugation during their early contacts with Roman ambassadors and before the arrival of Roman military. Thus, the Dobunni tribal area became a 'civitas', or unit of Roman administration.

It was noted that the tribe was one of the few pre-Roman coin minters. Before around 200 to 300 AD, as all Insular Celtic tribes, they followed heathen traditions. There is some evidence this was later related to a cult of a Romano-British goddess with a focus on worship of the natural world and particularly of rivers.

Many of the basic features of living in Iron Age Worcestershire continued from the previous Bronze Age. The Dobunni were a large tribe of farmers and craftsmen living in small villages of thatched round houses surrounded with a fence or ditch mainly in the Severn and Avon fertile flood plains and the Cotswold escarpment.[4]

---

[4] Celtic languages are phonetic. The Celtic Iceni tribe (probably pronounced E-KEN-E) inhabited a territory roughly equivalent to modern day Norfolk, and is best known for one of their queens, Boudicca (probably pronounced 'BO-DEEC-AH'). The Icknield Way, an ancient track later used by the Romans linking East Anglia to the Chilterns, may have derived from their tribal name.

Table 6 Words of Celtic Origin found in the Place Names of Modern Worcestershire	
Celtic Word	**Modern English Meaning**
afon	river
bryn	hill
cwr	corner, edge, limit, corner
dwfr	water
ffridd	common land, scrubland
gwen	white
heddioc	barley field
mamm	breast, mother
moel	bare
mynydd	mountain
onnen	ash tree
rhyd	ford
pen	head of
wyre	winding, spreading

By the late Iron Age some of these villages would have coalesced into larger settlements such as at Bath, Cirencester and Gloucester - the main towns of the Dobunni tribe. Their coins often had a branched emblem on the reverse side and there is evidence from these coins that the kingdom was sometimes divided into north and south zones.

The first Christian communities in southern Romano-Celtic Britain appeared in the early years of the 3rd century AD and Christian conversion intensified with the legalisation of the Christian religion under Constantine the Great in the early 4th century. There are a number of references to Christianity in Britain at this time. The list of Bishops attending the council of Arles in 314 AD mentions several from Britain. Gildas wrote that Christianity was flourishing in Britain in the 5th and 6th centuries and Bede also writes of Christian churches in Hereford and Gloucester around 540 AD. So, it is likely that the Dobunni were practicing Christianity well before the appearance of the Anglo-Saxons in the area. It is possible that at this time Celtic Christian worship was occurring at high status locations such as settlements on hill forts.

The Sounds of the Landscape of Brittonic Celt Origin

As we have seen across Europe and England, the most robust Celtic place name survivors are those describing the natural enduring features of the landscape. This is also a recognisable pattern for Celtic names in Worcestershire. We have already seen the reasons for the importance of rivers and water to ancient people and this is particularly so of the Celts. Celtic paganism was a polytheistic religion, an important aspect of which were water deities. There is abundant evidence for the veneration of water by the Celts, including the pattern of items offered, some useful and some valuable, deposited in pits, wells and lakes. One of the unsavoury features of these rituals is the not uncommon finding of skulls particularly in pits and wells. Most places sacred to the Celts, however, including pools, springs, rivers, wells and lakes were often unmarked by any structures. Yeates suggests the Dobunni deified rivers and, indeed as we shall see, the Celts often gave names to even the smallest of streams. The majority of contemporary English river names are derived from Brittonic Celtic origins and this is also the case for many rivers and streams in Worcestershire, as shown in Table 7.

Table 7 River and Stream Names in Worcestershire of Celtic Origin		
Modern English Name	Celtic Word Origin	Meaning
Avon	Afon	river
Arrow	Afon	river
Croome	Cromba	crooked
Dowles Brook	Dulas	blackish
Elmley Brook (formerly the Dufor)	Dyfr	water
Leadon	Llydan	broad
Laughern Brook	Llywarn	fox
Stour	Steu	the strong one
Teme	Tamesis	the dark one
Wynd Brook	Wen	white
Wyre Brook	Wyre	winding

The Brittonic Celtic language spoken by the Dobunni, as a branch of the Indo-European family of languages, is distantly related to other languages within this great family. Among these related languages was Sanskrit, spoken and written around 3,500 to 4,000 years ago on the Indian subcontinent. Thus, some current river names in Worcestershire of Celtic origin contain the same roots as current river names found today in India and, indeed, have similar meanings! The Teme, Celtic 'tamesis', in Sanskrit 'tamus' or 'tamasa', the current name of a tributary of the Ganges, and the Tiber that flows through Rome, all have the same root and meaning 'the dark one'. The River Stour that runs through Stourport, is recorded in 686 AD as Stur, in 866 as Sture, in 1300 as Stoure. The river name has a common root, 'steur' with the river Stura in Italy and the river name Sthavard from Sanskrit. All these rivers are associated with the same meaning - 'the strong one'.

The earliest record of a name given to the River Severn dates from 115 AD - Sabrina. Later names are Saeferne in 757, Habren around 800, Saefern in 896, Saverne around 1140, Sauerne in the Doomsday Book, Hefren around 1150, and Seuerne in 1205. The etymology of the name Sabrina is unclear and may represent a hybrid name with Common Brittonic and Old Latin elements. There were former river names in Bedfordshire and Ireland recorded as the 'Sabrann'. It probably shares a common origin with the modern French river names Sevre and Sevres. The Modern Welsh name for the river is Afon Hafren. Some experts have suggested a tentative relationship with the Modern Welsh word 'haf' meaning summer. Yeates suggests the earlier Celtic female name given to the river might reflect its veneration as a goddess by the Dubonni tribe. Evidence of Romano-Celtic religious beliefs also suggest the worship of water sources and rivers as part of an animistic paganism. The Severn and Wye were believed to be 'sister rivers' born from the same mountain father, now called Plynlimon (the Welsh name is 'Pumlumon' meaning five peaks and is related to the Scottish hill names Lomond Hills and Ben Lomond). Another nod to shared origins.

There are many river and stream names of Celtic origin in modern Worcestershire. The Avon, from the Celtic word, 'afon', meaning river, has cognates are also found in Cornish Celt as 'afon' and Gaelic as 'abhann', all meaning river. In all, there are ten rivers in England all named the Avon. The Worcestershire Avon is documented as 'Afon' in 704 and 'Afene' in 780. The change from 'f' to 'v' is from the Old French influence spoken by the Normans. Some toponymists have suggested that not only do they all derive from the Brittonic Celt word for river, 'afon', but also, they may have all had additional distinctive names. One in England might have been discovered. It has been proposed that the Brittonic Celt name for Warwickshire was

Caer Wrangon and that the river passing through was formerly known as the 'Afon Wrangon'. The name 'Afon Wrangon' survives in South Wales.

Dowles brook, a tributary of the Severn in Wyre Forest derives from Celtic 'dulas' meaning 'blackish', similarly of Celtic origin is the **Lem brook**. Both the **Ennick** and **Inkford** brooks may derive from the Celtic 'ennick' and 'hen' meaning old. However, I think some brooks with this name, as in **Hen brook**, a tributary of the Salwarpe near Stoke Prior and Upton Warren, probably derive from the Old English word 'hen'. In this context used as a general word for water-fowl, as in Moorhen or Marsh Hen. There is a Henmarsh with the same origin near Pedmore. **Kyre**, near Kyre Park and House, has Brittonic Celt origins. Recorded as Chure, Cuer and Cura in the 11th and 12th centuries. It is from the Celtic word 'cwr', meaning a border, edge, limit or corner. The manor lies on the boundary of the counties of Herefordshire and Worcestershire which here forms a sharp triangle. It may also have been the name of the nearby stream. In 1275 the locality was known as Cure Wyard from the Wyard family, the early Norman lords.

There are a number of streams derived from the Celtic names for water 'dubro' and 'dwfr' as in the Doferic, the former name for **Shrawley** Brook and the Dofer, the former name of **Elmley** Brook running through Doverdale. Dover, the Kent seaport, is over 170 miles from Doverdale just north of Droitwich but they are linked by a shared origin, as is Wendover in Buckingham. The rivers that run through these three places were called by the Brittonic Celt name, 'dwfr', which means water (compare with the Modern Welsh name for water 'dwr'). This shows, as we have encountered previously, the tendency of ancient cultures to name a place by the generic word in their language for a feature of that place.

The Anglo-Saxons, like many cultures before them, loaned the word, probably not knowing what it meant, and wrote it as 'dofer'. The places then all took their names from the river. The modern spelling of Dover also indicates the Norman, Old French, influence with the change from 'f' to 'v'. Doverdale also reveals something else about the evolution of place names - mistakes are made by transcribing errors. In 706 AD recorded as Dourdale, in 817 AD Doferdael and in the Doomsday (1086) as 'Lunvredele'. The latter is a blunder by an overworked or careless cleric!

Carrant Brook flows from Bredon into the Avon at Tewkesbury. In 778 written as 'Carent', 875 as 'Kcerent', and in 977 as 'Karente'. It is believed to derive from the Celtic word 'caranto' meaning 'friend'. The river seems to have been deified in the Romano-Celtic period as there has been found some evidence of ritual activity along its course including a shrine complex. There is a river in France called the 'Charente' which may represent a cognate.

Croome D'Abitot, **Earls Croome** and **Hill Croome** are villages between Croome Court and the Severn. All three places are named after the brook that flows through them. The brook, in turn, is derived from the Brittonic Celt word 'cromba' meaning 'crooked' and is cognate with the Modern Welsh word 'crwm'. All lay in the Royal Forest of Horewell which extended from Pershore in the north, to Strensham in the south and the River Severn to the west. Major deforestation began here in 1229, although remnants of the forest still remain.

Laughern Brook is recorded as Lawern in 757 and Lawerna in 1253. The name is of Common Brittonic Celt origin and is related to the Modern Welsh 'llywarn' and both the Old Breton and Old Cornish word 'louuern', all meaning 'fox'. The village of Laughern gave its name to the brook. The river Leadon, recorded as 'Ledene' in 972 and 'Leden' in 1248 is also of Brittonic Celt origin, and derives from the word 'litano' meaning broad, having the same meaning as the Modern Welsh word 'llydan'. Ledbury takes its name from the river upon which it stands. The source of the river, above Acton Beauchamp, was formerly in Worcestershire. The **River Arrow** rises in the Lickey Hills and has long marked the boundary between Worcestershire and Warwickshire. There are two rivers named 'Arrows' in Ireland. The name has probably the same Celtic derivation as 'afon', in this context meaning 'stream' and so related to the name Avon into which it flows. The River Avon in 704 is listed as the 'Afon' and in 780 as 'Afene'. The 'Avon' is one of the most common river names in England and evidently related to the Welsh, 'afon', the Cornish, 'avon' and the Irish, 'abhann'. It is fascinating to note that the previous Celtic residents of the area called the local hill 'Bre', as we have previously noted, meaning 'The Hill'. Similarly, I have heard local residents around 2,500 years later referring to the Avon as 'The River'! A recurring theme of human nature, some things never seem to change. Thus, many of the rivers and streams of Worcestershire, and indeed England, whisper and gurgle their ancient names that hint of their international and intercontinental connections and origins.

As we have seen widely over England, there are several hill names in Worcestershire that can tell us some interesting stories. **The Malvern Hills** is an excellent example of a tale told by at least four cultures and thus four languages. The word is derived from two Brittonic Celtic words 'moel' meaning bare and 'fryn' meaning hill (compare with the Modern Welsh name for hill, 'bryn'). We do not know what more ancient languages, such as Proto-Celtic and precursor languages have contributed to these words! The grammatical order, adjective then noun, reflects an Old English word order, therefore, Anglo-Saxon influence. In the 11th century, the name 'Malferna' has the sound of Old Latin influence. In the 12th century the name appears as 'Malverne', thus a Norman (Old French) influence as neither Brittonic Celtic or Old English had a 'v' in their alphabet. In the 16th and 17th century the Old English word 'much' is appears, meaning great or large, as in Much Malvern.

The story of the evolution of **Bredon** hill is truly fascinating and tells us so much about the people of the past and their ways. We do not know exactly when the first Celtic speaking people of the Iron Age appeared in Worcestershire. There is evidence of the Iron Age Hallstatt culture in south east England around the 6th century BC. It seems a reasonable speculation that this could have been as early as 500 BC. When they arrived in the area, they called the hill, 'Bre', one of the generic words used for hill in Celtic. This was a pattern of naming used by many cultures in the past and probably reflects that people tended to settle in one place and stayed and farmed there. So, the only hill that really mattered to them was the hill nearest to them and they called it 'The Hill' in their language. We can pin point the appearance of the Anglo-Saxon Hwicce tribe to the area more exactly. They arrived towards the end of the 6th century AD, sometime after 577 AD. They named the hill Breodun, 'dun' meaning hill in Old English, as written in Anglo-Saxon charters of 772 AD. Middle and Modern English have also added the word 'Hill'. Thus, three successive cultures, each probably unaware of the meaning of the previous cultures' language, created an accretion of elements to form a tautology - Hill, Hill, Hill! You will notice the change over time from 'dun' (Old English loaned from Celtic meaning 'fort') to 'don' meaning 'hill' in Old English. We have seen previously; place names change for all types of reasons including irrational ones. However, I wonder if the initial spelling alludes to an old Iron Age Celtic fort which was later used by the Anglo-Saxons, abandoned and later the suffix changed to 'don' becoming plain 'hill'?

Crookbarrow Hill at Whittington, near Worcester, is both fascinating, mysterious and impressive. The consensus view appears that it is mostly natural but with some human made features. However, it has never been excavated but some experts have suggested it may have been a burial mound. It rises steeply 20 meters above the valley floor, is an oval shape in plan,

75 m long and 45 m wide. Indeed, Silbury Hill, near Avebury, Wiltshire, the largest Neolithic artificial mound in Europe is higher at 39.3m. There is evidence of prehistoric activity at Crookbarrow including the find of a Neolithic scrapper. A Romano-British settlement has been found nearby and some Roman coins found on the hill. Some historians have theorised it could have functioned as a Roman military signalling post because of its strategic, lofty position. In recent years, so close and so easily identified from the M5, the hill has become something of an icon, indicating the arrival or marking 'a milestone' of a long car journey. To celebrate this high public interest, the hill was the subject of a radio programme in October 2019, called after a characteristic of one of its features and, indeed, one of its eponyms - One Tree Hill. However, its official name is just as intriguing. The first element derives from the Brittonic Celt word 'cruc', meaning 'barrow, cairn or hillock'. The Modern Welsh equivalent is 'crug'. 'Berewe' is a Middle English word which itself derives from Old English, 'beorg' or 'beorh', meaning mound, tumulus or hill. So, again, this is a hill named by the Brittonic Celts and later added to by the Anglo-Saxons and again by Middle and Modern English, so becoming a hybrid name and a tautology - calling out Hill, Hill, Hill in three different languages! I am intrigued that the locals refer to the hill as 'The Tump' or 'Whittington Tump'. This might be an example of a local folk memory from Celtic times as the equivalent in Welsh is still 'Y Twmp'.

The name of the **Lickey Hills** may or may not be of Brittonic Celt origin! Some toponymists have suggested the name has a similar origin to the Modern Welsh 'llechi', meaning stones, possibly alluding to the exposed rocks of the hills. Another proposal is it is related to the Old English listing of 'Leckheye' of 1255 meaning of 'the place at the forest enclosure'.

The **Wyre Forest**, ('wyre' meaning 'winding or spreading'), in Worcestershire and the Forest of Arden ('ardu' meaning 'high') mostly in Warwickshire, but also in parts of Worcestershire and Staffordshire, similarly reflect their Brittonic Celt names. The Ardennes or Ardennes Forest spreading mostly within Belgium and Luxembourg but also partly in Germany and France, has the same etymology. It reflects the extensive influence of the Celts of Western Europe in the 1st and possibly part of the 2nd millennium BC. In Roman times the area was known as Arduenna Silva ('silva' is Latin for 'forest'). This probably derives from a Gaulish cognate of the Brittonic Celt word 'ardu' as in the Modern Welsh word 'ardd' also meaning 'high ground'.

The features of the landscape that surround us, the rivers, mountains, hills, valleys and forests have long been recognised as important, useful and venerated by our ancestors, named by them and have much to tell us!

Settlement Names of Celtic Origin in Worcestershire

The Celtic settlement place names that have survived in Worcestershire are mostly found in the west of the county. Place names of Celtic origin east of the River Severn can still be found but are rare. There are historical reasons for this that will become apparent later. Table 6

Travelling west up the Teme valley there are some interesting place names with a notable distribution pattern. The place names within the fertile valley are of Old English, therefore, Anglo-Saxon origin. However, several villages and topographic features of Celtic origin are located on the higher ground to the north. These include **Menithwood**, a hamlet with a hybrid name, from Celtic 'mynydd' meaning mountain. Nearby is **Oney Coppice**, a Celtic name meaning 'ash tree' a name shared by tributary of the River Teme higher up the Teme valley. The village of **Pensax** is also a hybrid name, composed of Celtic 'pen', head of or hill and 'seax' the name the Saxons called themselves. The grammatical order of the elements points to a name given by the Celts to their neighbours. This may well reflect a time when the incoming Anglo-Saxons were still a minority cultural group. The name, however, has survived so it is likely the Anglo-Saxons continued to be in the minority for an extended period. Place names of this type in England are rare, but one example is Nansawsen in Cornwall meaning 'valley of the English'. Interestingly, place names reflecting similar situations are commoner in southern Scotland and are found as 'Pennersax', Glensaxon' and 'Glensax'. The nearby **Penn Hall** is also a hybrid name. In 1221 written as 'Penhyll' and 'Penhull, the 'pen' is Celtic meaning 'hill' and the element 'hyll' Old English, both meaning 'hill'. So, another tautology literally meaning 'Hill, Hill'! Just north is the village of **Mamble** recorded in 957 as Momela gemaera and in Domesday (1086) as Mamele. The derivation is from the Brittonic Celt word 'mamm' meaning breast or mother and takes its name from the breast-like shape of a hill, as does the city of Manchester. There is a hill in the High Peaks of Derbyshire, called Mam Tor and Moel Famau, the highest point on the Clewydian range in Flintshire, north east Wales probably has a similar derivation.

Patterns in the distribution of place names when two or more different cultures live in close proximity have been ascribed to social stratification. Fellow-Jensons studied the distribution of farmsteads of Scandinavian and Anglo-Saxon origin in north west England. The Scandinavian settlements were located at altitudes of over 800 feet on poorer agricultural soils and the Anglo-Saxon farmsteads lay below on more fertile ground. Perhaps a reflection of social dominance or a 'first come first served' basis. The pattern of place names in the Teme valley may also reflect centres of separate but not necessarily opposing cultures. So, a significant number of place names around the Teme valley reflect a snap shot in time of the expansion of Anglo-Saxons and early in their contacts with the local Celts. As we shall see, this area may not have been a 'Wild West' frontier but indicate a point of increasing contact, cooperation and assimilation of cultures.

There is a noteworthy road sign on the main A433 road through the Teme valley pointing north to the higher ground. It has a similar composition to many bilingual road signs in modern Wales, where the Welsh name always appears above the English equivalent. The Teme valley sign reads '**Frith**', and immediately below 'Common'. This is similar to a tautology as the first word originates from the Celtic word 'frythe' and indeed means common land. Therefore, the sign literally reads 'Common Common' derived from two languages! Figure 5

In the extreme south west of the county lies **Pendock**, a Celtic name composed of 'pen', head of, and 'heddioc', the barley field.

Pensham is a catch. The element 'pen' may initially give an impression of a Celtic origin, but the etymology does not. In 972 recorded as Pedneshamme and in the Domesday as Pendesham. This is derived from Old English, meaning 'the homestead of a man or people called Pedens' often related to a water meadow. **Welland**, due west of Upton-Upon -Severn, was written Wenelande in 1189 and Weneland in 1239. This is a hybrid name, the last element derived from Old England. 'Wen' is derived from the Celtic word 'gwyn' meaning 'white'. The stream running through the village, now Wynd Brook, was recorded as 'Wenbroc' in 963, so the village has probably taken the name of this stream. There is an **Assarts Common** nearby. I have mentioned this word earlier, derived from Old French, in relation to Mesolithic and Neolithic clearings, used respectively, to hunt wild animals and graze cattle.

The Rhydd is an interesting hamlet on the west bank of the Severn between Worcester and Upton-Upon-Severn. It is derived from the Celtic word, 'rhyd', meaning a ford or shallow crossing site of a river. There are some useful features present in this locality which help confirm the meaning of the name. **Rhydd Green** lies just west of the river with two good roads converging to it and which was probably a grazing area for cattle before they crossed. There are Scots pines on the eastern bank of the river and on the eastern horizon. These trees were characteristically planted along drovers' ways as directional markers on their long journeys. A thoroughfare, now a mettled road leads at right angles from the B4244 to the west river bank. A footpath is situated on the opposite side of the river leading east through Sheepcote Farm and passing by two more 'Greens', Kerswell Green and Birch Green. A common feature found in hydro-geology is that the shallowest part of a river is found at around the mid-point between two bends - exactly where The Rhydd is situated. There appear no Anglo-Saxon references to this name, so this suggests the name has later origins probably alluding to a crossing point of the River Severn by the Welsh drovers steering their cattle to the markets of Oxford and London as late as the 17th to 18th century. Although the water tends to be too deep for crossing now, before 1840s the river was tidal north of Worcester. The ford here is thought to have been a prehistoric crossing on a route to the hill camps on the Malvern Hills, possibly linking them with hill camps on Bredon. Indeed, the Celtic fort at Worcester dated to 400 BC was built near a ford, itself part of an ancient Neolithic track, as was the tidal ford crossing the river at Gloucester. There is still a Ferry House that stands on the river at The Rhydd and this ferry was working until 1914. As at Cleveland, it was also a distributing point for river-bourne coal and bricks for Malvern Wells and Great Malvern in the 19th century.[5]

There is also a **Rhydd Covert** near the eastern side of the River Severn on the opposite Bewdley Bank from Bewdley.

One needs to work hard to identify Celtic settlement names east of the river. As we shall see in the next chapter, the initial phase of Anglo-Saxon expansion into the area was confined by the River Severn. This formed the early western boundary of the Hiwicci tribe with the Celts still occupying the lands west of the river. One of the more obvious settlement names of Celtic origin lies on the River Avon, **Wyre Piddle**. The village is situated near the confluence of the rivers Piddle (from Old English for 'narrow stream') and the Avon. Recorded in 12th century as Pidele, 1290 as Wyre Pidele, 1327 as Pydele and 1420 Wyre Piddle. 'Wyre' is a word of Brittonic Celt

---

[5] Navigation at the rock bar of The Rhydd was a hazardous operation at low water, for the trows could not sail over, and it was necessary to get horses to haul the vessel through, or the owners were obliged to double the men by using two companies of hauliers. A channel was blasted in the rock bar but, when a strong tide was running, it was very dangerous. The trow 'Prince' struck the bar in 1847, and went down. There was also a ford crossing in historical times two miles upriver at Kempsey

origin meaning 'winding'. There is a **Wyre Brook** in the Teme valley near Newnham Bridge. There is a recognisable pattern found in the etymology of place names that a more ancient name appears and then disappears from the sequence of recorded names as we shall see with the etymology of Evesham and the Wyre Forest among others.

Some settlement names of Celtic origin east of the River Severn may represent occupancy by Celtic people long after the Anglo-Saxon invasion. Andrew Harris refers to **Walmer Farm** on the western border of the Parish of Hanbury as evidence of Celtic occupancy post-invasion. 'Wal' is an Old English word found quite commonly in modern England as in Walsall, derived from the Old English words 'Walh' and 'Halh', meaning 'Valley of the Celts'.

There are several Thrifts, **The Thrift** or **Thrift Woods** found in Worcestershire, some lying east of the River Severn. Thrift has the same meaning as Frith from Middle English and both are derived from the Celtic word 'frythe'. All mean common land of less agricultural worth, often scrub land on inclines so more difficult to cultivate. They tend to occur on the periphery of settlements, standing higher and quite isolated from the community. This, perhaps, is a reason for their survival.

The Archeological Evidence of Celts in Worcestershire

The most prominent features of Worcestershire's Iron Age landscape were the hill forts of which there are around ten that have been located. There is evidence of these on British Camp, Wychbury Hill, Hanbury, several on Bredon Hill, Woodbury Hill, Berrow Hill Camp, Conderton Camp, Headless Cross and Gadbury Bank. A promontory fort has been located by the Severn at Kempsey. The common finds at this time from move away from the tools and weapons of the Bronze Age to those of coins and brooches. In Pershore a large Iron Age hoard of 1,494 gold and silver coins were found near a large associated settlement, speculated to have been a shrine of the Dobunni tribe. Terret rings have been found near Bewdley, used as rein guides on chariots and carts and linch pins near Worcester which held chariot wheels in place. Discoveries point to a pottery industry in the Malvern Hills and salt extraction at Droitwich. A gold coin hoard was discovered near Droitwich dated to 20 and 50 AD and also a Dobunni coin has been found at Hanbury Hill fort.

The names of Worcestershire settlements and surrounding landscapes abound with a rich dialogue if we care to listen to them. They continue telling their story of the times before the next guardians of Worcestershire appear.

The View from the Malvern Hills in Celtic Times

If you were to stand on what the Brittonic Celts called Moel Bryn long before the Roman invasion, two features of the vista might strike you. Firstly, the impact of humans on the landscape would be more evident than ever. The creation of more clearings for cattle and settlements had given the landscape an increasingly mosaic pattern. These settlements of round houses mostly in valleys and flood plains had become a more permanent feature. Many of the hill forts would be in view as there is some evidence, they would have been visible to each other, suggesting they were centres of organisation and power.

Secondly, the human activities of daily life would be more evident. During the Iron Age the population of Britain rose substantially to around one million probably secondary to improved varieties of crops and more efficient farming techniques. Midsummer Hill Iron Age fort is thought to have been a settlement for around 1,500 people. Tracks busy with pedestrians and horses and carts might be seen passing through Wyche Cutting taking salt from Droitwich towards Herefordshire and South Wales. The main flint route between North Wales and Wessex passed just north of the Malvern Hills and trading of local produce, including pottery from the nearby works, might be seen. Busy in their tasks some may have walked quite near to you!

The Distribution of Celtic Languages in Pre-Roman Britain

Brittonic Celt — Pictish — Goidelic Celt

Figure 1 The Distribution of Celtic Languages in Pre-Roman Britain

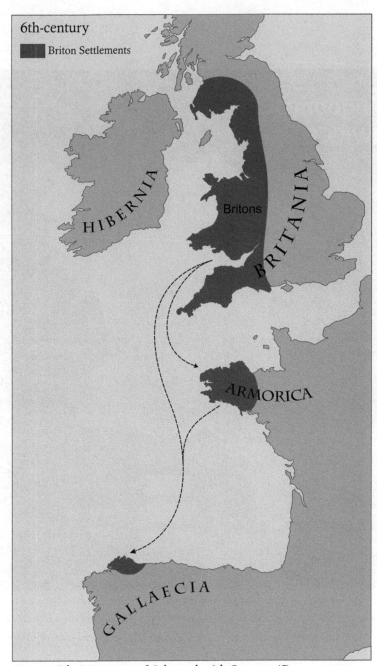

Figure 2 The Migrations of Celts in the 6th Century AD

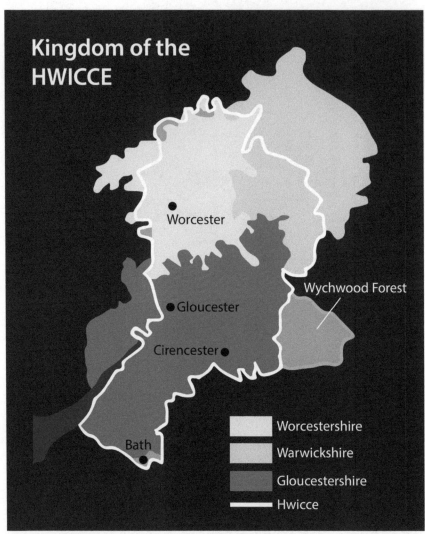

Figure 3 The Boundaries of the Kingdom of the Hwicce which are closely related to the Dobunni tribal territory, a Roman civitas and define the area of the early Diocese of Worcester. Thus, spanning and connecting well over two thousand years of history.

Figure 4 Looking south from Upper Bentley to Bredon Hill, seen in the distance. The name tells us much about how cultures named places in the past.

Figure 5 A road sign in the Teme valley showing a tautology. The Middle English word 'frith' has the same meaning as 'common' in Modern English and is derived from the Celtic word 'frythe' also meaning common land.

Figure 6 A representation of the hobgoblin Puck at Rudyard Kipling's home, Batemans, above which stands Pouk Hill. Variants appears in many place names in Britain reflecting a widespread belief in the supernatural.

Chapter 18 Roman Worcestershire

THE successful Roman invasion of Britain began in 43 AD lead by the politician and general Aulus Plautius, appointed by the Emperor Claudius. Aulus Plautius would become the first governor of the new province of Britannia. The Dobunni tribe negotiated an early peace settlement with Roman ambassadors before the arrival of the military. This was in contrast to many other Celtic tribes including their western neighbours, the Silures of South East Wales. However, excavations of the hill forts at Midsummer Hill, Bredon, Conderton and Croft Ambrey all reveal evidence of violent destruction by fire around 48 AD, presumably instigated by Romans to prevent them from functioning as defensive positions. The Dobunni tribal area, from the distribution of finds, was probably concentrated around Gloucestershire but extended to cover modern Worcestershire, parts of west Warwickshire and North Somerset. This area became the boundaries of a civitas under Roman civil administration. Although overall military and political responsibility of the province of Britannia lay with the Roman governor, some elements of local administration were delegated to high status members of Celtic tribes. These freedoms came with responsibilities including the payment of taxes.

The Romans were masters of identifying the best defensible, strategic and sustainable locations. They established a fort, Cair Guiragon, on the banks of the River Severn in 50 AD, near present-day Worcester. However, the Celts had also built a well-chosen nearby position for a fort about 450 year earlier. Situated on a ford of the Severn with an ancient flint track leading to North Wales to the north west and on the eastern bank a track to both the southwest Britain and to the north of Britain. This later ancient track became the cobbled stone road Icknield Street between Glevum (Gloucester) and Viroconium (Wroxeter) in Shropshire. The settlement was then probably known as Vertis and would eventually become Worcester.

The Dobunni tribal area, therefore, was soon removed from the Roman military front line. Thus, there is relatively little archeological evidence of Roman military presence in Worcestershire. There were some small road defences and bridge remains found at Kempsey. This may have belonged to the Roman Second Legion Augusta which were strategically situated at Isca Augusta at Caerleon, South Wales to counter the threat from the Silures. Signs of iron works and pottery kilns have been excavated in Worcester but no municipal buildings found. A small defence structure has been excavated near the river, probably to defend the crossing. Two Roman forts and a high-status villa with mosaics have been found at Dodderhill, Droitwich. This was also the site of industrial salt production and called Salinae by 100 AD. Roman villas are more numerous in the south west of Worcestershire, the Cotswolds, Gloucestershire in the south of the Dobunni tribal area where there is more evidence of an emerging Romano-British culture. Romano-British farmsteads have been identified scattered across Worcestershire. Roman brooches and well over 5,000 coins have been found in the county. Nearly 4,000 Roman radiate coins were discovered as a hoard associated with remains of a villa in the Bredon Hill area in 2011. Other high-status artefacts include a bronze dolphin brooch and a bronze figure of a lion.

Over the next 350 years British society underwent profound changes towards a Romano-British culture. Within the Dobunni territory this transformation is reflected in the founding of two Roman forts and settlements which were to become major Romano-British centres. In 48 AD the Romans built a fort near a ford of the River Severn at Kingsholme which grew to become Colonia Nervia Glevensium or Glevum (Gloucester). The nearby Dobunni fort, ford and subsequent site of a Roman settlement on the east side of the Severn gives obvious parallels to the developments of those at Worcester. A Roman Legion (Legio II Augusta) was based in Glevum before their invasion of Wales in 65 AD and the transfer of their centre of operations to Isca Augusta in Caerleon. In 97 AD, the area was designated a 'colonia' by Emperor Nerva, so became a town for retired soldiers, only one of four such towns in Britain. Thus, Glevum enjoyed the highest status the Empire could bestow and a basilica and forum were built together with many high -status villas with mosaic floors. The river crossing and thus a main route to South Wales, the proximity to the Fosse Way and to the military front line gave Glevum strategic importance. A Romano-British temple to the Celtic deity of can still be seen there. It has been estimated to have had a population of around 10,000 people which had a huge impact on the surrounding area. Many legionaries were given farmland in the countryside around and also could be called up to arms as a Roman auxiliary force. There is a concentration of Romano-British farms and villas in the surroundings, such as Chedworth and Woodchester. Chedworth villa is one of the largest in Britain demonstrating the best in Roman refinements and impressive mosaic floors. A living relic to these times is a 2,000-year-old population of snails, the protected species helix pomatia, the French or Edible snail, introduced by the Romans!

Similarly, Corinium Dobunnorum, a Romano-British hybrid name, now Cirencester, was founded by the building of a fort in 44 AD near the Dobunni hill fort and tribal oppidum at Bagendon. This became the capital and an important site of Dobunni food and wares production, trade and coin minting, indeed, the Dobunni economy thrived within a Romano-British culture and was based primarily on beef and wool. Three main roads crossed at Corinium Dobunnorium, the Fosse Way, Akeman Street and Ermin Street which facilitated its position as the second largest walled city area in Roman Britain. It also boasted a forum and amphitheater, and a fine basilica second, in Britain, only to Londinium.

The Romans founded the town of Bath, Aquae Sulis, between 60-70 AD around the thermal springs in the valley of the River Avon, where they built a spa and temple. The area was within the southern borders of the Dobunni tribe, its southern boundary probably defined by the River Axe. There is archaeological evidence that the springs were already the site of worship by the Celts to the goddess Sulis. She was believed to have been a life-giving mother goddess and an effective agent of curses. The etymology of the name Sulis is uncertain but the consensus is that it may be cognate with the Old Irish word 'suil', meaning 'eye' or 'sight'. The Romans identified the deity with Minerva, their goddess of wisdom and defensive warfare. Overlooking and predating Aquae Sulis were Iron Age hill forts at Solsbury Hill and Bathampton Camp.

The population of Roman Britain has been estimated from between 2.8 to 3 million by the end of the second century and around 3.6 million by the end of the fourth century. The urban population was about 240,000 at the end of the fourth century and were culturally diverse and included people of ethnic origins from many places in, or associated with, the Roman Empire. However, the vast majority of the indigenous Celts lived in rural areas. Latin was mostly confined for use within the military, politics and administration and Brittonic Celt spoken widely. British Vulgar Latin emerged and there is some evidence this survived, particularly in western Britain, for hundreds of years after the end of Roman rule. However, Latin was the official written language of government, religion and high-status individuals not the 'common people'. So, although Latinised in official written sources, the Celtic place names continued to be used. As in England generally, therefore, very few true Roman Latin place names survive in Worcestershire.

The Romans introduced many technologies and a new culture to Britain. They did not, however, introduce new place names other than Latinise all those they came across. These names were 'un-Latinised' by the next culture to appear in Britain - the Anglo-Saxons. Thus, very few Roman names still remain from this period.

Some place names on the boundaries of Worcestershire and Gloucestershire may seem of Roman Latin origin but are all derived from Old or Middle English origin. Aston Magna, Worcestershire, is derived from the Old English 'east' and 'tun', meaning 'the eastern farmstead'. Thus, 'Estona' in 1209, 'magna', Latin meaning 'great', was a later addition. Aston is a very common place name and has often been further qualified for easier identification. Similarly, Ampney Crucis, Gloucestershire, is recorded as simply Omenie in 1086 and Amenel Sancti Petri in 1275 and Weston-sub-Edge, Gloucestershire as Westone in 1086 then Weston sub-egge in 1255, meaning 'the western farmstead under the edge or escarpment'. During this part of the Medieval period Latin was the language of the church and administration and thus had a significant influence on place names.

Vigo is a small area north east of Bromsgrove. There are many localities called "The Vigo" in the Midlands and I have passed this one many times and always thought if I had remembered my spade, I should dig up a splendid Roman villa! However, there are no early records so it is likely a relatively recent name introduced to commemorate the naval victory at Vigo in Spain, in 1702, of an Anglo-Dutch expedition over a French and Spanish fleet in the early years of the War of the Spanish Succession.

The View from the Malvern Hills in Roman Times
The vista from the Malvern Hills at this period would have been a predominantly agricultural landscape with less woodlands than in the past. Numerous small Romano-British farms would be apparent. Chris Dyer estimated about 60 even within the woodland landscape of Hanbury. However, significant woodlands still existed, such as the vast Forest of Arden identifiable to the north east towards the Lickey and Clent Hills. Bounded

by the Saltway from Droitwich on its southern boundary, Icknield Street to its west, Watling Street to the north and the Fosse Way to the east, no Roman roads traversed this huge forest in the heart of southern Britain. It is likely smoke would be seen rising from sites of industrial activity from the iron and pottery works at Vertis (Worcester) and the salt industry of Salinae (Droitwich). The small fort at Kempsey and the signalling station on Crookbarrow hill could be spied. If you were lucky enough, you might witness the Roman army on the move. Perhaps a cohort (480 legionaries) or even a legion (5,000 legionaries) striding up Icknield Street, their highly polished metal helmets with horse hair crests, metal chest plates, wooden and metal shields glistening in the sunlight. You might view out front, the standard, a long pole carrying the legions flag-like badge of identity and perhaps hear the faint sound of the cornicens's trumpet or cornet giving instructions to the marching formation.

Chapter 19 Anglo-Saxon Worcestershire

THE expansion of the Anglo-Saxons across southern Britain has been documented from a number of primary sources including two early accounts. Gildas, a Christian British (Celtic) cleric wrote around 500 AD and the Venerable Bede, an English monk from the monastery at Jarrow, Northumbria wrote his Historia Ecclesiastica Gentis Anglorum (Ecclesiastical History of the English People) which he completed in 731 AD. The Anglo-Saxon Chronicles, a collection of annals in Old English also describe the history of the early Anglo-Saxons in Britain. The originals, probably from Wessex in the reign of Alfred the Great and dated from the 9th century, have been lost. Fortunately, multiple copies were distributed to monasteries across England and nine manuscripts survive.

The Celtic kingdom of Ceint (modern Kent) fell in 456 AD. Linnuis (modern Lincolnshire and Nottinghamshire) was subsumed by 500 AD and Rhegin (modern Sussex and Hampshire) by 510 AD. Ynys Weith (Isle of Wight) was taken over by 530 AD and Caer Colun (modern Essex) by 540 AD. The Anglo-Saxon Chronicle records the Anglo-Saxon kingdom of Wessex was founded in 494 AD. We are told in the Flores Historiarum, written in the early 13th century by Roger of Wendover at the Abbey of St Albans, that the Angels had expanded from East Anglia to the Midlands by 527. It says "Pagans came from Germany and occupied East Anglia, that is, the country of the East Angles; and some of them invaded Mercia, and waged war against the British". It is likely the first king of Mercia was Icel, also spelt Icil, the son of Eomer (of Beowulf fame), the last king of the Angles in northern Germany. By the time of his death, he was king of most of both East Anglia and Mercia.

Some regions, such as those west of the River Severn held out for decades and perhaps the upland areas of the Chilterns. Rheged, consisting of modern

Northumbria, Durham, Cumbria and parts of southern Scotland was in Celtic control into the late 8th century. According to Guildas, initial strong Celtic resistance was followed by successive defeats. A great British victory was recorded at the Battle of Mount Badon around 500 AD, probably in the South West of modern England, after which Anglo-Saxon expansion was temporarily stemmed. However, the British subsequently wasted their resources by internal disputes and conflict which became the inspiration of Gildas's book De Excidio Britanniae, or The Ruin of Britain.

The emerging Anglo-Saxon kingdoms vied for power and influence over the next few centuries. There were also many sub-kingdoms and small independent tribal areas. Tribes south of the Humber estuary were included in the Tribal Hidage, a list of 35 tribes compiled between the 7th and 9th century, however, many of these tribes were to be coalesced by more powerful neighbours. The kingdom of Kent under Aethelberht wielded significant influence over other Anglo-Saxon kingdoms in the late 6th century. The Mercian Supremacy covered the period between the 7th to early 9th century based on their military successes. Wessex was at the height of its powers in 6th century and again in the 9th century.

Historians are often sceptical of the exact dates and events given by many of these sources of evidence, written decades or even hundreds of years after the events and by authors who may have been aware or unaware of their bias or prejudices. Thus, although historians are dubious whether or not the Battle of Dyrham, or Deorham, recorded by Gildas and probably in south Gloucestershire, actually took place in 577, there was certainly an expansion of Wessex Saxons north west into the heartlands of the Dobunni tribal area. This successful campaign was led by Cealin, the king of Wessex, and subsequently the Dobunni lost their control of the Romano-British capital of Caer Baddon, Caer Ceri (Corinium Dobunnorum now Cirencester), Caer Gloui, (Glevum now Gloucester) and Aquae Sulis (Bath). This created a wedge between the Celts of the south west peninsula of Britain and the Celtic tribes west of the River Severn.

The Anglo-Saxon Chronicle tells us that the kingdom of the Hwicce (also recorded as Hwiccii) was established after the battle of Dyrham of 577 AD. It is possible that the tribe previously inhabited the area along the Thames valley, a part of the Kingdom of Wessex at the time. Bede records that a number of Saxon tribes migrated from the Thames valley into the new kingdom of the Hwicce after the defeat of the Dobunni, including the Feppingas, the Wixans and the Stoppingas. It is possible that these Anglo-

Saxon tribes replaced some Dobunni tribal groups who moved west of the Severn or possibly emigrated to the coastal areas of the Western European mainland. The Stoppingas migrated into the area around the Forest of Arden, which is now Wootton Wowen, Warwickshire and the Feppingas and Wixans into Worcestershire. We know of other tribal groups within the Hwicce sub-kingdom including the Weorgoran, occupying the area around Wyre Forest and the Husmerae, inhabiting ten hides of land around present-day Stourport-on-Severn. Figure 3

The Hwicce name is likely derived from Old German. The 'hw' seems a reduction of 'kw' or 'gw' as 'k' and 'g' are interchangeable and previous forms may have been 'kwicche' or 'gwicce'. The latter is similar to Gewissae, a name used in 519 to describe the West Saxons in the early years of their emergence as a kingdom. The Gewisse are known to have inhabited the Thames valley as early as the 420s and may have been Germanic mercenaries used by the Celts. The root cognates with 'witch' and Ekwall suggested the two tribes might have had a common origin. Yeates suggested the name Hwicce is related to the meaning of a sacred vessel used in pagan ceremonies. Both the Dobunni tribe before their conversion to Christianity, probably in the 4th century AD, and the Hwicce, before their conversion in the 7th century, were heathens. Thus, Yeates describes both these peoples in his 2008 book 'The Tribes of Witches'. Early forms of their name are written as prouincia Hwicciorum (province of the Hwicce) in 730, Hwiccium in 800 and Hwicca maego (boundary of the Hwicce) the 9th century. Interestingly, there are examples of Hwicca used as a personal name in Wichnor, Staffordshire, documented as 'Hwiccenofre' , Witchley Green in Rutland appears as 'Hwicceslea' and Whiston in Northamptonshire, as 'Hwiccintune' derived from Old English 'Hwiccingtun'.

The Hwicce have been described as a peaceful tribe of farmers, craftsmen and weavers, many of which lived within the Severn and Avon valleys. Their boundaries, however, match those of their predecessors the Dobunni, except that initially, the western border was defined by the River Severn. This frontier between Anglo-Saxons and Celts is reflected in the distribution of Celtic place names in the county even today. There are very few settlements of Celtic origin east of the River Severn but an increasing number found west of the Severn.

There is evidence of assimilation of the indigenous population by the Hwicce with close cooperation and inter-marriage and it is possible that the Hwicce did not entirely subjugate the Dobunni. The Dobunni were known to have already developed well organised Christian institutions and these systems seemed to have survived the influx of pagans and even absorbed the new comers into their existing church structure. Survival and continuity of Celtic Christian institutions and worship post-Anglo-Saxon invasion is suggested by two place names within the Hwicce territory known to contain the Old English word 'eccles' loaned from the Celtic word 'eglwys' meaning 'church'. Bede is not complimentary of the Celtic British clergy complaining of "their unspeakable crimes" and their reluctance to preach the faith to the Angles or Saxons, citing their refusal to assist Augustine in his mission of Christian conversion. However, the archeological evidence, including the small number of pagan burials, indicates that the British played an important role in the conversion of the Anglo-Saxons. So, there is evidence of territorial, religious and cultural continuity between the two tribes. It is difficult to be definite as to who assimilated who as there is a possibility that there were very many more Celts than Anglo-Saxons living in the area at least in the initial stages of the expansion of the Anglo-Saxons. This assimilation, integration and intermarriage is thought to have occurred more in the north and in the west of Anglo-Saxon England, including Mercia. However, it seems a complex process as many Insular Celts received fewer social privileges than most in Anglo-Saxon England and even the Anglo-Saxon monk, Bede, tells us the Celts 'being slaughtered or in perpetual servitude'. However, there were also high-status Celtic and Christian Celtic missionaries who exerted significant influence on the incomers. Indeed, many of the early kings of both Wessex and Mercia had Celtic names. These included Cerdic who founded the Wessex royal line in 519 and a number of his descendants such as Bretwalda Ceaslin and King Caedwalla who died in 689. In Mercia several kings bore Celtic names, notably King Penda.

Much of what is known about both the Anglo-Saxon and early Anglo-Norman periods pertains to high status individuals and families. The scope of evidence and written materials that have survived are charters, wills, land grants, and laws. These materials reveal information mostly about the upper classes. The lower classes, having little to bequeath or devise, left less of a legacy and without records. Anglo-Saxon charters and other sources tell us that Eanhere and his brother Eanfrith were kings of the Hwicce in the mid-7th century. Osric, possibly the son of Eanhere, and his brother, Oshere also ruled over the tribe towards the end of the 7th century. It is thought that Osric founded two monastic houses, one which is now Bath Abbey the other becoming Gloucester cathedral where he is buried. These confirm two of the most important sites under Hwicce influence. Several sons of Oshere seemed to have ruled during the early 8th century including Aethelheard, Aethelweard and Aethelric. In the mid-8th century Eanberht is said to have ruled alongside Uhtred and Ealdred. In 770 Ealdred considered himself ruler of the Hwicce but was considered a 'dux' or duke by King Offa of Mercia. In a 778 charter, Offa gave land to Ealdred, however, after his death, Offa then integrated the Hwicce into the kingdom of Mercia.

The Wessex connections to the Hwicce did not last long and may have ended, as recorded in the Anglo-Saxon Chronicles, as early as 584 at the battle of Fethanleag and certainly by 603. In 628 at the Battle of Cirencester the Mercian army under King Penda defeated the Saxons of Wessex. Bede comments "after reaching an agreement", the Mercians took control of the Severn valley and the minor kingdom of the Hwicce. The Hwicce then became a client or sub-kingdom and therefore subordinate to their powerful northern neighbours.

Several sources record the appearance of the Angles in the east of present-day England and their divergence and founding of kingdoms in Northumbria, East Anglia and Mercia. The name Mercia is a latinisation of the Old English 'mierce' or 'myrce' meaning 'border people'. The kingdom of Mercia was founded by king Icel, the leader of the Iclings, around 527, with their capital in Tamworth. In the reign of Penda, Mercia became a powerful military force which reached its zenith under King Offa. By the end of the 8th century, known as the Mercian Supremacy, most of the land south of the Humber was under their control. This influence was curtailed in the early 9th century when Wessex grew in power again. Mercia was weakened further by constant Viking (mostly Danish) raids and a brief period of Viking supremacy followed in 879. However, Anglo-Saxon control re-emerged by the end of the 9th century when King Alfred of Wessex defeated the Vikings. Wessex and Mercia were united and with further victories over the Vikings the first kingdom of all the Anglo-Saxons appeared and Alfreds's grandson became the first King of England in 937.

The archaeological evidence suggests that some Angles occupied the lands north of the Thames and migrated westwards appearing in present-day Warwickshire. The inflow of an Anglian culture in the upper Warwickshire Avon valley early in the 6th century is suggested by pagan burials and place names found in the area. Thus, Worcestershire may well be a county with truly Anglo and Saxon mixed origins in addition to the Celtic component. Indeed, historians are reinterpreting the successive invasions and migrations into Britain and accumulating more evidence of assimilation and therefore continuity of populations. It is interesting that the Angles and Saxons inhabited the same juxtaposition in southern Britain as they did in their continental homelands. In this case, this may well be co-incidence. However, there is a tendency in human history in general that migrations across Euroasia tend to occur along the same or similar lines of latitude. This theory, suggested by Diamond and others proposes that populations at similar latitudes experience similar climates making it easier to adapt to crops, the domestication of animals and consequently adapt new human technologies to new locations. This has also been supported by evidence from genetic population studies.

The local Celtic church gave way to the Anglo-Saxon Church under the jurisdiction of Rome. The first bishops of the Diocese of Worcester, founded in 679-680, bore the title Episcopus Hwicciorum, and indeed in 693, Oschere was called rex Huicciorum. The early boundaries of the Diocese of Worcester reflect the continuity between the original Dobunni tribal territory, probably emerging around 400 BC, the creation of the Roman civitas around 48 AD and the founding of the Diocese in 679 AD of the Hwicce sub-kingdom.

There are more pagan place names found north of Worcestershire within the area of the old kingdom of Mercia which in the 7th century a pagan Mercia was surrounded by Christian states. Weoley now a district of the city of Birmingham is probably one and 'Tyesmere' meaning 'two lakes' may be another sacred site to a pagan god but the location is yet to be determined. There are more pagan place names found north of Worcestershire within the area of Anglo-Saxon kingdom of Mercia which in the 7th century Mercia was surrounded by Christian states. So, the survival of place names such as Wednesbury, Wednesfield and Weeford may be related to the relatively late conversion to Christianity of the Mercian establishment and the death of the old pagan war-horse Penda. This conversion was facilitated by Northumbrian and Irish monks and possibly supported by the Hwicce establishment. His son, Peada, was Christian and founded an abbey at 'Medeshamstede', modern Peterborough.

The Genetic Ethnic Evidence from Population Studies
Remarkably, recent genetic population studies have also hinted of the genetic ethnic continuity of the people of England and Worcestershire. One of the exciting recent additions of enquiry into the past has been the application of new molecular genetic techniques of gene sequencing that can reveal subtle

genetic differences between populations and also demonstrate continuity of populations over time. These techniques include bioinformatics, the use of powerful computers to analyse large amounts of information quickly and identifying a haplotype in an individual's chromosomes that tend to be inherited together from one parent.

The 2015 People of the British Isles (PoBI) project by Leslie and colleagues on the fine scale genetic structure of the British population revealed a rich and detailed pattern of genetic differentiation. The results showed remarkable concordance between genetic clusters and geography in the British Isles, showing clear signals of historical demographic events. The 2015 People of the British Isles (PoBI) project by Leslie and colleagues on the fine scale genetic structure of the British population revealed a rich and detailed pattern of genetic differentiation. The results showed remarkable concordance between genetic clusters and geography in the British Isles, showing clear signals of historical demographic events.

Based on two separate analyses, the study found clear evidence in modern England of the Anglo-Saxon migrations we have discussed in the preceding chapters. Many of the genetic clusters show similar locations to the tribal groupings and kingdoms around the end of the 6th century, after the settlement of the Anglo-Saxons. This finding suggests these tribes and kingdoms may have maintained a regional identity for many centuries. The majority of eastern, central and southern England is made up of a single, relatively homogeneous, genetic group with a significant DNA contribution from Anglo-Saxon migrations (10-40% of total ancestry). This settles a historical controversy in showing that the Anglo-Saxons intermarried with, rather than replaced, the existing populations. Another regional pattern in genetic make-up which mirrors historical and geographic factors is there are separate genetic groups in Cornwall and in Devon, with a division almost exactly along the modern county boundary. Another impressive result of the study was the genetic confirmation of the cultural differences in populations that existed in the Celtic north and Anglo-Saxon south of the Landsker Line in south west Wales.

It is likely, given what we know of early Anglo-Saxon times, a significant percentage of the population of Worcestershire are descendants of the Hwicce and to some extent the Dobunni tribes.

Anglo-Saxon Place Names in Worcestershire
In contrast to the faint and distant echoes of the Celts emanating from the names of ancient hills, forests, rivers and streams, the Anglo-Saxons left

us with more solid, practical details of their lives in the settlements and surroundings they named. They were, like so many before them, pioneer folk who expanded into Worcestershire appearing from the south and the east. They named their settlements mostly in their own language of Old English and these are the names that have stuck. This is because of the very large amount of written evidence in the form of charters and documents preserved in the archives of the Bishops of Worcester, the monasteries of the county and the publications of the Worcestershire Historical Society.

We have already met these Anglo-Saxon folks who migrated into Worcestershire in the historical account. We can also get to know them better by listening to the echoes that resonate from the place names they were busy coining in the region. The place names of modern Worcestershire generally mirror those in many parts of England being predominantly of Anglo-Saxon origin. The rate of Anglo-Saxon expansion from the south east of Britain meant that the period of Old English place name formation occurred later in Worcestershire, mainly during the 7th to 8th centuries, compared to the 5th to 6th centuries in the east and south east. In Worcestershire an even higher proportion of place names derive from Old English. During this period Mercia was a powerful kingdom and from the 9th century the power and expansionism of the kingdom of Wessex guaranteed continuous Anglo-Saxon dominance in the area. Raids or incursions by the Danes were seldom welcome and mostly repulsed. This Mercian power is demonstrated by the fact that after their assimilation or dispersion, the Celts did not name any new settlements within Mercian boundaries and the Danes very few. Settlements were named by the Anglo-Saxons in Old English and a few by anglicising earlier Celtic names. So, the Old English place names of Worcestershire were overwhelmingly first coined by the Hwicce advancing from the south and with some influence from the Angles from the east and north.

A linguistic study of the Hwicce has concluded that after their assimilation into the kingdom of Mercia, they spoke an Anglian dialect of Old English. These different dialects are demonstrated by a comparison of place names and from a comparison of written sources, for example, the variations found in the Lord's Prayer written in the Old English of the Saxons of Wessex and the Angles of Mercia.

For convenience and easy reference, I have categorised the meanings of place names of the county loosely into some defined groups but there is, however, some overlap between a few of these place names. These categories can be dipped in and out of depending on your own interests into the many aspects of

Anglo-Saxon life they describe and their proximity to where you live.

The Old English Folk Names of Worcestershire

We now meet the Anglo-Saxon folks from the echoes of the places they named after themselves. There were far more Anglo-Saxon tribes than there were major and minor kingdoms in early Anglo-Saxon southern Britain. There were 35 important enough to be listed in the Tribal Hidage, an assessment of the number of hides (as defined by the area of land that could support one family) in each kingdom or territory. This document was probably compiled in Mercia during the 7th or 8th century. Wessex had by far the largest at 100,000, Mercia 30,000 and the Hwicce, 7,000 hides. This represented a similar size economy to the kingdoms of Essex or of Sussex. This suggests that the Hwicce were a large and successful tribe.

Many place names across the south Midlands region are recorded in the dative form of their name. Many of these Germanic names of Anglo-Saxon England usually contain two elements (dithematic) and they often had a freestanding meaning. The meaning of some Anglo-Saxon names are known but many have been lost. Table 8 lists these place names that originated from Anglo-Saxon personal folk names and their meanings where known. Table 9 is a list of personal Anglo-Saxon names whose meanings are unknown. Examples of these personal folk names found in many of the original settlement names of Worcestershire include Ecgwine, whose prefix means 'sword' or 'blade' and suffix 'friend', the prefix of 'AElfweard' means 'elf' and the suffix 'guard' and the prefix of Flaede means 'purity', 'glory' and 'beauty'. The Anglo-Saxons used only one personal name which is equivalent to our Christian names and some were nicknames such as 'Callow', 'the bald one', 'Cran', 'the lanky one' and 'Strenge', 'the strong one'. Table 10 lists some of the meanings of the attested names of the kings and queens of Anglo-Saxon Mercia and the Hwicce tribe. Some of these personal names have been given to towns and villages in Worcestershire. Some of these suffixes, such as 'wulf' are so common they may have signified a male name only and lost any literal meaning.

One of the loudest calls that resonate from place names in the region come from the large and successful Hwicce tribe themselves. The Cotswolds straddle a huge area of almost 800 square miles and include parts of the counties of Worcestershire, Gloucestershire, Oxfordshire and Wiltshire. In 780 they are documented as 'monie quern nominant incolae mons Hwicciorum', 'the hill which is called by the inhabitants the hill of the Hwicce'. In 964 written as 'in monte Wiccisa', but after 1231 recorded as

'Coteswold' and later 'Codstun', the settlement of a man called Cod.

An early reference to the tribe appears in 730 as 'Huicciorum'. Bede refers to Worcestershire as 'Provincia Huicciorum', and in 800 is listed as 'Hwiccium' and 'Hwicca maego' towards the end of the 9th century. Covering the south east border of the Hwicce tribal kingdom, now in west Oxfordshire, was the extensive 'Hwiccewudu' 'the forest of the tribe called Hwicce', first mentioned in 841. It was recorded in the Domesday Book as Wychwood Forest and was designated a Royal Hunting Forest. The woodlands are thought to have supplied timber for the Droitwich salt industry as the Hwicce royalty had a monopoly on salt production in the Droitwich area. Wychwood Forest is now reduced to 1,240 acres and includes a National Nature Reserve and a Site of Special Scientific Interest (SSSI). There are a number of settlements in the area that were previously within or adjacent to the forest including Wychwood, Shipton-under-Wychwood, Ascott-under-Wychwood and Milton-under-Wychwood in Oxfordshire and Whichford, (in 1130 recorded as Wicheforda, 'ford of the Hwicce'), in Warickshire.

Bredon has been mentioned previously as a fascinating Brittonic Celt-Anglo-Saxon hybrid name. In 772 it appears as Breodun in Huic, meaning 'Bredon in the territory of the Hwicce'. In all early forms note that the original Old English suffix 'dun' which meant 'hill' had not yet been corrupted to 'don', which in the original Old English meant valley!

Wychbury Hill, near Stourbridge, on the north west border of Worcestershire, the site of an Iron Age fort and the first element of **Wychavon,** the name of a local government district, may be reminders of the local indigenous Anglo-Saxon tribe, the Hiwicce.

A possible portal connecting the past to the present is found in the name of the village of **Wychbold.** In 692 the settlement name is recorded as Uuicbold, and again 123 years later in 815, also as Uuicbold, then in 831 as Wicelbold. The prefix has been related to the Hwicce tribe. Indeed, there are several references to the tribal name as 'Huicciorum', the earliest in 730 by Bede. The suffix, 'bold' is also Old English and has the meaning of 'a superior house or palace'. A charter of 692 implies a high-status ownership and in 815 was the residency of Coenwulf, a king of the Mercians who is mentioned again in 831. It is, therefore, probable that the location was a permanent residence of the kings of the Hwicce, who were tributary to the

Mercian kings at that time and also an occasional residency of the Mercian kings themselves. However, more recently experts have suggested it more likely that the prefix 'Wic' or 'Wich' is probably derived later from its vicinity to Droitwich, so becoming 'the palace near Wich'. I think, however, the signpost 'Royal Wychbold' would be quite a remarkable entree to this unpretentious Worcestershire village. All someone has to do is find the foundations of the palace!

Worcester is mentioned in many Anglo-Saxon charters and was probably the capital of the Hwicce sub-kingdom. The earliest charters are dated 691 and name the settlement 'Uueogorna civitate' and 'Weogorna civitate'. In 717 'Wigranceastre' and 'Wirecestre' in 1086 as recorded in the Domesday Book. The 'caester' derives from the Anglo-Saxon word for a former Roman fort. The first element of Worcester is probably derived from the Weogora tribe and is likely itself derived from the Celtic name meaning 'people of the winding river'. It has been suggested by historians that the original Celtic name for the settlement was Caer Wrangon or Caer Wigornia. The earliest record of the Wyre Forest is in 816 and was written 'Weogorena leage', meaning 'the forest of the Weogran'. Similarly, the earliest documented name for the county was 'Wireceastrescir', the suffix 'scir' meaning 'district' and which later became 'shire'. The place name appears in the 10th century when the Wessex Saxons took control of Mercia and divided the assimilated kingdom into roughly equal parts.

In Anglo-Saxon times, people were known by a personal name or a nickname but had no surname. There are very many towns and villages in Worcestershire, as there are in England, named after these first Anglo-Saxon pioneers. So, you will be getting to know men called Peden, Headd and Tidbeorht and a woman known as Flaede. As we meet these men and women bear in mind that if your relatives lived in Worcestershire for many generations as suggested by their inclusion in the first National Census of England in 1801, then these people may well have been your ancestors and contributed to some of your genes. Thus, you may have some physical, psychological and physiological features in common with them!

Several Worcestershire place names are derived from the Old English name of Hwita's people or the modern cognate name of 'Whites' people. These include **Whittington**, in 816 was written 'Huitmgton', and in 989 as Hwitinlun, meaning 'the town of the sons of Hwit'. One of the five Lenches was recorded as

'Hwitan Hlince' in the 11th century and a Whitlenge (Whitlench), mentioned in the Domesday Book in 1086 and on a map of Hartlebury of 1840.

Witton, within Droitwich is recorded as 'Wittona' in 714, in 1043 as 'Hwitonam', in the 12th century as 'Witton Petri Corbezun' and in 1340 as 'Wytton St Peter'. These forms tell us this is 'hwit-tun' or 'white town'.

The Anglo-Saxon name of Brem is notable. Birmingham was originally known as Bremingeham (soft 'g'), 'the home of the descendants of Brem'. The meaning is 'renowned or illustrious'. A Brem fought for the Normans at the Battle of Hastings. The earliest recorded name for **Bromsgrove** is similarly Bremesgrcefan in 804, Bremesgrcef in 821, Bremesgraf and Bremesgrave in 822 and Bremesgrave again in 1275. The 's' suffix attached to 'Breme' was also used in Old English to denote possession. Bromsgrove was also founded by Brem or the followers of Brem. The original suffix 'grcefan', 'grcef' and 'graf' denotes a 'grove' with the meaning of a coppiced wood. These are also associated with the Old English word 'grafan', to dig. Gelling and Cole proposed that place names with this suffix are associated with managed woods surrounded by ditches to deter browsing animals. There is well documented evidence that the large Domeday estate of Bromsgrove provided significant quantities of fuel to the saltworks at Droitwich. Leland describes the fuel for the saltworks as 'young pole wood, easy to be cloven'.

The name of the town of **Evesham** is derived from a folk name but that has not always been the case. The etymology of the settlement can be followed quite closely as there has been good preservation of many of the early charters. The earliest record of the settlement is in 709 as Homme. Homme, Hamme or Ham, a habitual place name, was used by the Hwicce, in both Worcestershire and Gloucestershire, to denote a settlement on a riverside meadow, especially one on the bend of a river. There are many 'hams' on the Severn, Avon and indeed on smaller rivers and brooks in the county, such as Eastham and Newnham Bridge. Evesham, like many major towns of England, is almost encircled by a large loop of a river, in this case, the River Avon. Also, in 709 the town is documented as 'Eveshomme', in 714 both as 'Homme' and as 'Eouesham'. However, in 854 as 'Ecguines hamme'. In the 11th century, the town reverts to 'Eofeshamme' and again in the 12th century as 'Eoveshame'. We can make some sense of this metamorphoses by explaining that Ecguine was the first Abbot of Evesham and the third Bishop of Worcester from 693 to 717, so was commemorated in the name of the town in 854. Eof was Bishop Ecgwine's herdsman. Ecgwine records that the Virgin appeared to Eof holding a book and with two maidens in attendance. Ecgwine also experienced this vision later and interpreted it as a command to build a monastery on this spot. Pope Constantine duly authorised the foundation of the Abbey which, at this time, was called 'Eofeshamme'. There is no 'v' in the Old English alphabet so the 12th century spelling of 'Eoveshame' reflects the influence of the Old French spoken by the Normans.

TABLE 8 Some Anglo-Saxon Folk Names of Known Meaning in Worcestershire		
Modern Place Name	Original Personal Name	Anglo-Saxon Meaning
Abberley	Eadbeald	'prosperity' and 'bold'
Abberton	Eadbeoht	'wealth, fortune' and 'beorht' - 'bright'
Alfrick	Ealhred	aelf' - 'elf' and 'raed' - 'counsel'
Alton	Eanwulf	'ean' unknown, 'wolf'.
Badsey	Baeddi	'battle' ?
Bengeworth	Beonna	'bear'
Bricklehampton	Beorhtwulf or Beorhthelm	'bright' and 'wolf' or 'helmet, protection'
Bromsgrove	Brem	'renowned', 'illustrious'
Chadwich	Ceadda	'battle' (from Celtic root 'cat' or 'cad')
Eardiston	Eardwulf	prefix unknown, 'wolf'
Evesham	Eof	'noble'?
Evesham	Ecgwine (name in 854)	'sword' and 'friend'
Fladbury	Flaede (f)	'purity', 'glory', 'beauty'
Grimley	Grima	ghost' or 'spectre'
Huddington	Huda	'mind, spirit heart' also a nickname for 'Hugh'
Ombersley	Ambr	'immortal'
Pinvin	Penda	unknown, but probably Celtic origin
Sedgeberrow	Secg	more likely 'warrior' or 'sword' but also 'ocean' and 'sedge'
Strensham	Strenge	'strong'
Tutnall	Totta	'thunder' and 'stone'
Warndon	Waerma	'snake' or 'serpent'
Whittington	Hwita	'white'
Wolverley	Wulfweard	'wolf' 'guardian'
Wolverton	Wulfhere	'wolf'

TABLE 9 Some Anglo-Saxon Folk Names of Worcestershire of Unknown Meaning	
Worcestershire Settlement Name	Personal Name meaning unknown
Bishampton	Bisa
Bredicote	Brada
Doddenham	Dodda
Dodford	Dodda
Dormston	Deormod
Eckington	Ecca
Feckenham	Fecca (possible)
Habberley	Heathuburg (f)
Hadzor	Headd
Hartlebury	Heortla
Inkberrow	Inta
Kempsey	Cymi
Kenswick	Caefea
Kersoe	Cridda
Martin Hussingtree	Husa
Mucklow	Muca
Oddingley	Odda
Offenham	Offa or Uffa
Pedmore	Pybba
Pensham	Peden
Peopleton	Pyppel
Perdiswell	Preed
Powick	Pohha
Shelsey Beauchamp	Sceld
Teddington	Teotta
Tibberton	Tidbeorht
Trimpley	Trympa
Wribbenhall	Wrybba

Table 10 The Names of the Hwicce Royalty and their Meanings		
NAME	PERIOD OF REIGN	MEANING OF NAME
Aethelred	675 - 704	'noble' and 'wisdom or counsel'
Aethelbald	715 - 757	'noble' and 'bold'
Beornred	757	'warrior' and 'wisdom' or 'counsel'
Ecgfrith	796	'sword' and 'peace'
Beornwulf	823 - 826	'warrior' and 'wolf'
Wiglaf	827 - 839	'fight' or 'battle' and 'what or who is left'
Wigmund	839 - 840	'fight' or 'battle' and 'protection' or 'defence'
Wigstan	840	'fight' or 'battle' and 'stone'
Beorthwulf	840 - 852	'bright' and 'wolf'
Burgred	852 - 874	'fortress' and 'wisdom' or 'counsel'
Ceolwulf	874 - 883	'keel (of a ship)' and 'wolf'
Æthelflæd (female)	911 - 918.	'noble' and 'beauty'

That is, however, not the end of the story in the evolution of Evesham's identity. An unusual feature of the naming of Evesham has been the recurrent appearance in documents of a previously strange and undecipherable inclusion. In 709 the settlement was also designated as 'Cronochomme'. In 717 recorded as 'Cronuchhomme' and again in 860 as 'Cronuchamme'. Some toponymists have given the prefix a possible but unknown Celtic word origin. The name may originate from the Old English words, 'cran', 'cranuc', 'cron', 'cronuc', 'cren' and 'crenuc' - all meaning crane, but later also became to mean a heron. These forms may be related to another Old English word meaning 'to cry hoarsely'. So the name of this large beautiful and unmistakable bird is perhaps an echo of their cry heard by Anglo-Saxon ears. Thus, 'Cronuchamme' means 'water meadows where the cranes live'. There are hundreds of place names in England, of both Old English and Old Scandinavian origin, which signify that they were once frequented by cranes. These include Cranford, Cranbrook and Cranmore. These magnificent birds had a wide distribution in Anglo-Saxon England and were concentrated in areas of low wetlands including the Avon valley. The average Anglo-Saxon male stood at 172 cm and female 160 cm compared to the average modern-day English male at 175 cm and female 164 cm. The trumpeting calls of the Common Crane, animated courtship dance and height of up to 130 cm would have meant they could not have been ignored by anyone working in the fields nearby.

Fladbury may represent the first strike for 'Women's Lib' in the county! In 692 written as Fledanburg, in 778 Flaedanbyrg and in Domeday Fledebirie. Thus, the village has the elements of Old English 'Fleade' and 'burgh', 'the fortified settlement of a woman called Flaede' as documented in the charter of 692. Flaede is a shortened version of several names including Aethelflaed.

It might come as a surprise, but Anglo-Saxon England between about 580 to 1066 was a comparatively bright period for women to fulfil their destinies. Anglo-Saxon society allowed women not only a high family status but also the widest liberty of intervention in public affairs. These rights included land ownership, marriage and child custody, professional opportunities, political leadership and participation in the legal system. Women had similar rights to men within the same social class during Anglo-Saxons times. This was in stark contrast to the limited roles that their descendants would play in Norman society. Thus, history shows that the values and advances that we hold dear now (and that includes technical and organisational medical advances) were not achieved in a smooth and upward trajectory but waxed and waned by the influences of chance and the other preoccupations of humans at the time.

Before the Norman Conquest, people did not have hereditary surnames. They were known by a personal name or nickname. When communities were small each person was known by a single name, but as populations increased and society became more complex, a further identification was required. This started the practice of connecting a name with what the persons role was in the community such as Cuthbert the Carpenter or Wilfred the Weaver.

Kidderminster is appears in Domesday of 1086 as Chideminstre and in 1155 as Kedelministre and Kiderministra in 1167 and well documented variations. We know there was a monastery founded here in 736 by king Aethelbald of Mercia, a site which was said to be favourable because of shelter from the surrounding hills and a plentiful supply of water. The folk name may be either 'Cydda's minister' or 'Cyddla's minster'.

Ombersley appears in 706 as Ambreslege, 714 as Ambresleie and 817 as Ombersetene gemaere. The first two records suggest the folk name Ambr, so 'the woodland clearing of Ambr'.

Feckenham, is recorded as 'Feccanham' in 804 and Feccanhom in 960. In the Hwicce dialect this means 'a settlement at a water meadow on a river or stream' and in this case probably 'of a man called Fecca'.

Inkberrow is documented as 'Intanbeorgas' in 789, 'Intanbeorgum' in 822 and 'Inteberge' in 1086. Thus, meaning 'Inta's mound or hill'.

Phepson is a tiny hamlet just north of Himbleton and south of Hanbury. The Venerable Bede records the group of settlers whom he called the Feppingas migrating to this location and likely before 730. Bede makes it plain that they were an Anglian tribe as he tells us that Diuma, the Bishop of the Middle Angles and the Mercians died there. In 956 documented as 'Fepsefnatune' in 1108 'Fepsintune', and in 1275 'Fepsintone. The Feppingas were an Anglo-Saxon tribe who moved from the area around Thame in Oxfordshire, then in Mid-Anglia. Another group he describes are the Stoppingas who migrated to Wootton Wowen. Indeed, the element 'setena' may derive from the Old English 'sittan' meaning 'settlers' or literally "to sit down'.

Bede also mentions the Wixan tribe migrated to the area around Bishampton at the end of the 6th century. They left their name in the form of the nearby **Whitsun Brook.**

Bishampton was included as 'Bisantune' in the Domesday Book of 1086 and also in the 14th century as 'Bishamtons' and 'Bisshopeshampton' so implying the original meaning as 'the settlement of a man called Bisa'.

Bredicote, three miles east of Worcester, is documented as 'Bradigcotan' in 840, 'Bradingccotan' in 978. The suffix derives from Old English 'cote' meaning 'cottage' and the prefix probably an Anglo-Saxon personal name 'Brada'.

Abberley is listed in the Domesday Book as 'Edboldelege' and appears in documents as 'Aldoldelega' in 1180 and 'Abbedeslegh' in 1216. Thus, meaning 'the woodland clearing of a man called Eadbeald'.

Abberton, situated just north of the Lenches, is a small village whose earliest record is in 972 as 'Eadbrihtincgtun' and thus 'the settlement of the people of Eadbeorht', consisting of the personal name then, 'inga' meaning 'people of' and 'tun' settlement, homesteads or village. The Old English word 'tun' eventually became the Modern English habitative name of 'town'.

Alfrick , six miles west of Worcester, is recorded as 'Alcredeswike' and 'Alfrewike' in the 13th century. This translates as 'Ealhred's wic'. Wic or Wick has the meaning of a farm producing a specialised product, often a dairy farm.

Besford, three miles south west of Pershore appears as 'Beilesford' in 972, in 1282 as 'Beford', and in 1275 as 'Beseford', which means 'the ford near Betti's house'.

Alvechurch, just north of Redditch, was written 'Elfgythe cyrce' in 780 and in 1323 as 'Alvievecharche'. 'Cyrce' means 'church', and is dedicated to St Lawrence. It is possible that the woman called 'Elfgyth' founded it.

Bayton, west of Bewdley, is recorded as 'Beitone' in 1080 and six years later in the Domesday Book as 'Betune', with a watermill. So, the likely interpretation is the settlement of 'Baege or Baega'.

Bengeworth, a district within Evesham, is well documented. In 709 as 'Benigwrthia', in 714 as 'Bemncgwrihe' and 'Benincguurihe', in 780 as 'Benincwyrthe'. The settlement is mentioned in another six charters including in 979 as 'Bennicworte' and the Domesday Book as 'Beningeorde'. Old English 'worth' means a farming settlement surrounded by a wooden palisade. The prefix derives from a personal name, so giving 'the farm of Beonna's people'. As is often the case, there are other variants of this personal name that appear as 'Bennington' or the 'sons of Benna' in Hertfordshire.

Frankley has a straightforward etymology. The suffix 'ley' derives from the Old English 'leah' meaning 'woodland clearing' with the personal name of 'a man called Franca'.

Hadzor in the Domesday Book appears as 'Hadesore' so 'Headd's hill or slope'.

Hartlebury has several recordings as as 'Heortlabyrig' in 817, 'Huerteberue' in Domesday and 'Heortlanbyrig' in 1320. Thus giving 'the stronghold of a man called 'Heortla'.

Catshill has a difficult etymology! The name has been documented as 'Cateshull', and as 'Kateshull' in Old English. It may represent the personal name of 'Caet' or 'Gael's' hill, or equally 'the hill where wild cats are found'.

Clows Top, between Bewdley and Tenbury is over 240 m (725 ft) above sea level. Near here are High Clows and Clows Cottage. In 1633 written 'Clowes Topp'. The Cloibe or Clouse was a Worcestershire family name as early as 1332.

Cropthorne, 3 miles south east of Pershore is well recorded as 'Cropponthorn' in 780, 'Croppanthorn' in 841, 'Croppethirne in 964 and 'Cropeiorn' in 1135. It has been proposed that this is a personal name meaning 'Croppa's thorn' and it was recorded by Nash that 'a great bush on the top of the fields dividing Cropthorne and Charlton is stated as the boundary'. The charter of 780 describes Cropthorne as 'regaled vicum' and a charter of 841 was written and signed at Cropthorne by Berhtwulf, king of the Mercians, on Christmas Day, his queen Ssethryth and many nobles being present and party to the charter. It seems likely that Cropthorne was a royal residence during this period. Some toponymists, however, have suggested that the first element is derived from Old English 'croppa' meaning 'a cluster' or 'bunch' which is also a possibility. There was a settlement called 'Croppedune' nearby the location of which is unknown, so this has been interpreted as meaning the name of the hill was 'Croppe'.

Huddington is written as 'Hudigtuna gemaera' in 840 and in the Domesday Book as 'Hundintune' meaning the farmstead of the people of Huda'.

Impney, is listed in the 13th century as 'Ymenege' and 'Imenye' meaning 'Imma's island'. The old meaning of island included 'land surrounded by marsh'. There was a mill here in the 12th century. 'Ey' is a loan word into Old English from Old Scandinavian. Well over half of Modern English words are loaned from other languages.

Lulsley, between Knightwick and Broadwas, lies on the River Teme. It is recorded as 'Lolleseie' and 'Lulleseia' in the 12th century and these earlier firms point to the combination of a personal name and a description of the locality in a lowland setting - 'Lull's island'.

Kempsey has been recorded since the 8th century as Kemesei, Cymesig, Kymesei, Kemesige and Chemesege. These all mean 'Cymi's island'.

Kenswick appears in the Domesday Book as Checinwiche and in the 13th century as 'Kekingwick' and 'Kekingewic' which gives 'the wic of the people of Caefea'.

Martin Hussingtree is listed as 'Meretun' and as 'Husantreo' both in 972 and meaning 'the farmstead by the lake' and 'the tree of Husa'. They are both of Anglo-Saxonorigin and may have been two separate places that united or two easily identified features of the landscape.

Oddingley is written as 'Oddingalea' and 'Odduncalea' in 963 and in the Domesday Book as 'Oddunclei'. This translates as they woodland clearing of the family or followers of a man called Odda'.

Offenham appears as 'Offeham' in 709, 'Uffaham' in 714 and 'Offenham' in 1086. The name means 'the homestead of a man called Offa or perhaps Uffa'.

Pedmore, near Stourbridge, in the Domesday Book is recorded as 'Pevermore', in 1176 as 'Pubemora' and in the 13th century as 'Pebbemore'. This translates as 'Pybba's moor'.

Pensham at first glance might lead you to suspect a Celtic origin from 'pen', meaning 'head of'. The locality is not high ground and the inclusion of an 's' points to an Anglo-Saxon personal name in possessive form. In 972 recorded as 'Pedneshamme' and in the Domesday Book as 'Pendesham' (the village is situated in a large loop of the River Avon). Thus, we have 'Peden's homestead'. Peden, which derives from Peada, was also the name of a king of Mercia who was the son of the old war-horse King Penda.

Pinvin derives from the name Penda, a renouned king of Mercia. Recorded as 'Pendefen' in 1187 meaning 'the place at or by Penda's fen'. Penda and his family gave their name to several settlements in the Midlands including Pinbury and Peddimore.

Powick, two miles south of Worcester, appears in 972 as 'Poincguuic' and 'Poiwic' in 1086. Thus 'the specialised farm (probably dairy) of the family or followers of a man called Pohha'.

Puck Hill, written as such in 946, is a ridge that lies just south west of Hanbury and now hosts a section of the Wychavon Way. It is not an uncommon place name in the Midlands but the origins were not originally intended to refer to any person of this world. A belief in good and evil spirits was almost universal in the Middle Ages, and Puck seems to have been the chief of the local tribe of elf's or hobgoblins. It is Old English with variants Pook, Pouk, Puca and Powk, but has deeper origins. Cognates are Pwca in Welsh, Pucanwyl in Scottish Gaelic, Puki in both Old Norse and in Icelandic. Shakespeare choose Puck in "A Midsummer Night's Dream" as Oberon's servant and jester. Rudyard Kipling, in his historical fantasy choose Puck too as the variant Pook, a hill so named near Bateman's, his beautiful home and gardens in East Sussex. Puck, I think, is one of Shakespeare's most enjoyable characters with his fun-loving, quick-witted and mischievous nature. What fun to meet him on Puck Hill on the evening of the summer solstice to exchange witticisms, jokes and riddles! Figure 6

Puxton, near Kidderminster, has a similar derivation but is used here as a personal name. In 1275 five families were assessed under the name of 'Pouke' which was also used as a nickname and implies this hobgoblin was not believed to be particularly evil just mischievous and acceptable! Indeed, there is a record of a Jordan Pouk living in Hanbury in 1275.

Place names that include **Hob** are also common in Worcestershire and include Hob Hill, Hob Hole, Hob Well, Hob Moor, Hob Green, Hob Croft and Hob Lane. The name again refers to a spirit or hobgoblin and is a rustic synonym of Rob Robin Goodfellow or Puck.

Sedgebarrow was written 'Segcgesbearuue' in the 8th century and 'Seggesbarue' in 1086. 'Secg' was an Anglo-Saxon name for 'warrior' and also used as a personal name.

Strensham, to the west of Bredon and situated on the west bank of the Severn appears in 972 as 'Strengesho' and in 1212 as 'Strengesham'. This prefix is a personal name from the Old English word 'strenge' meaning 'strong' and is probably a nickname. The suffix of the earlier name originates from the Old

English word 'hoh' meaning 'a spur of land' and the suffix of the later name, 'ham', is characteristic of a settlement near a water meadow adjacent to the river.

Teddington is documented as 'Teottingtun' in 780, 'Teotintun' in 964, 'Teottincgtun' in 969 and 'Teotintun' in Domesday. These suggest 'the farmstead of the family or followers of Teotta'.

Tibberton, 4 miles north east of Worcester, is listed as 'Tidbrihtincgtun' in 978 and as 'Tidbertun' in the Domesday Book, 'Tybrytone' in 1275 and 'Tyburton' and 'Tyberton' in 1307. This gives the original meaning of the name as 'the farmstead or village of the sons or descendants of a man called 'Tidbright' or 'Tidbeorht'.

Trimpley is found in the Domesday Book as 'Trinpelei', giving 'the place at the woodland clearing of a man called Trympa'.

Tutnall is recorded as 'Totehel' in the Domesday Book and in 1262 as 'Tottenhull'. 'Hyll' or 'hull' is Old English for 'hill', so this has the meaning of 'the place on the hill of a man called 'Totta'.

Upton Snodsbury in 972 is documented as just plain 'Snoddesbyri' and in the Domesday Book (1086) as 'Snodesbyrie' and in 1280 had become 'Upton juxta Snodebure' so now meaning 'the higher farmstead and stronghold of a man called Snodd'.

Warndon is listed as 'Wermedun' and also 'Warmendone' in the 11th century suggesting 'Waerma's place by the hill'. There exist other Anglo-Saxon documents relating to Dorset that imply ownership by a 'Werme' as in 'Werm's boundary' and 'Werm's Hill'.

Wilden is recorded in the 12th century as 'Wineladuna', 'W1nelduna' and 'Wiveldon'. Winela, a form of Winel, is an Anglo-Saxon personal name and 'dun', a hill, giving the meaning 'Winela's hill'.

Wolverley is recorded in 866 as 'Wulfferdinleh' and in the Domesday Book of 1086 as 'Ulwardelei'. This, thus means 'the woodland clearing of the family or followers of a man called 'Wulfweard'.

Wolverton is well documented and the name is nothing to do with canine predators. Written as 'Wulfringctun' in 977, 'Wulfringtun in 984 and in the Domesday Book as 'Ulfrintun' and means 'the farmstead of the family or followers of Wulfhere'.

Wribbenhall is recorded as 'Gurberhale' in 1086 and 'Wubbenhale' in 1160. This is an Anglo-Saxon personal name and the Old English 'halh' meaning 'nook of land', so giving them nook of land of a man called Wrybba'.

Wormington is actually just in Gloucestershire. In the Domesday Book listed as 'Wermetun', 'Wirmiton' in 1200, 'Worminton' in 1220 and 'Wurminton' in 1236. This translates as 'the place of the family or the followers of a man called Wyrma'. Wyrma is a form of Wyrm. I include the place name as the surname is one characteristically found in Worcestershire and recorded in the early National Census.

Bricklehampton, may be a unique place name in the English speaking world according to the linguist David Crystal. While you are mulling over this name, I will explain its etymology. Situated in the Evesham valley between Pershore and Evesham, it was written as 'Brihtulfingtun' in 972 but then 'Bricstelmestune' in 1086. The origins of the name may be either 'the farmstead of the people of Beorhrwulf' or 'Beorhthelm's Farmstead'. And the answer to the question? This 14-letter village name may well be the longest one-word place name in the English-speaking world that does not repeat any of its letters.

Conderton, south of Bredon, is towards the southern border of Worcestershire. In 875 it is written as 'Cantuaretun' and in 1201 as 'Canterton'. The Celtic name for Kent in the pre-Germanic invasion period was 'Cantiaci' (always a hard 'c' in the Celtic language). The Jutes from what is now Denmark occupied Kent and the Isle of Wight. It is fascinating to reflect that all these events and people are connected with this place name over a period of up to around 2,500 years. It means 'the farmstead of the Kentishmen'.

Comberton lies three miles south east of Pershore. Written in 972 as 'Cumbrincgtun' and in 1086 as 'Cumbrintune', the first element is derived from Old English 'Cumbre'. The word can be used as a personal name or a noun describing Celts or Welsh, rather like 'walh' meaning 'foreigner', which may have been a less polite name. Another example is the Old English derived name of Cumberland or 'land of the Welsh'.

Westmancote, just south west of Bredon Hill, appears as 'Westmonecote' and 'Westmancota' in 1275 and may mean 'the cottages of the western men'. If so, then these may possibly have been Welshmen. The Doomsday Book records an Under-tenant of the land by the name of Wesman.

After the Conquest of England, the Norman barons introduced identifying surnames which the indigenous population initially often used but then equally often dropped at will. Eventually, they began to be retained and passed down the generations, so by the beginning of the 15th century most English families were using hereditary surnames. These surnames were originally related to trades, places of origin and even nicknames.

Many surnames that can be traced back to the 14th century are thus related to ancestors' occupations or place of birth. Very few Anglo-Saxon personal names of the Medieval Period have survived into modern times, indeed, they may well have been a social disadvantage under Norman rule. The most common male surviving names are Edward ('Eadweard', meaning 'rich' or 'blessed' and 'guard'), Edwin ('Eadwine', 'rich' or 'blessed' 'friend') Edmund ('Eadmund', 'rich protector') Edgar ('Eadgar' 'rich spear'), Alfred ('Aelfraed', 'elf counsel') Oswald ('Osweald', 'god rule') and Harold ('Hereweald', 'army, brightness'). Female Anglo-Saxon names still in use include Audrey ('Aeoelbryo', meaning 'noble' and 'strength') and Godiva ('Godgifu', meaning 'god' and 'gift').

Some of the commonest surnames listed in Worcestershire in the First National Census of England of 1801 include Smith, Hill, Green, Hall, Turner, Cooper, White, Williams, Harries, Johnson, James, Wright, Clarke, Webb, Baker, Robinson, Lowe, Wormington and Allen. The list also includes many surnames usually associated with a Celtic origin such as Jones, Davies, Price, Morris and Evans. Of course, these Celtic names in Worcestershire may have arisen from migration. However, a significant number of the inhabitants of Worcestershire recorded in the 1801 census would be likely of mixed Anglo-Saxon Celt origins. The surname Dodkin is first found in Worcestershire where they held a family seat. The surname derives from the Anglo-Saxon personal name Dodd or Dodda and means 'son of Dodd or Dodda' as appears in Dodford.

Many of these surnames appear in charters relating to homesteads and farms as the property was often named after the first family who owned or lived there. This is true all over the county and a local example is **Webbhouse Farm**. The Webbe, Wibbe or Wybbe family held an estate in Hanbury and in 1275 William Webbe was in residence. Webbe is a trade name meaning 'weaver'.

No full contemporary record of the Hwicce royalty survives. However, a list has been compiled by historians from a variety of primary sources. Table 10 includes the Anglo-Saxon meaning of their names.

I deal with **Tardebigge** last as it is difficult, an enigma and perhaps unique in Worcestershire. Some of the calls of place names are powerful and their meanings decipherable and some of their echoes have become so faint and distorted over time that they are now unintelligible. Tardebigge is in the latter category. Situated between Bromsgrove and Redditch, the village presents some fascinating and unique features and one of these is the degree of challenge in understanding what the name is saying! Relatively isolated and set at 165 m elevation it provides wonderful panoramic views of the Ridgeway and Warwickshire hills, the Gloucestershire Cotswolds, May Hill in Herefordshire, the Malvern and Abberley Hills, the mid-Severn valley and often Hay Bluff in Powys around 45 miles away. The village history is unique as it is the only place in Britain that has belonged to three counties. Situated initially within Staffordshire from 1100 until 1266, in Warwickshire (as part of the Bordesley Abbey Estate) until 1844 and finally came to rest in Worcestershire. Documented as 'Tardebigg' in 974, as 'Tczrdebicgan', in the Domesday Book appearing as 'Terede(s)bigga' in 1317, during the 10th century written as 'Tarde bicg', later as 'Terdebiggan', in the 12th century as 'Terdeberie' and 'Terebigge', in 1283 'Tyrdebrigg' and in 1375 as 'Turdbice'. Despite the consistency of early forms, they are very difficult to define or categorise. The terminal is like nothing in Old English or any Celtic language. There have been suggestions that it may be derived from an Old Scandinavian 'bigging' which appears as 'biggin' in the northern England, but the frontier of Danelaw lay over 30 miles to the east. An Anglo-Saxon charter of 911 documents a battle between Anglo-Saxon Mercians (led by a son of a Mercian king) and Danes (led by King Cnut) but there is no record of Scandinavian residency in the area. The 'cg' in the suffix of some of the name variants may point to an Old English root but some toponymists have favoured a Celtic origin. Some experts have concluded it may represent an Anglo-Saxon personal name, 'Tyrdda', a name which is thought to be associated with the village of Tredington 24 miles to the south east. The village is included in the Dictionary of British Place Names and suggests a possible Brittonic Celt origin from 'tarth' meaning 'spring' and 'pig' meaning 'peak'. However, most toponymists seem to agree this this is one of those place names which remains obscure and has even been postulated to be related to a pre-Celtic, possibly an Old European (pre-Indo-European) language! If true, this would mean the name originates from at least 3,000 to 4,000 years ago!

Worcestershire Place Names Describing the Landscape

Many of the Old English place names of Worcestershire describe the Anglo-Saxon landscape and what the people noticed, what was important to them in their daily lives and what they valued most for survival. Thus, place names provide us with a rich insight into their surroundings. These place names are interpreted with a varying degree of certainty and some, with no further pointers or evidence emerging, are frankly impossible and at best a partly informed guess. However, some are so straight forward because they shout so loudly and clearly you almost feel you know the place before you get there! You may have never visited Inkberrow, but you might guess it does not lie in a valley. Similarly, Longdon, I have never had the pleasure of visiting, but I feel I know the place fairly well and can, I think, image the surrounding views. This chapter reveals how you can too.

A very common element of place names in Worcestershire is the Old English word 'leah' meaning 'a woodland clearing'. The word later came to mean 'a homestead or farmstead in a woodland clearing'.

In Anglo-Saxon times, the Forest of Arden was one of the largest continuous woodlands in central England. It covered around half of Warwickshire, parts of Staffordshire and north east Worcestershire and stretched from Stratford-on-Avon in the south to Tamworth in Staffordshire in the north and included the area now occupied by the cities of Birmingham and Coventry. At this time, woodlands covered around 30% of England, compared to around 12% now.

Although, the forest has become a pale shadow of its former self, its previous glory is reflected in the number of place names that were situated within its boundaries. Towns reminding us of its wide expanse include Hampton-in-Arden (Borough of Solihull), Henley-in-Arden and Tamworth-in-Arden (Warwickshire). Henley-in-Arden was the most important and largest settlement in the forest at the time.

The expanse of this 'wildwood' is also reflected by the 85 towns and villages in Warwickshire that are situated within its ancient boundaries taking their name from the Old English 'leah' meaning woodland clearing and found as the suffix 'ley' in place names. Only four villages of Warwickshire outside the original forest boundaries have names ending in 'ley'. This also explains the high number of districts of Birmingham (from Bartley to Yardley, around 25 in all) ending in 'ley' originating within this dense woodland. An ancient mark stone, known as the 'Coughton Cross' is still present on the south west corner of the old Forest of Arden and can be found at the southern end of the frontage of Coughton Court.

Likewise, there are many place names of Worcestershire that contain the Old English 'leah'. These are particularly found in north east Worcestershire in the area touched by the Forest of Arden and the old Royal Forest of Feckenham, such as Bentley and Bradley Green. Also, concentrations of this suffix are evident in the north west around the area of the Wyre Forest, such as Wolverley and Arley, in the north, Hagley and Romsley and west of the River Severn, as in Astley, Witley, Shrawley, Ombersley and Martley.

Some of these woodland clearings inhabited by the early Anglo-Saxons were of natural origin and some were created by the Anglo-Saxons themselves. However, as we have seen, many preceding cultures contributed to their formation, including the Mesolithic, Neolithic, Bronze Age people and Celts. This might explain the fewer place names containing this element in parts of the county that had already been well cleared and farmed by the time of the arrival of the Anglo-Saxons, mainly the wider fertile valleys. Although a description of a feature of the landscape, a 'leah' also tells us that farming was taking place in the area, either as the cultivation of crops or as the grazing of livestock.

Astley, is just down river from Stourport-on-Severn and appears early as 'Aestleah', 'Eslei' I the Domesday Book, 'Estlege' in the 12th century and 'Estley' in the 13th century. The name derives from the Old English words 'east' and 'leah' giving 'the eastern woodland clearing'. From the Subsidy Rolls of 1275 there was a small monastery here. The 'monks of Estle' being assessed at two and a half marks.

Astwood Bank describes the place perfectly. In 1242 written 'Estwode', the elements are Old English 'est' meaning 'east' and 'wode' meaning 'wood'. It describes an area which formed the eastern extremity of the Feckenham Forest. It also lies on the Ridgeway and thus the latter affix 'bank'.

Leigh, 4 miles west of Worcester, is unusual in that the Old English word 'leah' is more often found as a second element and the first element is often a personal name or some other distinguishing attached word. However, in 972 it is recorded as 'Beornothesleah', so the 'woodland clearing of a man called Beornoth'. By the Domesday survey it had become the plain and simple 'woodland clearing' and has retained that meaning ever since.

Similarly, **Lye**, adjacent to Stourbridge and historically within the boundaries of Worcestershire, is listed as 'Lega' in 1275 and has exactly the same origin from Old Englidh 'leah'.

Harpley, near and west of Clifton upon Teme, is what it says on the label! In 1222 appearing as 'Hoppeleia' and in 1275 as 'Harpele', from the Old English 'hearpe', so meaning they harp shaped woodland clearing'.

Cleeve Prior, 5 miles north east of Evesham, is documented in 888 as 'Clife'. In the Domesday Book the scribes dispensed with the Old English 'f' and substituted with the Old French 'v' written as 'Clive' and 'Clyve'. This change was then taken into the Middle English name 'Cleeve' meaning 'Cliff' or 'steep decent'. Obvious in the similarly named Cleeve Hill, the highest point of the Cotswold escarpment at 330 meters above sea level, but flat, lowlands sometimes a name given to a mere rising of the ground. The settlement was the property of the Priors of Worcester and by 1291 had become 'Clyve Prior'.

Barnt Green has a similar meaning but different etymology and is a fairly common name in England. It derives from the Old English word 'bernet' meaning 'burning' thus giving 'the woodland place cleared by burning', possibly from a natural event such as a lightning strike or as a farming method.

The Hwicce tribe, as did many immigrants who came before them, occupied the previous cultures settlements and particularly the more rural and those with advantageous resources or a strategic position. These included Roman fortified settlements which were often also on the high ground where Celtic Iron Age hill forts had been located. Indeed, the hill forts were probably some of the most obvious and frequent prehistoric monuments that the Anglo-Saxons witnessed in Britain. This continuity can be seen at the church hill in **Hanbury**, a settlement originating in the woodland setting of the Forest of Feckingham and has a relatively rich amount of supporting documentation surviving

There are two settlements in England called Hanbury, the other in Staffordshire.[6] In Table 11 I have compared their etymologies. Both place names are derived from two Old English words, 'heah' meaning 'high' and 'burh' meaning 'fortified settlement'. In Anglo-Saxon times, 'burg' and later 'burh' was pronounced a hard 'burx', which is partly the reason the Old French speaking Normans had such an issue with the Old English language. Oftentimes, the evolution of a place name takes a slightly different course over the centuries and have later converged. Both are of high elevation, Hanbury, Worcestershire, 103 m above sea level and Hanbury, Staffordshire at 140 m above sea level. Both settlements have developed around a church. In Hanbury, Staffordshire the church of St Werburgh is named after a Mercian Queen who organised effective defences against the Danes.

If you stand on the hill of the present-day Church of St Mary The Virgin, Hanbury, you can imagine the outlook in Anglo-Saxon times. Around three times the afforestation of current times, and on a clear (and perennially unpolluted) day, a panorama of the middle Severn valley, the Cotswolds, the Malvern and Abberley Hills and parts of Oxfordshire, Gloucestershire and even Hay Bluff in Powys, Wales opens out. The remains of the embankment and ditch of the Celtic Iron Age fort can be clearly seen and there is evidence of continuity from Celtic into Roman times with a number of coin finds. It has been suggested there may have been a church here in the 4th century, and if so, this would have been for Celtic Christian worship. A copy of an Anglo-Saxon charter from 660 records a 'minister' at Hanbury and thus Christian worship has taken place continuously since at least this date and perhaps before. A grant of 50 'manses' was made to an Abbot Colmannus in 675 by the King of Mercia in his will. Another document from 836 records, Wiglaf a king of Mercia, making grants to the Hanbury monastery.

---

[6] Hanbury, Staffordshire has been the location of a noteworthy accident and a major catastrophe through the ages. The Domesday surveyors arrived to assess 'how many hundreds of hides, and what stock upon the land, or, what dues (the king) ought to have by the year from the shire'. They duly made a detailed assessment of the locality, then realised they were not in Hanbury but another village several miles away! The catastrophe is known as the 'RAF Fauld' explosion, one of the largest artificial explosions in the world at the time, occurred within the civil parish in November 1944. Between 3,500 and 4,000 tons of ordnance exploded in an underground ammunition store. The ensuing crater measuring 91 meters deep and 230 meters wide is still visible to the east of Hanbury and is known as the Hanbury Crater. Around 70 people died in the incident, many drownings when a reservoir was obliterated and a farm and houses flooded.

Under the Mercian kings, an enclosed royal hunting area in the centre of the village called Feckenham Park was formed. In the Domesday Book, the whole parish was within the Royal Forest of Feckenham. Before 1301, the forest boundaries covered around 184 square miles from Evesham in the south to Belbroughton in the north, Worcester in the west and Alcester to the east. However, this was a legal definition and the area was not entirely wooded. Much of the timber of the forest was used for salt production at Droitwich. The King had legal rights over game, timber and grazing within the forest. Courts were held and the forest gaol located at Feckenham where severe penalties were imposed on transgressors. Executions were carried out at Gallows Green between Hanbury and Droitwich.

There are several place names in England with similar origins to these two Hanburys, including the Highbury districts of London, Birmingham and Manchester. Also, the village of Handborough, Oxfordshire in 1086 is listed as 'Haneberge' with the same meaning of 'high fortification' as the two other Hanburys. The name is fully justified by all three locations with the commanding positions from their parish church's over the surrounding countrysides.

Table 11 The Two Hanburys in England		
Hanbury Worcestershire		Hanbury Staffordshire
Name	Date	Name
Heanburg	12th Century	Heanburh
Heanburh	13th Century	Hamburg
Heanbyrig	13th Century	Hambyri
Heanbyrig	13th Century	Hambury
Hambyrie	14th Century	Hanbury
Hambury	1430	Hanbury

So, place names even with similar origins evolve, diverge and sometimes converge again over time. A number of Henburys in Dorset and Cheshire also have similar derivations as the Hanburys. Indeed, the name may be another example of the tendency of cultures in the past to name a local feature with the generic word in that language for the feature. We have seen examples of this previously, such as 'bryn' in the Celtic language, 'hyll' in

Old English, giving the meaning 'The Hill' and 'afon', giving the meaning as 'The River'. In other words, the only 'hill' or 'river' that is important to the local inhabitants. This may also be the case for 'The High Fort', a perfect description for the inhabitants, most of which were born, lived and died locally.

Interestingly, the 7th century name of Hanbury in Worcestershire, 'Heanburg' has many cognates on the Continent. Heuneburg, in southern Germany, is the site of one of the most impressive Celtic hill forts in Europe. There are other close parallels between these two places which underlines connectedness and continuity as both guarded and controlled important commercial routes. Heuneburg overlooks the Danube and thus trade from the Mediterranean and Hanbury's hill fort, guarded one of the Saltways leading east from Droitwich and an ancient north-south road from Bromsgrove to the Cotswolds. Both are now known by their Germanic names but both would have had prior Celtic names. The Common Brittonic name of the Worcestershire Hanbury has been lost over time, although there is sufficient evidence to speculate that it may have included the Celtic suffix 'dunum', meaning 'fort'. However, at Heuneburg excavations have revealed one of the largest and most important early Celtic sites in Central Europe from the 7th to 5th century BC. The Greek historian Herodotus in his 'Histories' of the mid-5th century, wrote of a city to the north on entering the land of the Celts which he called 'Pyrene' situated on the river Istros. The 'Istros' was the Old Greek name for the Danube meaning 'swift, strong'. An increasing number of archaeologists now suspect that Pyrene refers to the Heuneburg hill fort site.

There are other place names in Worcestershire that have an element with the same origins to the Hanburys mentioned above. **Hanley Castle, Child, William** and **Hanley Swan** are all also derived from the Old English word 'hean' meaning 'high', so all meaning 'high woodland clearing'.

Bach or sometimes 'Batch' is a common terminal and occasional prefix in place names of Worcestershire, Herefordshire and Shropshire. The Old English, 'bcece' and Middle English 'bache', means 'a bottom of a valley, or hollow, with a stream running through'. Several places known by their modern name of 'badge' are derived from 'bach'. Badge Court near Elmbridge is such, the residence of the Earl of Shrewsbury and later renowned as the home of Helena Wintour, daughter of the Gunpowder Plot conspirator Robert Wintour. In 1275 'Bache', and 1325 'Bachecote' 'the cottage in a hollow'.

Cow Bach is the name of a field in Clent near St Kenelm's Chapel, named after the venerated Saint mentioned by Chaucer in the Canterbury Tales and by William of Malmesbury. The church marks the site where it is said St Kenelm (his original name was Coenhelm) was murdered while on a hunting trip in 821. This is now the starting point of the 60 miles St Kenelm's Trail to Winchcombe where his body is interred. The source of the River Stour is within the grounds of the church.

Batchley, a north west district of Redditch, has the same etymology as Bach. In 1464 written as 'Bacheley' so from the Old English root 'bcece' or 'bece' so meaning 'the farmstead in a clearing in a steep-sided river valley'.

There is a tendency for languages to develop a number of words for a natural feature (and indeed many other things) that were important to them and that are meant to convey subtle differences between these features or things. The 'knapp' as in 'The **Knapp** and Papermill Nature Reserve' near Alfrick, 'Cold Knapp' Wood in Dormston, Fidler's Knap in Elmley Castle and also Collier's Knap and Dornap both in Broadway are examples in Worcestershire and probably means a 'rounded hill'. Other words for hill in Old English in addition to 'dun', include 'hyll', 'hrycg', 'hrycg', 'hoh', 'heafod', 'ofer' 'beorh' and 'beorge' and probably all convey slightly different types of hill. The place name 'Knowle' has an origin from the Old English word 'cnolle' with a similar meaning.

Cook hill, is yet another variation on a hill description. Found as 'Cochilla' in 1156 and 'Cochull' in 1262 literally means 'hill hill' so yet another of the many tautologies found in place names.

Berrow Hill, is derived from the Old English words 'beorh' and 'beorge', meaning 'hill' or 'tumulus', with later Middle English variants of 'barrow' and 'berrow'. Thus, this feature of the landscape is described twice in another tautology of Middle and Modern English - Hill, Hill!

Blackdown, near Hagley has origins in the Old English 'blacan' and 'blcec' meaning 'black' and Old English 'don' which came to mean 'hill'.

Similarly, **Blackmore**, in 1314, is recorded as 'Blakemor' from Middle English, meaning the 'black moor' referring to the dark soil of the area.

Bradley Green, east of Droitwich, is recorded as 'Bradanlaeh' in 730 and 'Bradanleage' in 803. These are two common Anglo-Saxon place name elements meaning 'the place at the wide woodland clearing'. Unusually, in this case, they always seemed to stood alone as invariably the description is associated with a personal name. At the time of the Domesday Book, the settlement belonged to the church.

Broughton is a common English place name and in Worcestershire usually derives from 'Broctune' meaning 'the farmstead on or near a brook'. This is the case in Broughton Hackett, in Belbroughton and Brockhamton Estate on the Herefordshire Worcestershire border. **Broughton Green**, just south of Hanbury, was formerly known as Temple Broughton reflecting ownership by the Knights Temple. The hamlet is located on higher ground without a nearby stream so may be derived, as some are, from the Old English words 'beorg' and 'tun', meaning 'farmstead on a hill'. It is further confusing as a 'broc' is also the Old English name for a badger. Green is a later addition of the Middle Ages when it denoted common land which local people had specific rights, such as grazing of their livestock.

Less than a mile to the west lie **Goosehill**, Goosehill Wood, Upper and Lower Goosehill Farms and Goosehill Lane. One of the earliest appearances of the name is as Middle English 'Goshull' as documented in the Bishops' register - 'Above Goshull lay a common, free for all men of the country, whether bond or free, for their cattle'.

Callow is a common name in the Midlands and is represented in Worcestershire by several Callow Hills, one just east of Redditch, in the Wyre Forest, near Broadwas, Oddingly and Bredicote. There is also a Callow End, a village just south of Powick and near the west bank of the Severn. They all derive from the descriptive Old English word 'calwe' or 'calu' meaning 'bare' in relation to a hill and 'bald' in relation to a person.

Claines, a village just north of Worcester, in 1234 recorded as 'Cleinesse'. This originates from Old English, 'claeg-naes' or 'clayey point of land'.

Dunclent, written as such in the Domesday Book and as 'Dounclent' in 1315, describes perfectly its situation on the slopes below the Clent Hills. Old English 'dun' came to mean 'down' or 'lower'.

Hallow, west of the River Severn between Holt Fleet and Worcester, appears as 'Heallingan' in 816, 'Hallege' in 963 and 'Halheogan', in 1135. The name is from the Old English words 'hagan-halh', meaning 'the enclosure in a nook or corner or tongue of land', often between two streams. The manor was granted by Coenwulf, king of the Mercians, to the Bishop of Worcester in 816.

Sometimes you can know a place long before you visit! Inkberrow is one such village - it is not going to be situated in a valley and shouts out higher ground! The same is also true of **Longdon**, 2 miles south west of Upton-on-Severn, and one of the disappointingly long list of places I have never visited. However, it is likely to be a small settlement on a long and elevated hill. This makes sense flanked by Longdon Marsh to the west and Bushley Brook and the River Severn to the east. In Anglo-Saxon times the Severn was tidal way beyond Worcester and would have occasionally extended to the low ground below the village. In 972 and 1046 written as 'Langdune', and later as 'Longandune' and 'Langandune'. Thus meaning 'settlement on the long hill'.

Harbours Hill farm lies on a ridge between Hanbury and Stoke Prior and is now the site of a recently planted vineyard. I have always been puzzled by this place name so far away from the sea! Although the word derives from the Old English 'herebeorg' meaning 'shelter, lodgings, quarters', some similar place names derive from the Old English compound name 'eorth-burh' meaning 'earth fort' as in Arbury, Harbury, Harborough and Yarborough. However, at this location I have not yet found any other clues as to the origin. A challenge for some one! Please let me know!

Timberhonger Lane is on the south west periphery of Bromsgrove. I have often wondered on travelling passed about the derivation of this rather strange name. It has been written as 'Timber-hanger' and 'Timberdine'. The elements are Old English and originally meant and enclosure, a field or place surrounded by a bank or hedge'. Later, 'Timber' referred to large trees and 'hangra' to 'hanging trees', and thus came to mean 'the hanging wood of large trees'. The nearby lane and area take their names from the large copse of trees on the ridge above, which presumably due to the difficulty in cultivating the slopping land, has been continuously wooded from at least Anglo-Saxon times.

Bungay Lake Lane is a nearby and equally strange name so is worthy of inclusion as such. It may be related to the Old English word 'bungy' which meant 'puffed out, protuberant' and appears as 'Bungy' in 1275. However, there is a Bungay in Suffolk written as 'Bunghea' in the Domesday Book. It is probably derived from the Anglo-Saxon personal name 'Buna', 'ing', signifying 'family or followers' and 'eg', meaning 'island', thus the 'island of the family or followers of a man called Buna'. Bungay, became a family name and so the Worcestershire place name may be associated with ownership by a member of the Bungay family.

Witley is well documented and found as 'Wittlaeg' in 964, 'Witleah' in 969, 'Wihtlega' in the 11th century, 'Witlege' in the Domesday Book and 'Whitele Major' in 1275. Both elements are Old English, 'wiht' meaning to 'bend' or 'curve' so 'the woodland clearing by the bend'. This bend refers to the deep recess in the Abberley Hills at Great Witley. Some toponymists have suggested that the settlement name derives from the 'Wita', 'Hwit' or 'hwlt', meaning Old English 'white'. However, then you would expect 'Hwitanleage' or 'Wttankage'. It is true that many Witley's certainly mean 'white woodland clearing' but probably not this one.

Wickhamford is found as 'Wicwona' in 709, 'Wiquene' in 1086 and 'Wikewaneford' in 1221. The meaning is 'the ford at the place called Wicwon'. The name seems to have a similar origin to the nearby village of Childswickham. This village is recorded as both 'Childeswicwon'' and 'Wicwone'. 'Wicwon' has been tentatively related to the Brittonic Celt word 'guic' meaning 'lodge, wood' and also with 'guoun' meaning 'plain, meadow or moor'. Certainly, both are situated in a flat part of the Vale of Evesham but the etymology is not certain!

Ripple is one of the most southerly parishes in the county and lies just east of the River Severn. Its etymology is certainly consistent, in 680 ''Rippel', in 1275 'Ryppel'. The name may derive from the Old English word 'ripel' meaning the 'place at a strip or tongue of land'. The village lies on a long stream that flows into the Severn two miles to the south. There is also a 'Ripple' village in Kent.

Just to the east of the Teme valley lies **Shrawley Woods** on the western bank of the Severn. This is one of the largest small-leaved lime woods in England at around 500 acres, but probably extended on to the eastern side of the Severn in the past. Some trees found here are over 300 years old, although a few at Westonbirt Arboretum in Gloucestershire are estimated to be 2,000 years old, so were growing for almost 500 years before the Anglo-Saxons arrived! Shrawley is earliest recorded in 804 as 'Scraefleh', in 1150 as 'Escreueleia' and 'Schraveleg' in 1212. The Old English 'scraef-leah' means the place of 'the woodland clearing by a scraef'. A 'scraef' has several meanings including 'cave, den or novel' or 'hollow, ravine'. It may refer to a nearby topographic feature.

The Anglo-Saxon Water Ways of Worcestershire
The presence and behaviour of water, water courses and sources have always been of great importance to people and especially for farmers. Not surprisingly, there are many references to them in Anglo-Saxon place names.

The **River Rea** is a tributary of the Teme. The name derives from the root, 'ea' found in many Indo-European languages and means in Old English, 'a stream', 'to run' or 'to flow'. The 'r' is intrusive and found post-Norman conquest and survives even though documents refer to the 'ea'. The element is found in settlements in England near rivers such as in Eton, Berkshire and Eaton, Oxfordshire and are thus both 'water town' and both on the River Thames. The Worcestershire River Rea was recorded in 957 and 1007 as the 'Nen', a word of Celtic origin. The place names, Neen Savage and Neen Sellers take their name from the river. There are rivers named Nene in Northamptonshire and Hampshire.

Smite, in 978 is recorded as 'Smitan' and in 1275 is written 'Smite'. In the spirit of 'if it works don't fix it mode', it has not changed since!

In the charter, the word is used as a river name and also contains the phrase 'from the slough to the Smitan'. A 'slough' or 'sloh' means 'soft, muddy ground'. There is also a River Smite in Leicestershire, but the meaning of the word is unknown. 'Upper' and 'Lower' Smites were later additions to differentiate the places.

The **River Salwarpe** is formed at Bromsgrove from a confluence of the Battlefied and Spadesbourne brooks and flows over 20 miles to join the Severn at Hawford. The river is mentioned in numerous Anglo-Saxon charters, the earliest in 817 as 'Salouurpe' and in the Domesday Book as

'Salewarpe'. The name probably originates from the Old English 'salu-wearp' meaning 'dark-coloured silted land' and perhaps also influenced by the Old English word 'weorpan' meaning 'to throw up', as in throwing up silt. The Old English weird 'waesse' means 'alluvial land' often referring to areas subject to seasonal flooding. It has been postulated by some toponymists that as the river runs through Droitwich and receives the overflow of salt springs and that the prefix may be related to 'throwing up salt'. but this is now thought a less likely origin.

Bow Brook, running through the Parish of Hanbury, arises in Upper Bentley and flows 28.8 miles south across Worcestershire to join the Avon at Defford. It seems to have been known by many names at various times as documented in Anglo-Saxon charters. Surprisingly, the name does not derive from the obvious alternatives of rivers bends or a description of its beauty but to the Old English name 'boga' meaning 'bridge', probably a footbridge.

Holt Fleet, west of Ombersley describes two aspects of the surrounding landscape. The Old English meaning of 'holt' is a 'wood, copse, thicket' often of same species tress. The Proto-Germanic cognate is 'hulta' and modern German 'Holz'. The Old English word 'fleot' means 'inlet, creek, mouth of river'. The name probably refers to the small stream which joins the Severn here.

Hewell Grange in Tardebigge appears as 'Hewelle Grange' in 1300. The 'h' is intrusive as the word should be 'Ewell' deriving from the Old English 'ce-wylm' or 'ce-wielle' meaning 'a water-spring'.

Broadwas, on the river Teme 7 miles west of Worcester tells us another story about the landscape in Anglo-Saxon times. In 779 written as Bradeuuesse and Bradewasse. In 1108 recorded as Bradewasse and Bradewesham, and in 1275 Bradewas. 'Brddwasc' in Old English means 'broad wash' or land liable to flooding along the side of a river.

Badsey and **Impney** share common origins. They both contain a prefix of an Anglo-Saxon personal name, 'Badde' or 'Baeddi' and 'Imma' respectively. They both contain a suffix which is a loan word from Old Scandinavian into Old English. The element 'ey' means an 'island' in the sense of raised land and therefore relatively dry land, surrounded by marshy or 'watery land'. Impney, just north of Droitwich, in the 12th century is documented as 'Impney', 13th century as 'Ymenege' and also as 'Imenye'. This gives the Anglo-Saxon masculine name, 'Imma's island'. There is a reference to a mill there at the time. Similarly, Badsey, two miles east of Evesham, in 709 was written Baddeseia, in 714 Baddesege and in 860 as Baddesig and means 'Badd's island'. It belonged to the Abbey at Evesham.

Lode is a common terminal in place names on the River Severn. In Old English 'ge-ldd' and Middle English 'lade' means 'a way' or 'passage' as applied to a ferry or ford. **Clevelode** is a village on the west bank of the River Severn about five miles south of Worcester. Written 'Clyvelode' in 1275, 'Clivelade' in 1300, 'Clyvelode' in 1319 and 'Cleveloade' in 1595. 'Cleeve' in Middle English means 'cliff' or 'steep bank'.

Saxons Lode, on the east bank and down river from of Upton-upon-Severn, is recorded as 'La Lode' in 1275 with an Old French influence, later 'Sastanelode' and 'Sextonslade' and 'Sestanelade' in the 16th century. The prefix may well be the personal name of an early ferryman, perhaps, 'Saexstan'.

Bransford is interesting as it describes two landscape features in one place name. The village lies south west of Worcester and close to the river Teme. The first element likely derives from the Old English word 'braegen' literally meaning 'brain' in the sense of 'crown of the head of a hill'. So the name interprets as 'the ford by the hill'.

The stream known as the **Alve** flows in to the river Arrow at Alvechurch. Very many settlement names are taken from the name of the local river or stream, simply because the natural feature was invariably named long before the site was settled. However, this a rare exception known as 'back formation' as Alvechurch was named after a woman called 'Elfgyth'.

Defford, near Pershore, in 972 is recorded as 'Deopford', also 972 as 'Deopanforda' and 1282 as 'Depeford'. In Old English 'deop' means 'deep' and thus means 'place of the deep ford'. It lies in a half circle of the Avon.

Draycott, lies just south of Kempsey and east of the River Severn. It is written as 'Draycote' in 1275 and derives from the Old English 'dragu-cot' meaning 'the cottage by a portage'. A portage usually refers to the dragging of a craft over land between two rivers, but here more likely means, a detour over land to avoid an impassable stretch of river.

'Deadmans Ait' is almost an island field in Offenham, just up river from Evesham. 'Ait' is Old English for a small island and there are several 'aits' or 'eyots' found on the Thames. A local story suggests that it earned the name because of the slaying of stragglers here after the Battle of Evesham in 1265.

Twyford, near Evesham is a common name in England. In 714 documented as 'Tuiforde', in the 10th century 'Twyfyrde' so clearly from the Old English words 'twi' and 'fryde', giving 'the place of the two fords'. A similar etymology applies to Twynings, a village on the Worcestershire - Gloucestershire border. Situated between the rivers Severn and Avon and mentioned in 1016 as 'Tuinaeum', and in the Domesday book as 'Tueninge', the meaning is 'the place between to rivers'.

Shell Ford, in the tiny hamlet of Shell, crosses Shell brook between Himbleton and Bradley Green. In 956 listed as 'Scylf', later 'Scelves' and in 1275 as 'Schelve'. In Old and Middle English, the meanings are 'a shelving cliff', 'a slope' and sometimes 'table-land sloping on most of all sides'. Similarly, derived names are found in Shelf, Yorkshire, Shelf-hanger in Norfolk and in many places called Shelfields. The hamlet shares the same derivation as the first word of the Selly Oak district of Birmingham.

Stanford on Teme, takes its name from the river and the local ford.

Early forms include 'Stanfordesbrycg' in 1030, 'Stanford' in 1086 and 'Stanford on Temede' in 1317. The prefix is Old English meaning 'stoney'.

The Banquetting Orchard moated site is a scheduled monument adjacent to The Thrift woodlands between Lower and Upper Bentley. Surveyed in 1969 it contains the undulating earthwork remains of former tree planting and certainly some moats are known to be used for horticulture. It is thought to be the original site of the medieval, possibly summer, residence of the Pauncefoot family whose history is well documented from the 12th century.

Around 6,000 moated sites are known in England and by far the greatest concentration lies in central and eastern parts of England. There are easily over one hundred in Worcestershire. The majority served as prestigious aristocratic and seigneurial (feudal lord) residences between 1250 - 1350 so were a status symbol rather than a practical military defence. To be somebody, in that period, you simply had to have a moat!

Shatterford, four miles north of Kidderminster, in 996 is recorded as 'Sciteresforda', in 1271 as 'Sheteresford', as 'Shutterford' in 1577 and 'Shitterford' in 1673. It would be romantic if the village took its name from 'Scytere', an Old English word for an 'archer' or 'shooter', thus translating 'the archer's ford'. However, more likely the settlement is derived from the Old English word 'scitere' meaning, 'a sewer, a channel or stream used as an open sewer'. It is understandable that our cultural sensibilities and norms have corrupted the Old English root to something more acceptable, so the local residents are relatively lucky. Not so lucky are the residents of Shitterton, a hamlet in Dorset with exactly the same roots and meaning.

Worcestershire Place Names Related to Farming
Like many cultures before them since the arrival of the Neolithic people, most Anglo-Saxons were farmers, eking their living off the land and the environment. Many place names, therefore, reflect the importance of agriculture in their lives.

Pershore has long been associated with the fruit tree orchards of the Vale of Evesham but its name may well be of a more ordinary origin. In 972, Persoran, 1046, also Persoran, in 1066 Perscore and in 1275 Per sore - all pronounced 'Parshore'. The terminal derives from the Old English 'ora' meaning an 'edge' or 'bank'. Most likely, 'persc' or 'persh' is from Old English meaning 'osiers' (willows) for weaving. So, this can be interpreted as 'the settlement where the osiers grow'. A less likely origin is from the Old English word 'persoc', not a native word but borrowed from the Latin 'Persicus', meaning a 'peach tree', so becoming 'peach tree bank'. In fact, although intensively grown in Persia, the peach actually originates in China.

Pirton, about 5 miles south east of Worcester is found as 'Pyritune' in 972 and as 'Peritune' in the Domesday Book. The name is derived from the Old English word 'pirige' meaning 'pear tree' and 'tun', 'farmstead', so 'the farm where pear trees grow' or simply 'a pear orchard'. A local stream probably takes its name from the village in a process called back formation. The original name of the stream has been lost, but was probably Celtic.

The **Lenches** are interesting as they tell us much about Anglo-Saxon agricultural practice in an open field system. All five, Church Lench, Rous Lench, Atch Lench, Sherrifs Lench and Ab Lench are situated on the higher ground on the north side of the Vale of Evesham. 'Lench', 'Linch', 'Lynch' and 'Link' are common elements found in the place names of England. Their root is from Old English, 'kline', with also variants 'hlinc' and 'hlenc', meaning 'rising ground', 'a ridge' or 'ledge'. When the slope of a hillside, ridge or bank formed part of an open field, the individual strips were aligned along the contours. These stripes were then ploughed only in one direction and always to turn the sod of the furrow down the slope. The plough always returning the opposite way idle. This resulted, over time, in the soil gradually moving down the hill to the lowest part of one strip. So, over many years, the ploughed strips became long level terraces. The lower part of each strip was not ploughed so served as a boundary. The process began again lower down the slope in the neighbours strip, so a bulk of land formed between each strip along the contours. These bulks of steep rough banks made up of course grass, brambles and bushes and thus a haven for wildlife, were called 'lynches' or 'linces'. The name also came to refer to the ploughed stripes.

In Anglo-Saxon charters, the Lenches are mentioned as 'Lench', 'Hwitan Hlince', 'Lenc' and 'Lence' making them difficult to identify from each other. There are other similar place names in Worcestershire related to the same agricultural practices including Whitlench in Hartlebury, Evelench in Tibberton, Lench in Inkberrow and Malvern Link.

Ab Lench in the Domesday Book appears 'Aberleng' and then as 'Abbelench' in 1227. Although the prefix refers to ownership by the church, the name appears as 'Abbots Lench' as late as the 19th century, but it never had an Abbot.

Church Lench is the largest of the five Lenches. The Domesday Book lists the village as 'Circelenz' and the church at Evesham were the landowners.

Rous Lench was originally simply 'Lench' in the pre-Norman period and Sheriffs Lench was 'Lench Alnod' in 716. In 1291 listed as 'Lench Randulph' from the Old French of the Norman name 'Randulf'. Together with Atch Lench, they are included later under the Norman influenced names. Found as 'Achelenz' in the Domesday Book and 'Aches Lenche' in 1262. Some toponymists have proposed that Atch derives from the Old English 'hcecce' and the Middle English 'hatch', a half door which may be closed while the upper half is open. There is a Hatch Beauchamp in Somerset and Falstaff speaks of 'the manor of 'Yickt-Hatch' in the Merry Wife's of Windsor.

Sheriffs Lench was 'Lench Alnod' in 716 and 'Scherreuelenche' in 1221, in 1275 'Shirr evelench' in the 13th 'Shyrrevelench' and in 1332 'Lench Vicecomitis'. The Beauchamps, through Urse D'Abitot were hereditary sheriffs of the manor. The name reflects the village as the residence of the sheriff in order to distinguish it from the other Lenches.

Lenchwick, just north of Evesham, appears consistently as 'Lenchwic' in 709, 'Lencuuicke' in 714, and 'Lenchwyk' in 1275 and means the place of the 'specialised farm on a ridge or slope'.

Bannutt Tree Farm, one mile southwest of Upper Arley on the west bank of the River Severn, is both interesting and unique. The farm has been in Worcestershire since boundary changes in 1895 and the word derives from the Middle English 'banne-note' meaning 'walnut' dating from at least 1609. The word was used only for the growing tree and the timber known as 'walnut'.

Cockshull Hill, Cockshot, Cockshoot, Cockshut and **Cockshutts** are all names of hills in Worcestershire and several farms. They all describe the use of a trough to redirect a water source from a spring or small brook to a convenient place for farming or domestic use.

Church Honeybourne, is located about five miles east of Evesham and found as 'Huniburne' in 709 and 714 and in 840 as 'Hunig burn'. It is clear this is Old English and means the place of the 'honey brook'. The village probably takes its name from the nearby stream of the same name. 'Church' was a Middle English addition as it came under the ownership of Evesham Abbey.

Cow Honeybourne, lies just across the stream and the old Roman road of Ryckneild Street from its twin settlement and was in Gloucestershire before boundary changes in 1931 brought it into Worcestershire. 'Cow' is also Old English but a corrupted form of the word 'calewe' or 'calu' meaning 'bare, lacking vegetation'.

Honey was a natural and farmed resource of great importance at the time. Hive bee keeping was well established in England even before the Roman conquest. Rents were frequently paid in honey; it was used in the production of mead and the wax used for domestic use and in the celebration of Christian events.

All these elements are commonly used in English settlement names and, indeed, for names of streams. There are Honeybournes near Crowle and Wolverley and Honeybrook (in 866 'Hunig broc') near Wolverley.

Hunnington, is a village north east of Clent in the very north of Worcestershire, near the boundary with the West Midlands. The origin of the name is also from the Old English words 'hunig-tun', so meaning 'the farmstead where honey is produced'.

Pipers Hill lies on the northern boundary of the village of Hanbury and Stoke Prior and is a Worcestershire Wildlife Woodland Reserve populated mainly by beech trees. A charter of 770 includes 'inpipan' on the bounds of Stoke. The word derives from 'pipe' and was often used to describe water conveyed by a wooden pipe. Pipe, near Lichfield, is similarly named.

Loggerheads Corner, in Hanbury can be found in old OS maps of the area on a right-angled bend of the Saltway. It is a Midland dialectic name for the Common Knapweed, Centaurea nigra, which grows well on the neutral clay soil of the locality. However, this unusual name, otherwise meaning 'quarrelsome', is possibly related to the name given to the undersides of salt wagons. There was a blacksmith located 500 meters west from the corner.

Madresfield, in the Domesday Book listed as 'Madresfeld' and in the 12th century as 'Metheresfeld'. It is unclear whether this is an Anglo-Saxon personal name or the Old English word 'maethere' meaning the mowers field'. A 'feld' in Anglo-Saxon times referred to an unenclosed field usually for growing a mix of crops.

Rubury, on the northern boundary of Worcestershire, appears as 'Rowberrie' and 'Roughberrow' in the 16th century and is derived from the Old English 'ruh-beorg', meaning 'rough-hill'. Here, 'rough' is used in the sense of 'lacking good soil' for agricultural use.

There is a **Swancote** recorded about one mile north west of Chaddesley

Corbet. In 1275 written as 'Swanecote' and has nothing to do with swans. The Middle English 'swain' means 'swine herd' or 'herdsman', so translating 'the herdsman's cottage'. A 'swain' later became known as a 'countryman'.

Stocking, is a fairly common name found in Worcestershire for localities and fields, from the Old English 'stocc' meaning 'tree trunks, stumps' or 'lgs'. Often found in the vicinity of former woodlands, meaning 'the place grubbed-up or cleared of trees' or 'the place of tree-stumps' and is synonymous with 'ridding' and 'birch'. There are Breach Farms in Huntington, Belbroughton and Stoulton. They all have the same origin from 'birch' a Middle English word meaning 'newly enclosed or cultivated ground' usually found near ancient forests and wastes.

'Ridding' is from Old English 'hrydtng' and Middle English 'ryding' also meaning 'a clearing or assart land taken in to an estate from waste' as in **Ridding Farm**. It is common a common name in Staffordshire but less common in Worcestershire.

Stildon Manor, near Menithwood above the Teme valley, appears as 'Stilladune' in 958, 'Stilldune' in 1007 and 'Stilldon' in 1332. The prefix may represent the Old English word 'stiell' meaning 'a place for catching fish'. Usually, a wicker trap was placed into a stream. Dumbleton Brook is nearby and flows down to join the Teme between Stamford Bridge and Orleton. Thus, this translates, 'the hill where fishing traps are placed'. Another possibility is if the 958 name 'Stilladune' really represented 'Stilladune', then it becomes likely the meaning includes an Anglo-Saxon personal name giving, 'Stilla's Hill'.

Throckmorton, appears as 'Throcmortune' and as 'Throchemeron' with consistency and is probably related to the Old English word 'throc' meaning a piece of wood used to support a structure like a jetty. So perhaps, 'the place near the mere with a wooden jetty'.

Thrift is derived from the Celtic word fyrhth(e) meaning 'common land' and the later Middle English word 'frith'. There are several Thrift woods, one towards Upper Bentley, The Thrift and another near Crowle, Thrift Wood. Further afield, the name is found in north Gloucestershire and another on the Worcestershire Herefordshire border. All are wooded and on higher ground. Thrift can also mean land overgrown with brushwood, scrubland on the edge of forest, or 'barren land' of less agricultural use and often situated at higher elevations.

Wadborough, is a small village in the Vale of Evesham about two miles west of Pershore. The earliest known record is from 972 written 'Wadbeorgas' and appears in the Domeday Book as 'Wadberge'. The name derives from the Old English 'wad-beorg' meaning the 'hill where the woad grows'. Woad was formerly used for dying articles blue.

The Wynyards in Ombersley, Wynyate Farm in Ipsley and the former named places of Wingard in Baldenhall and Wyngard in Powick all allude to the previous sites of vineyards. Their root is the Old English word 'wm-geard' or 'vineyard'.

The Call of the Wilds of Ancient Worcestershire
The observations and recordings of the Anglo-Saxon newcomers are very useful in building up a picture of the landscape and the natural history of the environment of the time. The names reveal what they noticed, what was important and valuable to them.

Himbleton is first documented in 816 as Hymeltun, and in 991 Hymeltune and Himeltun. This is Old English for 'town of the hop plant'. The manor is bounded by a stream called, in the charters, Hymel broc, ' the brook of the hop plant.'. The plant referred to is the wild hop.

Hopwood, just north of Alvechurch on the northern boundaries of Worcestershire may have a different origin. Documented as 'Hopwuda' in 848, 'Hopwuda' in 934 and 'Hoppewode' in 1275. 'Hopu' is Old English for 'privet', so likely 'the privet wood'.

Crowle is noteworthy. It appears as Croglea in 831, Croelat and Crohlea in 1275. The prefix is OE croh, commonly translated as crocus or saffron. (as in Croydon). This translates as the leah (or field) of the crocus (or saffron). Saffron was anciently much in request for medicinal, colouring and flavouring. However, some experts have noted a reference to a local stream named Crohwealla (which must be Bow Brooke) in the sense of 'croh' or bend and thus 'leah on the winding stream'.

Bentley. The Old English word 'bent' is commonly used to describe a tract of country unenclosed and producing mainly coarse grass and heath and thus of less agricultural value. It first appears in 1327 as 'Bentelegh' and as 'Bentelegh' in 1429. Interestingly, The Thrift is found nearby and conveys the same meaning, 'scrub or barren land' and the coarse bent grass can still be seen in this locality today.

Broome is a small village 5 miles east of Kidderminster. In 1275 written as 'Brome'. This is Old English for the shrub 'Broom' and probably reflects the original settlements site on a heath. At this time Broome lay within the boundaries of the Forest of Feckenham.

Boughton, just east of Upton-upon-Severn, is documented in 1038 as 'Bocctun', in 1275 as 'Boctone' and in 1327 as 'Bocton'. So clearly derived from Old English 'boc' and 'tun', so meaning 'the town of the beech trees'.

Hill Furze, is an area just north of Fladbury, that includes a road of that name. Derived from Old English word, 'fyrs', it refers to exactly the same indigenous plant as 'gorse', a very spiny evergreen shrub with fragrant golden-yellow flowers common on heathlands with poor and acid soil. Similarly, Frisland, near Tibberton, and Frieze Wood near Madresfield have the same origins, meaning 'land where furze or gorse grows'.

Lindridge, in the Teme valley halfway between Abberley and Tenbury Wells, in 1275 appears as 'Linderugge'. The prefix derives from the Old English 'lind' or 'linde' meaning 'lime tree', thus translating the place at 'the lime tree ridge'. Lime is a word that can be traced back to Proto-German, 'lindo', 'lentus' meaning 'flexible' in Latin, Sanskrit 'liana' and in modern German 'lindenbaum'. The root is also found in the Modern English 'lithe' meaning 'supple, graceful' and German 'lind' which translates 'lenient, yielding'.

This settlement name is one of several that commemorates the small-leaved lime tree and its dominance locally in the past. Thus, **Line Holt**, east of the Severn and south of Hartlebury and **Upper** and **Lower Lindon** near Rock, all have the same etymology which also applies to **Linthurst** ('lime-tree wood') north east of Bromsgrove and further afield, Lyndhurst, Hampshire. In the Tempest, Act 5, Scene 1, Shakespeare wrote "in the line-grove which weather-fends your cell".

Lincomb, in Hartlebury although superficially similar in appearance, has a different etymology. In 706 written as 'Lincumbe' and in the 15th century as 'Lynckcombe', both elements are Old English meaning the 'valley of the flax'. 'Combe' is a common terminal in West Saxon but comparatively rare in Mercia. The word is from the Old English 'comb' or 'cumb' and has been thought loaned from the Celtic word 'cwm' meaning 'a hollow between hills' or a 'valley'.

The steep slopes of the Teme valley have helped to conserve species that are characteristic of the area including wild service tree and small-leaved lime. Indeed, about half of the broadleaved and mixed woodlands found here occur on ancient woodland sites. Thus, the area is important for woodland biodiversity and designated as one of the National Character Areas (NCAs). Traditional orchards are also characteristic of the sloping valley and lower hills, particularly cherry in the north and west. Some of the Norman manors have subsequently been transformed into park estates and the mounds forming ancient pales can still be seen. The valley's open fields were gradually enclosed in rectangular fields creating a landscape which has remained to present day.

Orleton, is just over the border in Herefordshire but is noteworthy as it continues the tradition of the descriptive and informative words the Anglo-Saxons gave to their settlements. Recorded as 'Alretune' and in 1275 as 'Olretune' from the Old English, 'alor', then from Middle English, 'olre', so literally meaning 'Alder Town'.

Ockeridge, in Little Witley, is recorded as 'Ocrugge' in 1332. 'Oc' or 'Ocke' is Old English for 'oak' and 'rugge' is Middle English, a cognate of 'hrycg' in Old English meaning 'ridge', thus giving the place as 'the oak ridge'.

Acton, three miles north of Ombersley, written 'Actun' in 1275, is a very common English place name often, therefore, qualified by an additional word and also derives from the Old English 'ac' or 'oc' so means 'Oak Town'. Oak was a very important timber, used in shipbuilding and construction. The roots were used as hafts for daggers and knives, the bark for tanning leather and in dyeing and the acorns for feeding swine called 'pannage'.

Upper and **Lower Sapey,** are situated above and west of the river Teme. In 781 appearing as 'Sapian', in 1086 as 'Sapie', in 1275 as 'Sapye' and in 1346 as 'Sapey Pychard'. Probably from the Old English word 'saepig' meaning 'sappy, juicy', which may refer to the local orchards. The Pritchard family held the manor in the 13th and 14th centuries.

The elm or wych elm trees are referred to in several Worcestershire place names including, **Wichenford, Elmley Lovett** and **Elmbridge.**

Larford, just south of Stourport-on-Severn and lying on the western bank of the River Severn is of Old English derivation and means the place at 'the ford with wild iris'.

Hagley is included in the Domesday Book as 'Hageleia'. 'Hag' in Old English means haws (the fruit of hawthorn trees) and so 'the woodland clearing where haws are found'.

There is a mention of **Redditch** in 1348, the same year as the outbreak of the Black Death - the deadliest pandemic in history. In 843 there is a charter relating to Alvechurch that mentions 'in readon sloe', 'to the red ditch'. In 1300 the settlement appears as 'Redediche' and in 1642 as 'Reddiche'. So, the alternatives are either from the Old English words 'hreod-dic' meaning 'the reed ditch' or 'read-dic' meaning 'the red ditch'. Most toponymists favour the former as the most likely. The later name, if correct, may have referred to the red clay of the river Arrow that runs through the town. The village lay within the boundaries of the Feckenham Forest.

Romsley, in north Worcestershire is a village situated on the east side of the Clent Hills. In 1270 appearing as 'Romesle' and in 1291 as 'Romesleye'. The name derives from the Old English 'hramsa', so meaning the place at 'the woodland clearing where wild garlic (ramson) grow'.

Rushock, is recorded as 'Russococ' in the Domesday Book and 'Rossoc' in 1166. The name is probably from the Old English word 'ryscuc' and this gives the settlement near the 'rushes'.

Rushwick, is named after the local stream which appears as 'Rixuc' in 963, so the 'specialist farm (often a dairy farm, but may refer to some other product including weaving) by the rushy brook'.

The natural world including topographic features, hills, lakes, rivers and streams and even large ancient trees were often used as boundary markers in the past. **The Three Shires Oak**, was one such boundary marker that stood at the junction of Staffordshire and detached portions of Shropshire and Worcestershire and which is now Bearwood, Smethwick. It was a very ancient tree and felled in 1904.

Suckley, about 10 miles west of Worcester, was first recorded as 'Succhelege' in 1156, as 'Suchelei', in 1275 as 'Sukkeleye' and in 1346 'Sukeley'. This is from an Old English word 'sucga' and related 'hegesugga' meaning 'sparrow' and 'hedge sparrow' (or 'Dunnock') respectively. Wonderful to acknowledge some of the earliest keen birdwatchers in the county who then named a woodland clearing after these streaky-brown, shy but busy little birds nearly 1,000 years ago!

Upper and Lower Arley, situated on the River Severn between Bewdley and Bridgnorth, the former village is written as 'Earnleie' in 996 and in the Domesday Book as 'alia Ernlege' and 'Emlege' respectively. There is no doubt they derive from the Old English word 'earn' meaning 'eagle' and thus 'the woodland clearing of the eagle'. The only doubt is whether they were referring to the golden or white-tailed eagle or indeed both, as in Anglo-Saxon times, their distributions overlapped.

Froxmere Court and Froxmere Farm, are found lie just north of Crowle, in 1275 they appear unchanged as 'Froxmere' and in 1327 as 'Froxemere'. In Old English 'frox' and 'frogga' both mean 'frog', so translating as the place of the 'frog pool'.

The **Atterburn** is a tributary of the Salwarpe, but in 1038 was known as the 'Oter burne', or 'brook where otters are seen'. Fortunately, their spread from the Welsh borders since 2010, means these delightful aquatic mammals can be sighted here again.

Barbourne, a north west suburb of the city of Worcester adjacent to the Severn is named after the stream that flows into the river here. In 904 documented as 'Beferburna' and in 969 as 'Beferic'. This is Anglo-Saxon meaning 'Beaver stream'.

Bevere Lock and Island are on the River Severn about three miles north of Worcester. Documented early as 'Beverege insula Sabrinae' and in 1240 as 'Bevereye', 'Beaver Island on the Severn'. There may also be a reference to Beavers in an Anglo-Saxon charter of 969 relating to land between Little Witley and the River Severn which mentions 'beferic' which may be related to 'beofer' (beaver) and 'ric' (Old English 'wooded stream' or 'ditch') so 'Beavers Ditch'. Indeed, this is the exact spelling of Barbourne in 969. Beavers were in decline in England by the 5th to 6th century and were not found in southern Britain by the time of the Norman Conquest. They had become extinct in Britain by the 16th century, but with their reintroduction in Devon in 2015, may be these place names will regain their full meaning.

There are a number of references in Anglo-Saxon charters to wolves in Worcestershire. Wolf-pits, 'seathe' are mentioned in **Bredicote** and **Broadwas** and a wolf 'hagan' ('haven') in Longdon and also a 'haia' in Longdon, 'in which wild animals are captured'.

In 1167, the sheriff paid three shillings to a hunter for destroying wolves in Feckenham Forest. In the 13th century wolves were still quite common in Worcestershire and, indeed, most parts of lowland England. However, at this time sheep farming became more lucrative due to the profits made from wool. Edward I (1272-1307) commissioned Peter Corbet in 1281 'to destroy all wolves from the counties of Worcestershire, Herefordshire, Gloucestershire, Shropshire and Staffordshire'. He must have done an excellent job as he was knighted for his services and wolves were no longer mentioned in charters of the region after this period. Corbet also included wild cats in his cull and their numbers reduced dramatically. There is a reference to 'Wolfho', Wolf Hill near Alvechurch in 1327. Although there were a few late sightings recorded above Suckley and Cracombe, by the early 18th century they had disappeared from Worcestershire.

There is good etymological evidence that **Wolverley** and **Wolverton** have origins in Anglo-Saxon personal names and not from wolves. Similarly, Wolferlow on an isthmus of a protuberance of Herefordshire into Worcestershire on face value may seem related to wolves. The etymology, however, shows that in 1086 it is listed as 'Ulferlau', in 1276 as 'Wolfrelowe', in 1291 Wolfrelawe', in 1340 'Walverslows' and in 1341 as 'Wolferlow'. So, the original meaning is likely to be 'Wulfhere's tumulus' possibly relating to the Mercian king. The Old English name meaning an ancient burial site may have been 'hlaw' or 'hlaew' which later appears as 'low' in place names. However, Wolvey just across the border in Warwickshire, appears as 'Wulfeia' in 1195. The name derives from the Old English 'wulf-hege' which means 'an enclosure to protect flocks from wolves or to trap wolves'.

Place Names Relating to Local Industries

Droitwich is synonymous with salt and the salt industry and there is evidence supporting large-scale production from at least the Iron Age and, therefore, hundreds of years before the Roman invasion. During the 1st century AD, it became one of several towns in southern Britain known as 'Salinae' or 'Salt Town'. The suffix 'wich' derives from Old English 'wic' or 'wick' meaning specialist 'farm or place' producing some specialist product, in this case, salt. In 716 'in wico emptorio salis quern nos Saltwich vocamus', meaning 'in the place for the sale of salt which we call Saltwich'. In 888 recorded as 'Saltwic', in 1017 'Sealtwic', appearing in the Domesday Book as 'Wich' in 1086. In 1313 plain 'Wich', in 1347 as 'le Dryght-wych' and in 1469 as 'Deriwyche'. All salt-towns in Anglo-Saxon England included the suffix 'wich', such as Nantwich, Middlewich and Northwich. 'Drit' and 'dryht' means 'dirty' or 'muddy', so the meaning of the name may be 'the muddy or dirty salt works'. However, Edward III (a French speaking king 1312-1377) granted the town the 'right' or in Old French "droit" to produce and sell salt which, of course, attracted a heavy taxation that benefited the king's coffers. So, the name may well be related to this royal grant. Most etymologises favour the 'dirt' meaning 'dirty' or 'muddy' proposal as the old salt town of Fullwich in Cheshire is recorded earlier as 'Fuleuuic', meaning in Old English 'foul place'. The alternative recorded names for 'Fuleuuic' town were 'Dirtwich', 'Droytwich' and 'Durtwich'. Interestingly, there were several other settlements named by the Romans bearing the name 'Salinis', one in Cheshire became later became known as Nantwich and Ptolemy mentions two more on the Continent.

Finstall is recorded as 'Vinstalstude' in 1295, 'Finstal' in 1328 an 'Vynestallstede' in 1368. The derivation is Old English and referees to the extraction and refining of salt. A 'finstallus' is a 'place where firewood is stored' which was then used to heat the brine and evaporate the water to produce usable salt. It was recorded that 300 cartloads of wood were required to obtain 300 measures (mitts) of salt.

Upper and Lower Wyche lie adjacent to the Wyche Cutting, a pass through the Malvern Hills. Some early toponymists had thought the names derived from the Hwicce, the Anglo-Saxon tribe, whose western border may have been defined by the north-south alignment of the Malvern Hills. However, more recently experts have concluded the villages are probably derived from the Old English word 'wic', and later evolved to 'wyche' possibly related in this context, to the use of the nearby pass for the transport of salt.

Worcestershire Place Names related to Sports and Hunting

The English nobility of the medieval period enjoyed their hunting and the sport was a major pastime with a detailed vocabulary to accompany all the various intricacies related to both the hunter and the hunted. A first-year stag was called a 'calf', a second year a 'brocket', a 'spayed', 'spadle' or 'spayard' in its third year, 'staggerd' or 'staggard' in its fourth year and a 'stag' or 'great stag' in the fifth year. If it were lucky enough to achieve maturity it was known as a 'hart'.

Huntingtrap Farm was the location of a tiny hamlet near Hadzor and Hadzor Common to the east of Droitwich. Documented as 'Hountingthrope' in the 13th and 14th century, the name means 'the hunting village' and would have been, at this time, within the boundaries of the Forest of Feckingham. It is unusual as the element 'trap' is very rare in Worcestershire and derives from the Old Danish word 'thorpe' which is common in north and east England, the previous area of Danelaw. It means 'a small settlement dependent on a larger nearby settlement.

Rochford, two miles east of Tenbury, consists of two hamlets, Upper and Lower. Included in the Domesday Book as 'Recesford', and in 1242 as 'Rochesford'. The derivation is from the Old English word 'raecces', meaning 'hunting dog', so the place by the 'ford of the hunting dog'.

Fox Lydiate, between Bromsgrove and Redditch is mentioned in a Forest of Feckenham manuscript of 1300, 'and thence to Fox huntley yates, and along Fox huntsey, common, called Rugwey, to Smethhedley' and again in 1377 as 'Foxhunt Ledegate'. We have met the Old English words 'hlidgeat' and Middle English 'lidyate' previously and usually means a gate, but can also mean just a gap or passage large enough to be navigable.

Gannow Green Moat, situated west of Frankley in north Worcestershire has a typical rectangular moat lying around 700 m to the east. 'Gannow' is derived from the Old English words 'gamen' and 'ho'. The first element means 'to game' or 'to play' and the second element alludes to a topographic feature meaning 'a ridge of land that sticks out', so giving 'the ridge where games are played'. The manor may well have been the venue for tournaments and sport and the 'green' may refer to a village area on which village games are played. It was excavated in 1961 and showed evidence of occupation from the 13th to 15th century and the site is now a Scheduled Monument. Set on relatively high ground, one of the nearby hills, Endmill Hill, has an elevation of 315 m above sea level. Not surprisingly, there was a mill near called Gannow Mill.

The frequently used suffix or second word 'Green' in a place name often refers to common land over which local people had rights, the most important of which were the grazing of their livestock.

There is a moated **Gannow Farm** and **Gannow Wood** between Inkberrow and Stock Green. In the 14th and 15th century the farm was known as 'Ganowe'. It is not included in the Domesday Book, so must have become manorial after 1086 and before 1290 when a statute 'Quia Emptores' was passed preventing the creation of new manors. This medieval homestead lay within the boundaries of the Royal Forest of Feckenham and has a well-preserved moat and undisturbed island which may well provide further information in the future. This was a homestead of complexity and high status reflected by the relatively rare figure of '8' moat plan and has been given a Heritage Category of Scheduled Monument. There are at least three other moated sites within 1.5 kilometres of Gannow Farm. There is an estate called 'Gannowe' in Holme Lacey, Herefordshire and a 'Gannovv' in Whaley, Lancashire.

Worcestershire Place Names related to Local Administration
Spetchley, nearly four miles east of Worcester, was written 'Spaeclea' in 967 and 'Speclea' in the Domesday Book. The name derives from two Old English words, 'spec' meaning 'speech' and, 'leah', so giving, 'the woodland clearing where meetings are held', and is a unique name. On the border between Spetchley and Wolverton there is a tumulus called 'The Low'. In 977 recorded as 'Oswaldes hlaw' and later 'Oswaldeslow', the name of a newly created hundred. Oswald was then the Bishop of Worcester and this may have been the site of a court. It was common for the ancient administrative units known as hundreds to meet on the boundaries of estates. They would

often choose raised ground such as a 'tumulus', the name given by Anglo-Saxons for an ancient relic they believed to be a 'burial place'.

The Burf, near Astley, is an unusual name for a local elevated feature meaning 'the raised land topped by a meeting place'. It was probably the venue for the local hundred, a sub-division of the county administration

There are many dialects in modern England and Anglo-Saxon England was no exception. There are many word variations characteristic of the Midlands dialect such as 'mardy' meaning 'sulky, whining or bad tempered'. Another example characteristic of the region and indeed a rare place name in Worcestershire is 'cank' as in **Cank Alley**, Hanbury and Cank, a former enclosure in Nunnery Wood. There is also a 'Cank Street' in Leicester and a Cank Hill in St Albans. In this latter context it may be Old English for a 'rounded hill'. In the Midlands dialect both in Hanbury and Leicester the word has the same meaning, 'to chatter, gabble, or cackle'.

Place Names Related to Military Defence
Military defence is an important part of the integrity of any kingdom and was a definite requirement in Anglo-Saxon England. There was competition and occasional conflict with other Anglo-Saxon kingdoms particularly over border disputes and expansionism. There were also the constant threats of harrying by the Welsh from the west and during the 9th and 10th centuries by the Danes from Danelaw to the east. **'Wassel'** is a common place name particularly for hills and elevated positions along the north west, north and north east borders of the Hwicce kingdom of Anglo-Saxon England. Wassell Wood on the eastern bank of the River Severn is the western most point of a chain of such names that include, Wassell Grove near Wychbury Hill, Waseley Hills and Wast Hills near Alvechurch. 'Wassell' is derived from the Old English word 'weardsetl' meaning a 'watch place' or 'watch tower'. Wassell Wood, a wooded hill overlooking the River Severn just north east of Bewdley, is surmounted by an earthwork enclosure.

Place Names Related to Religious Practices
Before the Dissolution of the monasteries, between 1536 and 1541, the Church owned a large portion of the county. Indeed, the Bishop alone about one-third. Thus, a significant proportion of place names reflect their ecclesiastical ownership.

There are two places in the county sharing the name **Churchill**. One, around four miles east of Worcester is found as 'Circehille' in the Domesday Book and as 'Cherchhull' in 1209. The village has the ancient church of St Michael on a hill and the name seems self-explanatory. The other Churchill lies east of Kidderminster and is recorded as 'Circhul' and as 'Cercehalle' in the Domesday and 'Chyrchull' in 1275. The village and church lie in a valley and do not seem to be related to any of the surrounding hills. Thus, in the English Place Name Society's Worcestershire volume the suggestion arose that this latter name may be related to the Celtic element 'cruc' or 'hill or 'tumulus'.

White Ladies Aston, about 6 miles south east of Worcester, is found as simply 'Eastun' in 977 and 'Estun' in the Domesday Book, and thus meaning 'eastern settlement'. By 1481 it appears as 'Whitladyaston', referring to ownership of the manor by the Cistercian nuns of Whitestones.

Crutch Hill and **Crutch Lane** may take their names from the Middle English, 'cruche' or 'cross', a wayside cross erected near here by nuns. However, Margaret Gelling in her book Signposts to the Past, suggests that Crutch derives from the Brittonic Celtic word 'crug' referring to a small hill, often abrupt in shape.

Ankerdine Hill, near Knightwick, on the Worcestershire-Herefordshire border appears in 1275 as 'Oncredham' and in 1327 as 'Ancredam'. 'Ancra' is an Old English word, 'an anchorite, anchoress or nun', so meaning 'the place of a nun'. As is often the case, the suffix has become corrupted to the common colloquial ending 'wardine' or 'dene'. There are similar place names in England, including the River Anker in Warwickshire upon which lay two hermitages and a nunnery and Ankerwyke in Middlesex meaning 'the anchorite's village'.

Settlements Related to Relative Positions

Many place names describe their position in relation to nearby settlements or landscape features. Sometimes a prefix is added to a settlement with the same name and in close proximity to differentiate them from each other. Some of the commonest are the additions of 'Upper' and 'Lower' to as in the Sapey's.

White Ladies Ashton, Astley and Astwood Bank have been mentioned already. **Aston Fields**, in Bromsgrove, is found as 'Eastun' in 767, so clearly the 'eastern settlement' in relation to its larger neighbour, then called, 'Bremesgraf' lying to the west. The original meaning for 'feld' in Old English was an open area of land, possibly cleared before the arrival of Anglo-Saxons.

Westwood Park, appears as 'aet Westwudu' in 972 and 'Westwod' in 1206, meaning the place of 'the western wood' in relation to the larger neighbour, Droitwich to the east, known at the time as 'Sealtwic'.

Northwick, is a northern district of Worcester, well described by the Anglo-Saxons in 964 as 'Norowica' or 'northern specialist settlement', usually applying to a dairy farm.

Similarly, there are several **Nortons** in Worcestershire, all having the same derivation of 'nord-tun' or 'northern farmstead'.

Sutton, is a common place name, one in the county lying a few miles south east of Tenbury Wells. All are from the Old English 'suth-ton' or 'the southern farmstead'.

A common place name or common element within a place name is the Old English 'nether' meaning 'lower' as in **Netherton** about two miles south west of Pershore. In 780 recorded as 'Neolheretune' meaning 'the lower farmstead'. There may well have been another farmstead near and above, possibly an 'Overton' from the Old English 'ofer' meaning 'over' or 'upper'.

Habitative Place Names in Worcestershire
Some commonly recurring elements found in place names describe the nature of the original settlement. These elements are very often further qualified by the addition of a second identifying name. One of the commonest is the Old English 'tun' which originally simply meant 'enclosure' and sometimes 'fence' and evolved into meaning 'enclosure round a homestead' and later 'village' and 'town'. In most cases, 'tun' means 'homestead' or 'village'. There are many examples in Worcestershire including some we have already mentioned as in Whittington, Upton and Bishampton.

Old English 'stoc' or 'stok' is also a common element of place names, meaning a small settlement dependant on a larger nearby settlement. Thus,

Stoke Prior in 770 is recorded as 'Stoke' and in 804 as 'Stocce'. Similarly, **Severn Stoke** is documented as Stoc in 972 and 'Stoche' in the Domesday Book. However, both were further qualified to 'Stok Prior' in 1275 and 'Savernestok' by 1212, respectively. The former because of a monastery built there and the later because of its proximity to the River Severn. The monastery at Stoke Prior was 'granted by Uhtred, regulus of the Hwiccii, to the monastery at Worcester' in 770 and belonged to them for 800 years.

'Ham' is a common element in place names originally meaning 'a home or homestead' and in the Hwicce dialect often meant 'a settlement in a water meadow near the bend of a river or stream'. As we have seen, the earliest surviving record of Evesham in 709 is simply 'Homme' before the later additions of personal names.

'Wic', meaning 'a specialised farm (usually dairy) producing a commodity, a trading settlement and often in a bay or river' is a common element in place names so often further identified by a second element as we will see in Droitwich which is early documented simply as 'Wich' on twenty-four occasions, in 888 'Saltwic' and again in 1027 'Sealtwic'. Thus, 'the town specialising in salt production'. It is uncommon to find a village name recorded simply as **Wick**, lying on the Worcestershire Avon. It appears as 'Wiche' in the Domesday Book.

Chapter 20 The Norsemen and Worcestershire

THE second half of the 9th century saw constant tension and conflict between the Danes, who controlled much of the east of southern Britain, and their Anglo-Saxon neighbours, the kingdoms of Wessex and Mercia. Between 866 to 874 King Burgred of Mercia was involved in almost constant battles with the Viking Danes. Viking raiders travelled up the Severn and on at least one occasion the monks at Worcester had to flee for their lives. During King Alfred's reign the city was chosen as the site of a 'burgh', or fortified town, as part of a strategy to defend Anglo-Saxon territories from Viking invasions.

In 895 AD the Danes harried as far up the river as Bridgnorth and created a winter camp which is now known as Danes Dyke. However, after a heavy defeat at Buttington, Viking influence in the area waned until the time of King Cnut the Great who by the time of his death in 1035 was king of the 'North Sea Empire' that included Denmark, Norway and England. In 1041 two, huscarls, or household bodyguards of Harthacnut, meaning 'tough-knot', together with the son of King Cnut, were killed in Worcester by the townsfolk while attempting to collect taxes. In the inevitable reprisals a military force ransacked and burnt the town, while the citizens took refuge on Bevere island. However, within ten years of Cnut's death, his heirs had died, and with the Norman Conquest of England, the Viking dynasty in England had died too. Thus, there is little evidence of permanent settlement by the Norsemen in Worcestershire, except perhaps for a few places.

Clent lies on the southern slopes of the Clent Hills which rise up to 316 m (1,037 ft) above sea level. The village appears in the Domesday Book (1086) as "Klinter". This may derive from the Old Scandinavian word 'klint' meaning "cliff" or 'rocky slope' and might be evidence of Old Scandinavian settlement in Worcestershire possibly via the River Severn. Some evidence from studies of place name settlements in Cumbria and the East Midlands within a multi-cultural setting suggests that Anglo-Saxon settlements are found in the fertile valleys and Scandinavian settlements at higher elevations on the poorer soils.

There are two settlements lying on the western bank of the River Severn that may have Viking origins or connections. **Grimley** is recorded as 'Grimanlea', 'Grimanlege' and 'Grimanleh' in the 9th and 10th centuries. The prefix represents the Old Scandinavian personal name of 'Grima', and the suffix derives, of course, from the common Old English word 'leah'. Likewise, **Greenhill,** just to the south has the same origin. Appearing as 'Grimeshyll' in 816, 'Grimanhyll' in 957 and as 'Gremanhil' listed in the Domesday Book. The oldest available name for the settlement contains the possessive 's', so again represents the same Old Scandinavian name 'Grima'. The literal meaning in Old English is the place at 'the hill of the ghost or spectre'.

Interestingly, history records many incursions and raids of Vikings into western England and indeed conflicts and battles with the Mercians over the 9th and 10th centuries. In 2015 a Viking hoard was discovered as far west as Eye near Leominster and dated to between the late 9th to 10th century. It consisted of Anglo-Saxon coins, a dragon heads bracelet, a silver ingot and crystal rock pendant. It is thought that the hoard was accumulated and buried by Vikings while raiding deep into Mercian territory around 879 and intending to return later. The new and exciting relevance of the find is that the coins point to a close alliance between the king of Wessex, King Alfred the Great and the king of Mercia, Ceolwulf II. Some of the hoard is now displayed in the British Museum.

Chapter 21 Norman Worcestershire

AS in England generally there were huge changes in Worcestershire society as a consequence of the Norman Conquest. This mainly affected Anglo-Saxon royalty, Ealdorman and Thanes (like landlords). The Anglo-Saxon commoners (Ceorls) mostly the farmers and craftsmen, slaves (Thralls) and Bondsmen (effectively slaves) would have raised their heads and noticed a new set of 'line-managers' who looked different and spoke a strange language - Old French. It was the implementation of a new type of feudalism based on manorialism and the new language that had the greatest impact on place names. William I set about allocating large tracks of land to his Norman lords and to the church. Place names often followed the family names of the Norman aristocracy or the bishops who held the land.

The first barony recorded in Worcestershire was at Salwarpe in 1086 when Urse d'Abitot became the Sheriff of Worcestershire (his descendants were the Beauchamps). He held considerable land in the county and became known as 'Urso of Worcester' and also responsible for the building of a new castle in Worcester by 1069. The Domesday Book records that over half of Worcestershire was owned by the church at this time.

Where place names were common it became customary, in the twelfth and thirteenth centuries, to add the family name of manorial lords for the purpose of identity. **Acton Beauchamp** is an early example, known simply as the Old English 'Aaciune' in 718 and in 969 as 'Actune', meaning 'farm or estate where the oak are found'. The Beauchamps were its early Norman lords. **Abbots Morton** in Anglo-Saxon times was similarly written simply 'Mortun' or 'the settlement by the marshy ground' and in 1086 as 'Mortune', a very common name at over fifty known locations in England. After the Conquest the land was bestowed to the Bishop of Evesham, the addition of 'Abbots' appearing and the ownership remained unchanged for over 800 years. Similarly, **Castle Morton**, about 4 miles south west of Upton-on-Severn also has the very common Anglo-Saxon element. In 1275 and in 1333 recorded with the Norman addition as, 'Morton Folliot'. There was a Norman castle built here and the Folliots held the land.

Shelsey Beauchamp and **Shelsey Walsh** are examples that face each other across the Teme, just north east of Clifton upon Teme. The former appears Pre-Conquest simply as 'Celdeslai', 'Caldeslei' and as 'Sceldeslega' and the second as 'Sceldeslaehge' and 'Caldeslei'. They both originally meant 'the woodland clearing of a man called Sceld'. Post-Norman Conquest, first listed as 'Sheldeslegh Beauchampe' in 1255 and its neighbour as 'Seldeslege Waleys' in 1275. The former was thus held by the Beauchamp family from the 12th century and the latter by Johannesburg Walensis or John the Welshman by 1212.

Naunton Beauchamp is about 4.5 miles north of Pershore. Documented as 'Niuuantune' in 972, 'Newentune' in the Domesday Book. The name is from Old English, 'niwe-tun' meaning 'the new farmstead'. By 1370 the place appears as 'Newenton Beauchamp' referring to the ownership passing to William de Bellocampo in 1167.

It is interesting to compare the different trajectories taken in the evolution of 'niwe-tuns' or 'new towns' in different regions. Generally becoming forms such as 'Newington', 'Newton' or 'Newnton' in many parts of England but in Worcestershire and Gloucestershire, in the territory of the Hwicce, always as 'Naunton', as in Naunton in Ripple and Naunton near Severn Stoke. However, this change seemed to take place after 1327, very likely related to regional dialect.

Chaddesley Corbett, was the seat of the Corbet family (from Old French meaning 'raven') the manorial lords from the 12th to 15th centuries. The settlement appears as 'Ceadresleahge' in 816 and 'Cedeslai' in 1086. The early names probably mean 'the woodland clearing (ley) of Cead (816 AD)'. Some experts have postulated that the name derives from the Celtic word 'cadeir' meaning 'chair' in reference to the shape of a local hill. In Anglo-Saxon times the land here was owned by a woman called Aldeva.

Bentley Pauncefoot, first appears as such in 1212 and refers to the landlord,

Richard Panzeauot, a Norman nickname that translates as 'round belly', held the manor in 1185.

Bewdley, on the west bank of the Severn west of Kidderminster certainly deserves its Old French name of Norman origin. Recorded as 'Beuleu' in 1275, 'Buleye' in 1315, 'Beudle' and as 'Beaudele' in 1335, from 'beau lieu' meaning 'beautiful place'. The riverside location must have enchanted the new Norman owners as it is unusual to encounter an old Anglo-Saxon settlement name that has been totally replaced by one of Norman origin. Recorded as 'Gurberhale' in the Domesday Book of 1086 and later as 'Wrubbenhale', from the Old English 'halh' so meaning 'the hook of land of a man called Wrybba'. Originally, the name applied to both sides of the river but is still retained in the name of the village of Wribbenhall on the eastern bank. Load Street in Bewdley refers to a local ferry and derives from the Old English word 'lode'. There are records of a ferry here in 1336 and of the use of coracles around the same time. It is likely, however, that these activities are of far more ancient origin as Julius Caesar described the use of coracles by insular Celts in the 1st century BC and archaeological excavations have discovered the probable remains of this light-weight craft in Bronze Age burial sites. Lax Lane descends through the town to the river and alludes to a local salmon fall. The word is cognate with the Old English, 'leax', the Middle English 'lax', the Old Scandinavian word, 'lax' and the German, 'lachs'- all meaning salmon. As we have discovered earlier, modern linguistic research has traced the word 'lox' to a Proto-Indo-European language which was uttered 8,000 years ago in the Middle East by some of the first Neolithic farmers – a startling insight into continuity and connectedness to the past!

Drakes Broughton was simply 'Broctune' in 972. William le Drake was the owner by 1275 and the name added thus distinguishing the village from the other settlements locally with the same name.

Elmley Lovett, first appears as 'Elmlege' in 780 and 'Elmesetene gemaere' in 817, 'Aelmeliea' in 1086 and first listed with the addition, 'Almeleye Lovet in 1275. By 1285 documented as 'Elmeleye Lovet'. The original Anglo-Saxon meaning is 'the woodland clearing among the elm trees'. The mature trees, often growing to 30 m columns, could not be missed. A local farmer once told me they were grand trees but you could not see very far with them around! By the 13th century the Lovet family, probably given as a nickname meaning 'wolf cub', held the manor.

Hampton Lovett, similarly derives from the Norman Lovet family. Early listings include 'Hamtona' in 716, 'Hamtune' in 1086 and the family name first appearing in 1291 as 'Hamton Lovet'.

Hampton is a common Anglo-Saxon name and usually means 'a farmstead near a water meadow'.

Stoke Bliss, lies between Tenbury Wells and Clifton upon Teme. The first element of which we have already seen is a very common name from the Old English word 'stoc' meaning 'a secondary settlement'. The addition appears in the 13th century as 'Stoke de Blez' referring to ownership by the de Blez family from Blay in Normandy.

Upton Warren, between Bromsgrove and Droitwich, was recorded as 'Uptone' in 714 and 'Uptune' and then 'Uptone' again in 1275. In the 13th and 14th centuries, the Warins and Fitzgerald-Warins owned the manor.

The addition of '**Rous**' to this **Lench** appeared in the 12th century in the form of 'Lench Randolph' from the Randolph family and later passed to the Rouse or Rufus family.

In 1275 **Sheriffs Lench** is written as 'Shirr evelench', in the 13th century as 'Shyrrevelench' and in 1332 as 'Lench Vice-comitis'. The Beauchamps, through Urse d'Abitot, were hereditary sheriffs and held the manor. Some of the meadows around are called 'Sheriffs Leasows'.

Chapter 22 The Ancient Ways of Worcestershire

THE topography of Worcestershire, the hills, valleys and rivers re-emerged after the end of the last Glacial Period and have remained very much the same in basic form over these last 11,000 years. It is useful to view this basic pattern as an upward pointing horse-shoe. On the left (west) the hill chain of the Malvern and Abberley Hills, uppermost the Clent and Lickey Hills, to the right (east) the long north-south orientated Ridgeway and to the south the wide-open valleys of the Severn and Avon and the confluence of the Teme valley emerging from the north west. Within these borders was a large tidal estuary and river system. The River Severn for much of its past was tidal to at least Bewdley, before the public works interventions of the 19th century. There were large areas of mud and marches, particularly in the lower reaches of the Worcestershire Severn, such as the flood marches around Longdon. Beyond these river valleys were vast forests punctuated by hills, ridges, natural meadows and later human made clearings.

These features help us to understand the challenges and patterns of the old thoroughfares in the county. This is the scene that the first Mesolithic hunter-fisher-gatherers would have witnessed. It is likely that animals using tracks through the swamps, meadows and forests would have been followed by these hunters. Some of these tracks would have eventually become more definite, particularly those more reliable and favoured along higher ground, hills and ridges. These routes gave access to lucrative hunting locations, to waterways, to nearby settlements and also to more distant places for trading. Some of these ancient paths, probably at least from the Iron Age, have been noted along the Malvern Hills, linking Midsummer Hill to Bredon Hill and another linking Bredon Hill to the Cotswolds. It is thought that some of these tracks have been in continuous use from Mesolithic and Neolithic times, utilised subsequently by Iron Age Celts, the Romans, Anglo-Saxons and more recently by drovers as late as the early 19th century. Several of these ancient trackways have been mentioned in preceding chapters. Artefacts found in Worcestershire from the Neolithic period originated from places as far afield as Cumbria, North Wales and the Continent. These finds reflect the long-range trading and ancient trade routes in existence in these times that often kept, where possible, to the high ground and ridgeways. These included a Neolithic saltway through the Wyche Cutting to South Wales and a flint track from North Wales skirting north of the Malvern Hills and crossing the ford at near modern Worcester.

The original, or at least, old names of some of these thoroughfares are known but many have been lost in time. However, toponymy can make a contribution to our understanding of these routes by the analysis of the names of settlements and landscape features located on river crossings and those lying beside these ancient ways. These routes give us an insight into how surprisingly interconnected our island has been since at least the Neolithic period.

Although fifteen **Roman roads** have been identified within Worcestershire, only one of the great Roman roads of the period, the Foss Way, ever passed through two outlying detached parts of the county to the south east. The two most important crossings of the River Severn during this period were at Glevum (Gloucester) to the south and at Wroxeter to the north of the county. However, during the 1st century AD the area we now call Worcestershire became important as a base for further military activity to the west and a number of roads have been detected. One was built by the 20th legion between the fort at Glevum (Gloucester) and Wroxeter near Shrewsbury. Ickneild (or Ryknild) Street was one of the most important Roman routes in the area connecting the forts at Glevum to Metchley (a fort on the site of the Queen Elizabeth Hospital and Birmingham University). Kempsey, the probable site of a Roman military camp, sits on this Roman road and in the 19th century a Roman stone slab milestone marker was found. The word 'mile' engraved on the marker derives from the Latin 'milia passuum' or 'a thousand paces'. The first line of the text is missing but it was dedicated to Constantine the Great, emperor from 306 - 337 AD, the first emperor to convert to Christianity. Also discernible on the road marker is the word 'INVICTO' or 'unconquerable'.

Roman interest in the region was not all military. They developed or improved many straight 'Saltways' emanating from the salt springs at

'Salinae' or Droitwich and there were also extensive ironworks at Worcester. Salinis is a Latin name recorded in the Ravenna Cosmography on a road leading north eastwards out of modern Gloucester. It means 'at the salt-pans' and is probably referring to the Romano-British settlement at Droitwich.

Another old Roman road identified is the Greensforge which runs between Kinver, Staffordshire and Droitwich via Kidderminster. Today, the course of the original Icknield Street is used by many modern roads and several sections retain their Old English name. In Worcester one of these is called Icknield Street Drive. There is an Icknield Street in Redditch, a 'Ryknild Street' in Lichfield and a 'Ryknild Road' in Derby.

In the 3rd century AD there was an increase in farm size and activity in Roman Britain especially in the larger villa farm estates. This would have included farms in the Cotswold and south east Worcestershire and also would have required an effective transport system. The increase in agricultural production in Britain in the 260s related to the unrest on the Continent due to a combination of incursions from 'Barbarians' through the Balkans and sporadic civil war. During this time the Empire lost the Agri Decumates a region of Gaul and Germany that was very important for the food supply for the Roman army on the Rhine. In 277 AD emperor Probus (276 - 282) lifted restrictions on wine production in Britain and the province became a vital 'bread basket' for the Empire.

All these Roman roads and and ancient ways are mostly now known by their Anglo-Saxon names. **The Saltways** radiating out of Droitwich have left their mark all over the county, and indeed, in the adjoining counties of Warwickshire, Gloucestershire and beyond. The local brine springs were unique in the area and the nearest alternative reliable saltworks were at Shirleywich in Staffordshire. Thus, all Saltways in the area can confidently be related to Droitwich. Salt was in great demand and a necessity in food processing and consumption in the past. Livestock were slaughtered in October and much of the meat salted for the coming winter, so fish and game were the predominant fresh meats. Before the building of a canal system in the county in 1767, all salt was transported by road or river. Pack horses were used to export the salt, often considerable distances and on the homeward journey they carried wood, the only fuel used to heat the brine to produce salt crystals.

There are numerous references to salt in Anglo-Saxon charters. The Old English word, 'sealtere' means a 'salter', 'a carrier of or dealer in salt'. 'Salters

Way, Salters Lane, Saltersford' are all found on sections of ancient saltways. 'Sealterford' is mentioned in 1109 near Redmarley and there is a Salters Lane south east of Tardebigge. Ogilby, in his Book of the Roads in 1675 mentions that one of the busier salt roads passed directly south via Martin Hussingtree. 'Seal Street', a portion of Icknield Street, is mentioned on the eastern side of Broadway in 1282, running almost due north-south and passing through Temple Guiting, Northleach, Coln St Aldwyns and meeting the navigable Thames at Lechlade. A saltway, documented in 1016 as 'Seal Stret' travelled east from Droitwich via Hanbury, Feckenham, Coughton, then south of Great Alne and hence to Stratford-on-Avon. 'Seal Stret', 2 miles east of Coughton, diverged to the south east, joined Icknield Street and then via Alcester, Bidford, Church Honeybourne arriving at Weston-sub-Edge. The road between Coughton and Stratford was also the London road to Shrewsbury, via Bromsgrove, Kidderminster and Bridgenorth.

Trench Lane, at Trench Wood, about 2 miles south east of Droitwich, runs between Dunhampstead ('Dunhamstyde in 814, so 'homestead on a hill') and Huddington. In 1327 it appears as a highway called 'Trench' and was known to be a 'salt way'. It is not an Old English word but has been loaned from Old French. One of the meanings is 'a lane that has been cut through a wood', and indeed, Chaucer uses the word in this sense. It may have joined the 'Lechlade Saltway' at Pershore via Pinvin. Old tracks of this name also appear at Ellesmere, Wem and Wellington in Shropshire.[7]

---

[7] The importance of Lechlade-on-Thames to many ancient cultures has been demonstrated by archaeological evidence. The remains of a Neolithic cursus, Iron Age and Roman dwellings have been excavated in the locality. The settlement is situated at the highest navigable point on the Thames and at the confluence of the rivers Colne and Leach. It is also at the convergence of several ancient long distance trading routes including the Welsh Way, an Iron Age track which was improved by the Romans and later used by cattle drovers, from the west. The Welsh Way linked the lowest crossing point of the Severn at Gloucester to Lechlade for onward transport by boat to Oxford and London. The Saltway, referred to in Anglo-Saxon charters as 'Sealt Stret', converged at Lechlade from the north and continued south to meet the coast in Hampshire. Lechlade is found as 'Lecelade' in the Doomsday Book of 1086, from the Old English 'laec' meaning 'boggy stream' and 'gelad' meaning 'a water course', so probably meaning 'channel or water-course of the river Leach'. An alternative possible meaning has been suggested as 'river-crossing or passage near the river Leach'.

Salford Priors lies just south west of Bidford-on-Avon at the confluence of the rivers Arrow and Avon on the Warwickshire - Worcestershire border. In 714 recorded as 'Saltford' and in the Domesday Book as 'Salford' and thus a definite 'ford over which salt is carried'. Interestingly, several place names in England have converged to this name but originate from the Old English words 'salh' meaning 'sallow' as in a species of tree. Salford in Oxfordshire has exactly the same meaning as Salford Priors, although the affix is related to early possession by Kenilworth Priory and Evesham Abbey.

The Ridgeway, is a common name in England for ancient tracks. Some, such as the now National Trail that joins Overtun Hill in Wiltshire to Ivanhoe Beacon in Buckinghamshire is known to have been in use for over 5,000 years by Neolithic travellers. On the eastern boundary of Worcestershire, The Ridgeway runs from the south side of Redditch to Evesham and was recorded in 1300 as 'Reggewey'. In other Anglo-Saxon charters the road between Evesham and Pershore appears as 'Rycgweye, Ricgweg and Rycgweye'. The road between Kidderminster and Bridgnorth is documented as 'Rycwei' in 994, again meaning 'Ridgeway'. In a charter relating to Wolverley, this same road is referred to as 'tha myclan strete' translating as 'the great street'. Other charters describe the road between Pershore and Worcester as 'Riavege' and Hricgweye' in 1368 and similarly the road between Stratford-on-Avon and Shipston-on-Stour is described as a Ridgeway. The original Old English word is 'hrycg-weg' but the initial 'h' was often omitted and ultimately discarded.

Broadway, 5 miles south east of Evesham, is recorded in 972 and in the Domesday Book of 1086 as 'Bradanuuege' and 'Bradeweia' respectively. In 1282 written as 'Bradtweial' and in 1275 as 'Bradtweye'. There is much consistency here and no catches, the place name originally means what it says on the label - the place at 'the broad way'. It is possible that this was one of the many ancient ways in an east west orientation. The later gives access to the Cotswold escarpment via Fish Hill. It is possible that the droving of stock through the village encouraged an unusually wide road.

Portway is also a name given to many old thoroughfares. In Old English 'port' means a 'haven' and also a word used for an inland settlement with a market. It appears in Anglo-Saxon charters as 'Portstrcet' and 'Portweg' meaning the 'town way' or 'market way'. There are many included in local charters such as, Port Street in Himbleton (probably a continuation of

Trench Lane), Port Street in Salwarpe (probably the Droitwich to Worcester road), Portweig in Hallow (Worcester to Tenbury), Port street in Oddingley (another reference to Trench Lane), Port Street in Battenhall (Worcester to Tewkesbury) mentioned in 1240, Port street in Waresley (between Kidderminster and Worcester, part of the Roman Way from Chester) and Portstreet in Teddington (Tewkesbury to Stow-on-the-Wold road) and a Port Street in Evesham.

Lydiate Ash. 'Lydiate' is a common name and derives from the Old English word 'hlidgeat' and later the Middle English, 'lidyate' meaning 'a swing gate'. This describes a gate between pasture and arable land or a highway, and in this location, 'near Ash trees'. There is also a Lydiates in Belbroughton. Sometimes, in Old English, it means 'a gap'.

Sharpway Gate is first recorded in two charters of 770. In one this hamlet between Hanbury and Stoke Prior is written as 'Sceap weg'. This would give 'Sheep's way, however, the charter is a copy and has several other misspelt words - may be a scribe having a bad day or an apprentice! In the second document the hamlet is referred to as 'Scearp weg' and is perfectly written in all other respects, thus doubtless the original meaning. Here 'sharp' seems to be used in the sense of two roads meeting at a sharp angle and 'Gate' a later addition.

Chapter 23 Post-Medieval Worcestershire

AS in England generally, there are relatively few places in Worcestershire that were named after 1500. Even 'new towns' are often named after a much older nearby settlement, as in the case of Redditch. It is heartening to see the new building developments in the county, be they residential, retail or manufacturing, given names that mark historical events, renowned local people or natural features. This practice helps keep relevance and continuity and indeed will help toponymists of the future. Weogoran Park is a new residential development around 3 miles south east of Worcester. The name is a nod to the Weogora tribe who are recorded in a charter of 691 as 'Weogorna civitate' which, of course, became the city of Worcester. Another new housing initiative, takes its name from the nearby Hen brook at Stoke Prior and a road name on a new residential development in Great Witley commemorates the nearby site of the 'Battle' of Woodbury Hill (a skirmish really), where in 1405 Owain Glyndwr, the Welsh pretender to an independent Wales faced the English king, Henry IV. Indeed, there are very many more similar examples in Worcestershire. These commemorations are to be applauded for keeping alive old place names and their original meaning.

Chapter 24 The Place Name Toolkit

THERE are a wide array of resources and methods of exploring the origins and meaning of the place names that surround you.

The internet is one starting point. You can get lucky by using a search engine, entering 'etymology, derivation or origin of', followed by the name of the place you are interested in followed by 'place name'. Sometimes you are very lucky and hit upon a free online publication that includes a systematic review of place names in a county or district. Otherwise, I would be a little wary of explanations from one-off internet websites, unless corroborated by other sources as they can be very much wide of the mark and not supported by expert consensus.

Some books on the place names of counties are free online, however, some were published many years ago and more recent evidence may have prompted a re-interpretation of the origin and meaning of some place names. W H Duignan's books on the place names of Worcestershire, Staffordshire and Warwickshire are also free online. They are extremely well researched and detailed, particularly on Anglo-Saxon charters and church documents but are now over one hundred years old and many place names have since been the subject of new evidence and re-evaluation. The British History Society via British History Online is a helpful supplementary resource providing insights into events, dates and the meaning of place names.

I like books you can hold in your hand, so it is easy to search for publications on the place names of England, Britain or particular counties from independent authors and these are often inexpensive. Indeed, many of these books second hand cost less than £10. They cover most counties of England and are a wonderful source of well considered and interesting information. For Worcestershire, the monograph, Worcestershire Place Names by Anthony Poulton-Smith is a very detailed, authoritative and a relatively new book of the meaning of place names with some fascinating facts about local history. I have listed in the references several other modern, very comprehensive books on the subject including Victor Watt's, The Cambridge Dictionary of English Place Names, Mills, A Dictionary of British Place Names and some old classics such as Ekwall's Concise Oxford Dictionary of English Place-Names. Another masterful book both insightful and detailed is Signposts to the Past by Margaret Gelling.

There may well be a wealth of knowledge, experience and enthusiasm available at your local history group or society that you can tap into and, of course, your local library is another port of call.

The English Place Name Society (EPNS) founded in 1923 and based at Nottingham University has an ongoing mission to provide a county-by-county guide to the linguistic origins of England's place names. The survey has so far covered almost all of the 48 counties of England and the society publishes a regular journal. The Key to English Place-Names is a useful web-based tool from the Institute for Name-Studies University of Nottingham and has a search function which allows you to find out the meaning and origins of place names in England by entering the name of a place or by browsing by county – 'kepn.nottingham.ac.uk'.

Thus, there are many individuals and organisations who have studied the meaning of place names and performed all the hard work for you. However, if you become very interested in the discipline of toponymy then further research using the services of your local County Council Library, Archive and Archaeology Service or nearest Cathedral Library and Archive collections are possibilities. They often provide support relevant to exploring place names in a county.

Chapter 25 Summary and Afterword

'The past is a foreign country; they do things differently there.'
The Go-Between L P Hartley

I have drawn on the study of place names as the main portal or bridge to explore the past. I have encouraged you to listen and to understand what these names are telling us by employing the resources mentioned in chapter 24. They can help us to discover more about the people who named and lived in and around them. Although often of ancient origin they are still present all around us today and they still communicate with us through maps, road signs and countless other records and documents. In this sense they seem alive and calling, the embodiment of living history.

I have attempted to make history interesting by exploring the lives of the ordinary folks who came before, the majority of whom lived off the natural resources that their environment and the land offered. I have tried also to make history relevant and intimate by encouraging you to search for the meanings of the names that the local folks in the past gave to the places that surround you now. I encourage you to visit them where there is public access and armed with the appropriate Ordnance Survey map. The study of place names can be an energetic pastime and could easily become an ongoing and enjoyable family activity, as place names relate to both the whole spectrum of life in the past and our own interests in the present. Place names are linked to many of our hobbies including history, geography, geology, languages, farming, engineering, religion and natural history to name but a few. By studying them you can discover for yourselves why our ancestors thought your local places important enough to name and why they used the particular descriptions that they did. The place names covered in the previous chapters may be many but are certainly not exhaustive. There are still local place names near you whose meanings are waiting to be discovered and may well surprise you. Becoming a 'place name detective' is a rewarding and fun way for the whole family to connect with local history. It can also be very satisfying to note the dates of place names mentioned in place name books derived from charters and various documents and correlate these with regional, national and international events that occurred at the same time. This gives both a sense of perspective and relevance.

The combined evidence now available from local written sources, from the general historical literature and from new scientific data, in combination with place name analysis makes a powerful team for understanding the past. Many of these insights have been gained by new and improving scientific techniques, from archaeology to dendrology and from ancient DNA analysis to genetic population studies. It is perhaps surprising how much of our ancient settlements, landscape and the daily lives of people can be reconstructed by using this inter-disciplinary approach. Perhaps we have the chance of seeing the past more clearly, irrespective of the stories the victors have told us. It is likely, with further developments of genetic techniques and the growth in genetic population studies, and particularly if mutations unique to specific populations are identified, more insights will be revealed about our ancestors. It seems, in our genes the past is permanently in the present, so too with place names.

Exploring the meaning of the names given to the places around you provides an understanding into the continuity of local populations. As a collective study it tells us what England has been and therefore by extension, who we are. Just as we acknowledge and respect those who surround us now, we can also extend to those who lived in the locality in the past. I have always thought it sensible that we develop a birds-eye view of humanity. To step back and look at the greater picture. Not just the here and now, but the then and before. It is the place where the differences between peoples, cultures, their languages and religions, become understandable and the commonality of our shared origins apparent. This is a powerful tool in the honourable aims to move towards mutual respect, peace, and an awareness of the context of our existence. Indeed, in the diversity of people and place names we can detect continuity, connectedness and unity through exploring their common origins.

The study of local place names can provide us with new insights by understanding the original intended meaning of a place, and thus give a refreshing change in perspective of our surroundings. They can give us a concept of temporal continuity and can highlight the challenges our ancestors faced. Rather like the study of art, it teaches us to look more carefully at the subject of our surroundings and what they are telling us. Toponymy can help us understand what people thought important around them, how they lived and draws a vivid picture of a locality in the past. They can help us imagine what people saw, heard and sensed. I ask you to pause, wonder and respect these people who we emerged from, these folks who came before. We owe them that.

The names of human settlements and the landscape in which they are set are resounding with the echoes of the 'Voices of the Past' and form an important part of our history. They stand as memorials of the people and events in the past. They throw light on the scenes and movements of former ages, and therefore, cannot be neglected in the study of the past.

I write this during our isolation from the Coronavirus Pandemic - 'The Lockdown'. The worst pandemic since the 1918 Influenza Pandemic which is estimated to have caused the death of between 17 to 50 million, many young adults. As of September 2020, after the first wave of Covid-19 and as I write these words, we are approaching the grim milestone of 1 million deaths worldwide. One of the characteristics of modern infectious diseases has been the increasing tendency of pathogens to 'jump' from animals to humans - the zoonoses. Recent examples of these emerging zoonoses are Avian Influenza, MERS (Middle East Respiratory Syndrome) from camels, Bovine Spongiform Encephalitis (BSE), Ebola virus, Nipah virus and West Nile virus. Indeed, six of the last ten new infectious diseases identified in humans over the last decade have derived from animals, as is the coronavirus, SARS-CoV-2, the virus responsible for COVID-19 Pandemic. This is very likely due to humans' continuing expansion and settlement into new and particularly tropical habitats. We continue to encroach into wilderness that brings us into contact with new pathogens and their spread has been facilitated by an ever-increasing global transport infrastructure. It makes me wonder if we know any more about the nature and implications of the modern world that we have created than the one that 'the folks who came before' created for themselves? Indeed, as science dispels the mists of the past, still our future is no clearer, partly for the same reasons - the ever-accelerating rate of change in technology and society. The adverse effects of these rapid changes are now increasingly manifesting themselves in damage to the planet, its biomass and in unintended effects on our quality of life.

Before and during the Early Medieval Period there were epidemics and some of these were zoonoses, such as the Bubonic Plague, and accompanied by extremely high infectivity and mortality rates. The environment was often hostile with extremes of weather, crop failures, food shortages and the constant threats from human conflicts and wild animals. In short, life was often extremely hard and life span and expectations low. Life seemed a short interlude between birth and death with the hope of everlasting salvation in an afterlife. Thus, this pandemic is nothing that our predecessors have not gone through and survived. Previous pandemics have, indeed, been associated with much worse mortality rates than this one, so far, but that does not comfort those who have lost loved ones now. However, our ancestors always rose to the challenge, otherwise we would not be here! So will, and indeed, must we. We owe ourselves and those who beget us that. I think they would understand.

From my study I am able to gaze upon the Malvern Hills, Midsummer Hill and British Camp. Those ancient landmarks that Palaeolithic and Mesolithic hunters used as directional markers, that Neolithic people farmed below, Bronze Age people used as seasonal meeting places and Celts defended with their hill forts. I am able to see many of the surrounding settlements and natural features of this beautiful Worcestershire landscape mentioned in this book that the Anglo-Saxons recorded so diligently and to which the Norman high status families added their surnames. It has been a fascinating journey into the deep past. Place names reflect the history of the people and by their study you can catch a glimpse of their world, in their eyes, imagine their challenges and how they lived. Place names can provide the detail to the locality and life to history. To stand by the river named 'the dark one', the stream called 'the strong one', the high ground known as 'the speech hill' or the view point literally meaning, 'hill, hill, hill' imagining how the creators of these names lived is an intimate and personal journey. The spirits of our ancestors are locked in the meaning of the places they named and that surround us today. They are waiting to be unlocked and can come alive again if we breath our energy and attention in to them. The very embodiment of living local history.

I do hope I have both awoken your interest and enthusiasm to explore these echoes of the past and provided the guidance in order to do so. I hope I have encouraged you to pause and listen to their calls and to work out what they are trying to tell us. By listening to the folks who came before they can bring history to your own locality and to your own door. Even places you thought you knew well appear refreshingly new if you arrive from a different direction. I hope I have encouraged you to visit these places, enjoy their wonder and beauty, their magic and mystery, stand where our ancestors have stood and imagine what they saw, heard and how they felt. This is not history of distant cold facts and figures but one of senses, imagination and intimacy based on what is known; history in your head, heart and at your feet! This is a challenge, as they lived long ago, spoke and certainly lived so differently from us. However, the rich reward is a better understanding of our ancestors and the gift they offer us of a new perspective on our current settlements and landscape, and of our origins. Which, I guess, is what a different language and culture is - a different way of viewing the world. Discovering the origins and meaning of place names changes our understanding of what England and indeed Britain had been, and therefore by extension, what it is and who we are.

Perhaps you have felt a stirring of continuity and connection between us and the folks who came before? Maybe we are more similar to them than we thought? Maybe, by understanding them, we learn more about ourselves? Happy and rewarding time travelling.

References

Foreword
Leslie, S. 2015 The fine-scale genetic structure of the British population Nature. 519(7543):309-14
Ekwall, E., 1959 The Concise Oxford Dictionary of English Place-names Fourth Edition Oxford Clarendon Press
Mills, A. D. 2011 A Dictionary of British Place Names revision Oxford University Press
Watts, V. 2004 The Cambridge Dictionary of English Place Names Cambridge University Press
Taggart C 2011 The Book of English Place Names Random House Group Ltd
Potter, S. and Sargent, L 1973 Essays on the Etymology of Words From Nature Collins, London
Gelling, M.1978 Signposts to the Past J. M. Dent & Sons Ltd
Gelling, M. and Cole, A. (2000). The Landscape of Place-Names Shaun Tyas Publications
Harari, Y N 2014 Sapiens A Brief History of Humankind Harper Publications

Part 1 The Foundations

Chapter 1 The Nature of Place Names.
Ekwall, E. 1959 The Concise Oxford Dictionary of English Place-names Fourth Edition Oxford Clarendon Press
Mills, A. D., 2011 A Dictionary of British Place Names revision Oxford University Press
Watts, V. 2004 The Cambridge Dictionary of English Place Names Cambridge University Press
Taggart, C., 2011 The Book of English Place Names Random House Group Ltd

Potter, S. and Sargent, L 1973 Essays on the Etymology of Words From Nature Collins, London

Gelling, M.1978 Signposts to the Past J. M. Dent & Sons Ltd

Gelling, M. and Cole, A. 2000. The Landscape of Place-Names Shaun Tyas Publications

Chapter 2 A Brief History of Languages

Pagel M, Atkinson Q D, Calude A, and Meade A 2013, Ultraconserved words point to deep language ancestory across Eurasia. Proceedings of the National Academy of Sciences of the United States of America, 110 (21), 8471-8476.

Campbell, M. C. and Tishkoff S. A. 2008 African Genetic Diversity: Implications for Human Demographic History, Modern Human Origins, and Complex Disease Mapping Annu Rev Genomics Hum Genet. 9: 403–433.

Tucci, S and Akey, J. M. 2019 The Long Walk Out of Africa Genome Biology, 20, 130

Bons, PD, Bauer CC, Bocherens H, de Riese T, Drucker DG, Francken M, et al. 2019 Out of Africa by spontaneous migration waves.

Bickerton, D. 2009 Adam's Tongue. New York: Hill and Wang

Botha, D. and Knight, C. 2009. The Prehistory of Language Oxford: Oxford University Press.

Lieberman, P. 2018 The Theory That Changed Everything: "On the Origin of Species" as a Work in Progress. New York: Columbia University Press.

Lieberman, P. 1984. The biology and evolution of languages. Cambridge, Massachusetts: Harvard University Press

Hauser, M. D. et al 2014 The mystery of language evolution. Frontiers in Psychology. 5: 401.

Burling, R. 2005. The talking ape: how language evolved. Oxford; New York: Oxford University

Pagel M, 2017 Darwinian perspectives on the evolution of human language, Psychonomic Bulletin & Review, 24 (1), 151-157

Pagal M, 2014 Frequency of Use and Basic Vocabulary, Multilingual Cognition and Language Use: Processing and Typological Perspectives

Pagel M, 2013 Linguistics and Evolution of Human Languages, in Princeton Guide to Evolution

Pagel M, Beaumont M A, Meade A, Verkerk A and Calude A 2019, Dominant words rise to the top by positive frequency-dependent selection, Proceedings of the National Academy of Sciences of the United States of America, 116 (15), 7397-7402.

Ostler, N. 2005. Empires of the Word. Harper Collins Publishers

McWhorter, John. 2002. The Power of Babel, A Natural History of Language. Columbia University. Arrow Books

Guy, G R. 2014 Lexical Phonology and the Problem of Variation. Annual Meeting of the Berkeley Linguistic Society.

Guy, G R 2019, Variation and Mental Representation. In Lightfoot, D and Havenhill, J. Variable Properties in Language: Their Nature and Acquisition. Washington DC: Georgetown University Press.

Gelling, M.1978 Signposts to the Past J. M. Dent & Sons Ltd

Forsyth, K. 1998 Literacy in Pictish in Literacy in Medieval Celtic Societies Cambridge University Press

Chapter 3 The Oldest Known Place Names

Ekwall, E 1928. English River-Names. Oxford: at the Clarendon Press

Krahe, H. 1963 *Die Struktur der alteuropäischen Hydronomie* ("The structure of Old-European river names") Wiesbaden,

Krahe, H. 1964. *Unsere ältesten Flussnamen* ("Our oldest river names") Wiesbaden,

Kitson, P. R. 1996 British and European River Names, Transactional of the Philological Society, November, Vol. 94, Issue 2

Davies, P. V., Price G., and Schrijver, P, 2017 Encyclopaedia of the Languages of Europe, (355-364).

Lowe J. J., Indo-European Caland Adjectives in *-nt- and Participles in Sanskrit Historical Linguistics, November 2014,127, 1

Hough, C., Place Names, Encyclopaedia of Language & Linguistics, 2006, 10.1016, (613-620)

Snir A et al. 2015. The Origin of Cultivation and Proto-Weeds, Long Before Neolithic Farming. PLoS ONE 10 (7): e0131422; doi: 10.1371/journal. pone.013142

Hammarström, H. Forkel, R. Haspelmath, M. eds. 2017 "Sumerian". Glottolog 3.0. Jena, Germany: Max Planck Institute for the Science of Human History.

Jamison, S. and Brereton, J 2014 The Rigveda: the earliest religious poetry of India, Oxford University Press, 4, 7-9.

Lefkowitz, M. 2003 Greek Gods, Human Lives: What We Can Learn From Myths. New Haven, Conn: Yale University Press.

Lawson, J. 2012 Modern Greek Folklore and Ancient Greek Religion: A Study in Survivals. Cambridge University Press. 2

Edmonston M C, 1953 The Mammoth and the Madyodon in the Folklore of Indians of North America, Journal of the Illinois State Archaeological Society, Vol. 3, No. 1 15-17

Strong, W D 1934 North American Indian Traditions Suggesting a Knowledge of the Mammoth. American Anthropologist. 36 (1): 81-88

Scott, W B 1887 American Elephant Myths. Scribner's Magazins. New York: c Scribner's Sons, 1: 474-476

Records of the Past Exploration Society, 1907 Pre-Indian inhabitants of North America, Part II, Man and the Elephant and Mastodon, Records of the Past, Washington DC 164.

Langford G E 1980 Pleistocene Animals in Folk Memory The Journal of American Folklore. 93 (369): 293-304.

Mayor, A. 2005, Fossil Legends of the First Americans. Princeton: Princeton University Press.

Nunn, P., 2016 Australian Aboriginal Traditions about Coastal Change Reconciled with Postglacial Sea-Level History. Environment and History, 22, 3.

Nunn, P., 2018 The Edge of Memory, Ancient Stories, Oral Tradition and the Post-Glacial World. Bloomsbury

Piccardi, L. Masse, W. B. 2007 Myth and Geology. Geological Society Special Publication 273. Geological Society, London.

Part 2 Populating Britain

Chapter 4 The Palaeolithic Hunter-Gatherers of North West Europe

Reyes-Garcia, Marti, V.N. McDade, T. Tanner, S. Vadez, V. 2007 Concepts and Methods in Studies Measuring Individual Ethnobotanical Knowledge, J of Ethnobotanical Knowledge, 27 (2), 182-203.

Barrera-Bassols, N. Toledo, V. 2005, Ethnoecology of the Yucatec Maya: Symbolism, knowledge and Management of Natural Resources. J of Latin American Geography 4:9-41

Berkes, F. 1999. Sacred Ecology: Traditional Ecology, Knowledge and Resource Management. Philadelphia Taylor & Francis

Wynn, T. and Coolidge, E.L. 2017 Cognitive Models in Palaeolithic Archaeology, Oxford University Press

Coolidge F.L. and Wynn. T. 2005 Working Memory, its executive functions and the emergence of modern thinking. Cambridge Archaeological Journal, 15(1), 5-26.

Chatwin B, 1987 The Songlines. London, Jonathan Cape

Bradley, J. 2010 Yanyuwa Families. Singing Saltwater Country: Journey to the Songlines of Carpentaria, Allen & Unwin

Kerrin, D., 2010. Aboriginal Dreaming paths and trading routes: the colonisation of the Australian economic landscape. Eastbourne, UK, Sussex Academic Press

Clarke, P.A., 2003. Where the ancestors walked: Australia as an Aboriginal landscape. Sydney, Allen and Unwin.

Clarke, P.A., 2009. Australian Aboriginal ethnometeorology and seasonal calendars. History and Anthropology, 20, 79-106.

Norris, R P and Harney, B Y 2014 Songlines and navigation in Wardaman and other Australian Aboriginal cultures. Journal of Astronomical History and Heritage, 17(2), 141-148.

Lewis, D., 1976. Observations on route finding and spatial orientation among the Aboriginal peoples of the Western Desert region of Central Australia. Oceania, 46(4), 249-282.

Norris, R.P., and Hamacher D.W., 2009. The astronomy of Aboriginal Australia. In D. Valls-Gabaud and A. Boksenberg (eds) The role of Astronomy in Society and Culture. Cambridge, Cambridge University Press. 39-47

Tindale, N.B., 1974. Aboriginal tribes of Australia. Berkeley, University of California Press.

Norris, R P, 2016. Dawes Review 5: Australian Aboriginal Astronomy and Navigation. Astronomical Society of Australia. 33, 39.

Fuller, R S, Trudgett, M M, Norris, R P, and Anderson M G 2014 Star maps and travelling to ceremonies; the Euahlayi People and their use of the night sky. Journal of Astonomical History and Heritage, 17 (2), 149-160

V Reyes-Garcia, A Fernandez-Llamazares, Sing to Learn: The Role of Songs in the Transmission of Indigenous Knowledge among the Tsimane' of Bolivian Amazonia. Journal of Ethnobiology Sept 2019, Vol 39, 3, 460-477.

Kents Cavern: A field guide to the natural history. Joyce Lundberg and Donald McFarlane. 2008. William Pengelly Cave Studies Trust

Jacobi, R. M and Higham, T. F. G: 2008 The 'Red Lady' ages gracefully: New Ultrafiltration AMS determinations from Paviland", Journal of Human Evolution.

Bahn, P. and Pettit, P., 2009, Britain's Oldest Art: The Ice Age Cave Art of Creswell Crags, London: English

Brace, S. et al 2015 Upper Palaeolithic ritualistic cannibalism at Gough's Cave (Somerset, UK) The human remains from head to toe. Journal of Human Evolution. Vol 82, 270-189.

Sikora, M. Pitulko, V. Willerslev, E. 2019 The population history of northeastern Siberia since the Pleistocene Nature, 570, 182-188.

Chapter 5 The Mesolithic Hunter-Fisher-Gatherers of Europe

Wohlleben, P. 2016 Destination North in The Hidden Life of Trees. Harper Collins Publishers

Wright, J. 2017. In The Beginning in A Natural History of Hedgerows Profile Books Ltd.

Vera, F. 2000. Grazing Ecology and Forest History. CABI Publishing

Brown, T. 1997 Clearances and clearings: deforestation in Mesolithic/Neolithic Britain. Oxford Journal of Archaeology, 16,2, 133-146

Clarke, G. 1954 Excavation at Starr Carr: an early Mesolithic site at Steamer, near Scarborough , Yorkshire. Cambridge University Press.

Mellors, P, Dark, P. (1998). Star Carr in Context: New Archaeological and Palaeoecological Investigations at the Early Mesolithic Site of Star Carr, North Yorkshire. McDonald Institute for Archaeological Research

Conneller, C, Milner N, Taylor, B and Taylor M. 2012 Substantial settlement in the European Early Mesolithic: new research at Starr Carr. Antiquity, 86, 334, 1004-1020

Taylor, M 1998 Identification of the wood and evidence for human working, in Mellars, P & Dark, P. (ed) Star Carr in context: new archaeological and palaeocological investigations at Early Mesolithic site of Star Carr, North Yorkshire: 52-63. Cambridge: McDonald Institute for Archaeological Research

Herring, Peter (2000). St Michael's Mount Archaeological Works, 1995-8. Truro: Cornwall Archaeological Unit.

de Beer, Gavin June 1960 "Iktin". The Geographical Journal. 126 (2): 160-167

Parry RF, Davies, JA (1928) Excavations at the caves, Cheddar. Proceedings SANHS 14(4):102–121

Parry RF (1930) Excavations at Cheddar. Proceedings SANHS 16(4):46–62

Orlando, L Ginolhac, A and Willerslev E June 2013 Recalibrating Equus evolution using the genome Nature, 499, 74-78

Welker, F et al 2020 The dental proteome of Homo antecessor Nature, 580, 235-238

Brace, S et al, Ancient dark skinned Cheddar man find may not be true. New Scientist. 21. February 2018

Brace, S et al 2018 Population Replacement in Early Neolithic Britain Nature Ecology & Evolution 3, 765-771

Haak, W et al. 2015 Massive migration from the steppe is responsible for Indo-European languages in Europe. Nature. 10, 1038.

Lacan, M. Keystrokes, C and Ludes, B. 2013 Review: Ancestry of Modern Europeans: Contributions of Ancient DNA Cell Mol Life Sci Jul;70(14):2473-87

Lazaridis, L 2018 Review The Evolutionary History of Human Populations in Europe. Curr Opin Genet Dev 53: 21-27

Chapter 6 The Neolithic Farmers Arrive

Harari, Y. N. 2114. Sapiens - A Brief History of Humankind Vantage Publication

Meikiejohn, C. Schentag, C Venema, A and Kay, P 1984 Socio-Economic changes in the Mesolithic and Neolithic in Western Europe, In Paleopathology and the origins of the agriculture Ed Cohen M N, 75-100, New York.

Cuncliffe, B. 2012 Britain Begins Oxford University Press

Oliver, N. 2011 A History of Ancient Britain Weidenfeld & Nicolson

Lacan, M. Keystrokes, C and Ludes, B. 2013 Review: Ancestry of Modern Europeans: Contributions of Ancient DNA Cell Mol Life Sci Jul;70(14):2473-87

Lazaridis, L 2018 Review The Evolutionary History of Human Populations in Europe. Curr Opin Genet Dev 53: 21-27

The People of the British Isles (PoBI) project 2015 Nature on the 19th of March 2015

McWhorter, J., 2002. The Power of Babel, A Natural History of Language. Columbia University. Arrow Books

Blood Groups of the Basques Nature 160, 505–506(1947)

Arredi, B. Polo I, E, Tyler-Smith, C. 2007 The Peopling of Europe, Anthropological Genetics: Theory, Methods and Applications, Cambridge University Press

Behar, D.M. Harmant, C and The Genographic Consortium The Basque Paradigm; Genetic Evidence of a Maternal Continuity in Franco-Cantabrian Region since Pre-Neolithic Times. 2012. American Journal of Human Genetics. 90 (3): 486-493.

Dupandunlop, I; et al 2004. Estimating the impact of prehistoric admixture in the genome of Europeans. Molecular Biology and Evolution. 2 (7): 1361-1372.

Cavalli-Sforza, L.L. 1997 Genes, people and languages
Proceedings of the National Academy of Sciences of the United States of America. 94 15: 7719-7724

Chapter 7 The Bronze Age Immigrants

Haak, W et al 2015 Massive migration from the steppe was a source for Indo-European languages in Europe. Nature. 522 (7555): 207-211.

Olalde, Iñigo; et al. (2017). "The Beaker Phenomenon And The Genomic Transformation Of Northwest Europe" Nature, 555, 190-196.

Lazaridis I, et al. Ancient human genomes suggest three ancestral populations for present-day Europeans. Nature. 2014;513:409–413

Novembre, J et al 2008 Genes mirror geography in Europe Nature 456 (7218) 98-101

Brandt G, et al. Ancient DNA reveals key stages in the formation of central European mitochondrial genetic diversity. Science. 2013;342:257–261

Skoglund P, et al. Origins and genetic legacy of Neolithic farmers and hunter-gatherers in Europe. Science. 2012;336:466–469

Schama, S. 2009 Vol. 1 At the Edge of the World 3000 BC to AD 1603 BBC Books

George, E. 2018 Ed Human Origins: 7 Million Years and Counting New Scientist

Chapter 8 The Migration of Celts to Southern Britain

Gibson, C and Wodtko, D S 2013 The Background of the Celtic Language: Theories from Archaeology and Linguistics University of Wales Centre for Advanced Welsh and Celtic Studies

Cuncliffe, B. 2012 Britain Begins Oxford University Press

Welsh, G. P. 1963. Britannia: the Roman Conquest and Occupation of Britain. 27-31

Oliver, N. 2011 A History of Ancient Britain Weidenfeld & Nicolson

Ostler, N. 2005 Empires of the World, A Language History of the World, HarperCollinsPublishers

Schama, S 2009 Vol. 1 At the Edge of the World 3000 BC to AD 1603 BBC Books

Delaney, F. 1886 The Celts Guild Publishing London

Laing, L. 1981 Celtic Britain Paladin Books

Leslie, S. et 2015 The fine-scale genetic structure of the British population Nature. 519(7543):309-14

Olalde, I. et al. 2017 "The Beaker Phenomenon And The Genomic Transformation Of Northwest Europe" Nature, 555, 190-196

Chapter 9 Roman Britain

Schama, S 2009 Vol. 1 At the Edge of the World 3000 BC to AD 1603 BBC Books

Leslie, S et 2015 The fine-scale genetic structure of the British population Nature. 519(7543):309-14

King, T. E. et al. 2007 Africans in Yorkshire? "The deepest rooting glade of the Y phylogeny within an English genealogy" European Journal of Human Genetics 15 (3); 288-293.

Martiniano, R., Caffell, A., Holst, M. et al. 2016 Genomic signals of migration and continuity in Britain before the Anglo-Saxons. Nat Commun 7, 10326.

Chapter 10 The Anglo-Saxons

Wmffre, I., 2007 Post-Roman Irish settlement in Wales: new insights from a recent study of Cardiganshire place-names

Cavill, P., 2016 A New Dictionary of English Field-Names English Place Name Society University of Nottingham

Leslie, S. 2015 The fine-scale genetic structure of the British population Nature. 519(7543):309-14

Martiniano, R., Caffell, A., 2016 Holst, M. et al. Genomic signals of migration and continuity in Britain before the Anglo-Saxons. Nat Commun 7, 10326.

O'Dushlaine, C. et al 2010 Genetic Differences Between Five Different Populations Human Heredity; 70: 141-149.

Schiffels, S et al 2016 Iron Age and Anglo-Saxon genomes from East England reveal British migration history Nature Communication. 7: 10408. Nat Commun. 2016; 7: 10408.

Schiffels, S. et al. 2016 Iron Age and Anglo-Saxon genomes from East England reveal British migration history, Nature Communications 7, Article number:10408

Schama, S 2009 Vol. 1 At the Edge of the World 3000 BC to AD 1603 BBC Books

Lewis-Stempel, J 2005 England: The Autobiography. Viking Publications

Chapter 11 The Scandinavians in Southern Britain

Schama, S 2009 Vol. 1 At the Edge of the World 3000 BC to AD 1603 BBC Books

Ekwall, E. 1959 The Concise Oxford Dictionary of English Place-names Fourth Edition Oxford Clarendon Press

Watts, V. 2004 The Cambridge Dictionary of English Place Names Cambridge University Press

Ekwall, E., 1918 Scandinavians and Celts in the North-West of England, Lund, 51-55.

Fellows-Jensen, G., 1985 Scandinavian Settlement Names in the North-West, Copenhagen.

Fellows-Jensen, G., 1972 Scandinavian Settlements in Cumbria and Dumfriesshire: The Place-Name Evidence, Copenhagen.

Gelling, M.1978 Signposts to the Past J. M. Dent & Sons Ltd

Cameron, K. 1965 Scandinavian Settlement in the Territory of the Five Boroughs: The Place-Name Evidence. University of Nottingham.

Bowden, G. R. et al 2008 "Excavating Past Population Structures by Surname-Based Sampling: The Genetic Legacy of the Vikings in Northwest England" Molecular Biology and Evolution Vol 25, 2, 301- 309

Goodacre et al. 2005 "Genetic evidence for a family-based Scandinavian settlement of Shetland and Orkney during the Viking periods", Hereditary. 95 (2): 129-135.

"Gene geography: Do you have Viking ancestry in your DNA?" Wellcome Trust. 2004.

Margaryan, A., Lawson, D.J., Sikora, M. et al 2020 Population genomics of the Viking world. Nature 585, 390-396

Leslie, S 2015 The fine-scale genetic structure of the British population Nature. 519(7543):309-14

Chapter 12 The Normans

Gross, C. 1900 The Sources and Literature of English History from the Earliest Times to 1485. Long mans, Green and Co.

Schama, S 2009 Vol. 1 At the Edge of the World 3000 BC to AD 1603 BBC Books

Golding, B. 2001 Conquest and Colonisation The Normans in Britain, 1066-1100 Pelgrave Macmillan

Chapter 13 Late and Post-Medieval England

Ekwall, E., 1959 The Concise Oxford Dictionary of English Place-names Fourth Edition Oxford Clarendon Press

Mills, A. D. 2011 A Dictionary of British Place Names revision Oxford University Press

Watts, V. 2004 The Cambridge Dictionary of English Place Names Cambridge University Press

Taggart C 2011 The Book of English Place Names Random House Group Ltd

Gelling, M.1978 Signposts to the Past J. M. Dent & Sons Ltd

Chapter 14 The Call of the Wild

Potter, S. and Sargent, L 1973 Essays on the Etymology of Words from Nature Collins, London

Aybes, C and Yalden, D Place-name evidence for the former distribution and status of wolves and beavers in Britain Mammal Rev 25: 201-227 1995

Wolf History, Conservation, Ecology and Behaviour Mammal Review 25. 4 (1995)

Gelling, M Anglo-Saxon eagles, Leeds Stud. Eng.18, 173-181

Evans R J and Whitfield D P The history of eagles in Britain and Ireland. An ecological review of place names and documentary evidence from the last 1,500 years. Bird Study 59(3): 1-15 Aug 2012.

Yalden, D.W. The Older History of the White-Tailed Eagle in Britain Derek W. Yalden August 2007 British Birds 471-480.

The Great Crane Project - Wildfowl & Wetlands Trust and RSPB 2010 - 2014, in Crane History

Record Year for Great Crane Project. 31 August 2018 Bird Guide

The White Stork Project 2016 Knepp Castle Estate

Chapter 15 The Diversity of Place Names in Modern England

Ekwall, E., 1959 The Concise Oxford Dictionary of English Place-names. Fourth Edition Oxford Clarendon Press

Mills, A. D. 2011 A Dictionary of British Place Names Oxford University Press

Watts, V. 2004 The Cambridge Dictionary of English Place Names Cambridge University Press

Taggart, C., 2011 The Book of English Place Names Random House Group Ltd

Potter, S. and Sargent, L 1973 Essays on the Etymology of Words From Nature Collins, London

Gelling, M.1978 Signposts to the Past J. M. Dent & Sons Ltd

Gelling, M. and Cole, A. (2000). The Landscape of Place-Names Shaun Tyas Publications

Part 3 The Place Names of Worcestershire

Chapter 16 Populating Britain

Allnatt, V. 2018 50 Finds from Worcestershire. Amberley Publishing

Sikora, M. Pitulko, V. Willerslev, E. 2019 The population history of northeastern Siberia since the Pleistocene Nature, 570, 182-188.

Russell, O., Daffern, H., Nash, A. 2018 Putting the Palaeolithic into Worcestershire's HER: An evidence-base for development management. Internet Archaeology, 47. (47)

Brooks, A., Pevsner, N. 2007 Worcestershire, The Buildings of England, London: Yale University Press.

Evans R J and Whitfield D P The history of eagles in Britain and Ireland. An ecological review of place names and documentary evidence from the last 1,500 years. Bird Study 59(3): 1-15 Aug 2012.

Yalden, D.W. The Older History of the White-Tailed Eagle in Britain Derek W. Yalden August 2007 British Birds 471-480.

Smith, C. 2002 Late Stone Age Hunters of the British Isles Published by Routledge

Brookes, A., Pevsner, N. 2007, Worcestershire, The Buildings of England (Revised ed.), London: Yale University Press

Zimmermann, A. Hilpert, J. Wendt, K P. 2009. Estimations of Population Density for Selected Periods Between the Neolithic and AD 1800. Human Biology, 81, 2.

Thomas J 1991 Rethinking the Neolithic, Cambridge University Press

Thomas J 2003 Thoughts on the 'Repacked' Neolithic revolution, Antiquity, 77 (295), 67-74

Chapter 17 The Celts in Worcestershire

Children, G. Nash, G., 1994. *Prehistoric Sites of Herefordshire*. Logaston Press

Smith, B. S. 1978 *A History of Malvern*. Leicester, UK: Leicester University Press

Julius Caesar, Commentarii de Bello Gallico 2.4

Cunliffe, B. 1991 Iron Age Communities: an account of England, Scotland and Wakes from the seventh century BC to the Roman conquest. 3rd edition, 170-175.

The Venerable Bede Ecclesiastical History of the English People

Hutton, R. 1991. The Pagan Religions of the Ancient British Isles: Their Nature and Legacy. Oxford, UK and Cambridge: Blackwell

Yeates, S.J. 2008 The Tribes of Witches Oxbow Books

Moore, T., 2006 Iron-Age Societies in the Severn-Cotswolds: Developing narratives of social and landscape change, BAR British Series 421, 2006

Laing, L. 1981 Celtic Britain Paladin Books

Rees, A. Rees, B. 1998 Celtic Heritage: Ancient Tradition in Ireland and Wales. New York, NY: Thames

Duignan, W. H. 1905 Worcestershire Place Names. Oxford University Press.

Hannah, A. 1993 Excavations at Tewkesbury Transactions of the Bristol and Gloucestershire Archaeological Society, 111, 21-75.

Historic England 2019 Motte castle site and medieval agricultural remains at Crookbarrow Farm, Whittington.

Fellows-Jensen, G., 1985 Scandinavian Settlement Names in the North-West, Copenhagen.

Fellows-Jensen, G., 1972 Scandinavian Settlements in Cumbria and Dumfriesshire: The Place-Name Evidence, Copenhagen.

City of Worcester. 2005. The First Settlers. Worcester City Council

Harris, A. 2018 A History of Hanbury. KopyKats Design & Print

Freezer, D. 1977 From Saltings to Spa Town.

Allnatt, V. 2018 50 Finds from Worcestershire Amberley Publishing

Dyer C. 1991 Hanbury: Settlement and Society in a Woodland Landscape Leicester University Press

Mawer, A., Stenton, F.M. and Houghton F.T.S. 1927 The Place-Names of Worcestershire English Place-Name Society Woolnough Bookbinding Ltd

Chapter 18 Roman Worcestershire

City of Worcester. 2005 The First Settlers. Worcester City Council.

Brooks, A., Pevsner, N. 2007 Worcestershire, The Buildings of England, London: Yale University Press

MacDonald, A., 1969 *Worcestershire in English History* (Reprint ed.), London: SR Publishers.

Allnatt, V. 2018 50 Finds from Worcestershire Amberley Publishing

Dyer, C 1991 Hanbury: Settlement and Society in a Woodland

Cunliffe, B. 1991 Iron Age Communities: an account of England, Scotland and Wales from the seventh century BC to the Roman conquest. 3rd edition, 170-175.

Chapter 19 Anglo-Saxon Worcestershire

Ekwall E., 1959 The Concise Oxford Dictionary of English Place-names Fourth Edition Oxford Clarendon Press

Yeates, S.J. 2008 The Tribes of Witches Oxbow Books

Snyder, C. A. The Britons, Blackwell Publishing

Heinrich H., 2003 *Ethnicity and Structures in* Hines. The Anglo-Saxons pp. 148–49

Attenborough F. L. The Laws of Ine and of Alfred in The Laws of the earliest English kings, 33-36

Hook, D., 1985 The Anglo-Saxon Landscape: The Kingdom of the Hwicce, 8-10; Sims-Williams.

St Wilfred and two charters dated AD 676 and 680, Journal of Ecclesiatical History, 39, 2, 169

Diamond, J., 1999 Guns, Germs and Steel: The Fates of Human Societies W.W. Norton &Co.

Ramachandran, S., and Rosenberg, N., 2011, Genetic Variation and Population Structure, American Journal of Physical Anthropology.

Leslie, S. 2015 The fine-scale genetic structure of the British population Nature. 519(7543):309-14

Mawer, A., Stenton, F.M. and Houghton F.T.S. 1927 The Place-Names of Worcestershire English Place-Name Society Woolnough Bookbinding Ltd

Smith, A.H. 1965 The Hwicce. In Frankiplegius; medieval and linguistic studies of Francis Peabody Magoun Jr., 56-65, New York

Gelling, M., Cole, A. 2000 The Landscape of Place Names Stamford, Shaun Tyas.

Clark, C. 1995 Women's Rights in Early England
Brigham Young University Law Review, 1, 4, 207 - 236.

Crystal, D. (18 May 2007) What's so special about Bricklehampton? The Guardian

Ekwall, E., 1959 The Concise Oxford Dictionary of English Place-names. Fourth Edition Oxford Clarendon Press

Watts, V. 2004 The Cambridge Dictionary of English Place Names Cambridge University Press

Mills, A. D. 2011 A Dictionary of British Place Names revision Oxford University Press

Taggart, C., 2011 The Book of English Place Names Random House Group Ltd

Burton, J. R. 1883 A History of Bewdley with concise accounts of the neighbouring parishes William Reeves Publications

The Victoria History of the County of Worcester: 1913 Volume III, 224

Bond C J, 1969 Bentley Pauncefoot Moated site at the Thrift, unpublished survey notes in SMR.

Horowitz, D. 2002 'A Survey and Analysis of the Place-Names of Staffordshire' Thesis submitted to the University for the degree of Doctor of Philosophy, Nottingham October 2003.

Yaldon, D. W. 1999 The History of British Mammals T & A D Poyser Ltd., London.

Green, H., et al 2012 Worcestershire Mammals Worcestershire Biological Record Centre Published by Aspect Design.

Mogger, O, Wragge, A, 1913 The Victoria History of the County of Worcestershire, 419.

Bond, C J, 1978 'Medieval Moated Sites' in Worcestershire: Selected Moats, Vol. Res Rep 17, 7.

James, K., 2016 Place Names of Stourbridge, The Black Country and their Environs: Origins, meaning and interpretation. The Black Countryman, The Black Country Society.

Chapter 20 The Norsemen and Worcestershire

Fellows-Jensen, G., 1985 Scandinavian Settlement Names in the North-West, Copenhagen.

Fellows-Jensen, G., 1972 Scandinavian Settlements in Cumbria and Dumfriesshire: The Place-Name Evidence, Copenhagen

Gelling, M.1978 Signposts to the Past J. M. Dent & Sons Ltd

Cameron, K. 1965 Scandinavian Settlement in the Territory of the Five Boroughs: The Place-Name Evidence. University of Nottingham.

Chapter 22 The Ancient Ways of Worcestershire

MacDonald, A. 1969, Worcestershire in English History. London: SR Publishers

Poulton-Smith, Anthony 2013 The Salt Routes Amberley Books

Chapter 23 Post-Medieval Worcestershire

Ekwall, E. 1959 The Concise Oxford Dictionary of English Place-names Fourth Edition Oxford Clarendon Press

Mills, A. D. 2011 A Dictionary of British Place Names, revision Oxford University Press

BV - #0188 - 170523 - C0 - 229/152/13 - PB - 9781913425784 - Matt Lamination